T5-DGS-900

ADVANCE PRAISE FOR

RECLAIMING TOM LONGBOAT

"Richly insightful and original, this gem of book will make a big impact—on scholarship, on the thinking of sport policy makers, and on public consciousness. It speaks to so many aspects of Canadian life beyond sport, and makes for fascinating and compelling reading about something that is so important, yet not well known, in Canadian history....Anyone seeking to understand and/or implement the Truth and Reconciliation Commission's Calls to Action 87–91 regarding Sports and Reconciliation will want to read this book."
—Nancy Bouchier, *For the Love of the Game*

"*Reclaiming Tom Longboat* provides important contributions to the fields of Canadian sport history and Indigenous studies in Canada. Researchers in Canadian sport history have only recently begun to pay serious attention the colonial biases inherent in sport and recreation practices, and this work provides an important alternate view as to how we can understand sport and physical culture as part of our shared history."
—Robert Kossuth, Associate Professor of Kinesiology and Physical Education, University of Lethbridge

"*Reclaiming Tom Longboat* weaves the stories of Indigenous athletes, non-Indigenous interest groups, government, and Indigenous political organizations together to provide a fascinating account of an important phase in the ongoing struggle to decolonize Canadian institutions."
—J.R. Miller, author of *Residential Schools and Reconciliation*

"A genuine project of reclamation that advances the rebuilding of Indigenous nations and nationhood."
—Christine O'Bonsawin, Associate Professor, History and Indigenous Studies, University of Victoria

RECLAIMING TOM LONGBOAT
INDIGENOUS SELF-DETERMINATION IN CANADIAN SPORT

JANICE FORSYTH

FOREWORD BY WILLIE LITTLECHILD

 University of Regina Press

© 2020 Janice Forsyth

All rights reserved. No part of this work covered by the copyrights hereon may be reproduced or used in any form or by any means—graphic, electronic, or mechanical—without the prior written permission of the publisher. Any request for photocopying, recording, taping or placement in information storage and retrieval systems of any sort shall be directed in writing to Access Copyright.

Printed and bound in Canada at Friesens. The text of this book is printed on 100% post-consumer recycled paper with earth-friendly vegetable-based inks.

Cover art: Canada's Sports Hall of Fame | Panthéon des sports canadiens, SPORTSHALL.CA | PANTHEONSPORTS.CA, Object ID: x981.637.1.25
Cover and text design: Duncan Campbell, University of Regina Press
Copy editor: Ryan Perks
Proofreader: Kirsten Craven
Indexer: Jason Begy Indexing

Library and Archives Canada Cataloguing in Publication
Title: Reclaiming Tom Longboat : indigenous self-determination in Canadian sport / Janice Forsyth.
Names: Forsyth, Janice, author.
Description: Includes bibliographical references and index.
Identifiers: Canadiana (print) 20200168479 | Canadiana (ebook) 20200168541 | ISBN 9780889777286 (softcover) | ISBN 9780889777309 (hardcover) | ISBN 9780889777323 (PDF) | ISBN 9780889777347 (HTML)
Subjects: LCSH: Indians of North America—Sports—Canada—History. | LCSH: Sports—Social aspects—Canada—History. | LCSH: Sports and state—Canada—History. | CSH: Native peoples—Sports—Canada—History.
Classification: LCC E98.G2 F67 2020 | DDC 796.089/97071—dc23

10 9 8 7 6 5 4 3 2 1

University of Regina Press, University of Regina
Regina, Saskatchewan, Canada, s4s 0A2
TEL: (306) 585-4758 FAX: (306) 585-4699
U OF R PRESS   WEB: www.uofrpress.ca

We acknowledge the support of the Canada Council for the Arts for our publishing program. We acknowledge the financial support of the Government of Canada. / Nous reconnaissons l'appui financier du gouvernement du Canada. This publication was made possible with support from Creative Saskatchewan's Book Publishing Production Grant Program.

This publication was made possible with the help of a grant from the Federation for the Humanities and Social Sciences, through the Awards to Scholarly Publications Program, using funds provided by the Social Sciences and Humanities Research Council of Canada.

*This book is dedicated to my dear friend
Jan Eisenhardt (1906–2004) and to all my
fellow recipients of a Tom Longboat Award.*

CONTENTS

FOREWORD

by WILLIE LITTLECHILD

M y name is Wilton 'Willie' Littlechild. I was born in 1944 and raised by my grandparents on the Ermineskin Cree First Nation at Maskwacîs in Alberta.

I was first awarded the regional Tom Longboat Award in 1965, and then won the national award in 1967. This was followed by another national award in 1974 and a regional award in 1975. Receiving the award is the most incredible honour: it is the highest recognition an athlete can receive in Canada. The first time I won, I was very embarrassed at the ceremony when media asked me, *So who was Tom Longboat?*, and I didn't know. So I began searching through old newspapers during his era and was surprised to find so many articles; the significance of winning the trophy became more meaningful to me the more I learned. Tom Longboat—Cogwagee— was such an outstanding athlete, an Olympian who contributed so much to the development of amateur sports in Canada. I needed to know more.

I traveled to his community at Six Nations, met family members, and visited his grave site to thank his spirit for his motivation and positive impact on my life. This experience was a lifetime influence that changed me; from then on, I wanted to work harder than ever to pursue excellence in school, sports, and later, work.

In the future, I hope to see the Tom Longboat Award given the same status and recognition as the other major sports awards in Canada. With this increase in profile for the award, my dream is that many more Indigenous children and youth will be motivated, as I was, to pursue sport and seek balance and excellence in life. I would like also to see a scholarship and/or bursary program(s) attached to the award to assist honourees in pursuing high-level training, competitions, and educational opportunities. Further, nominees for the Tom Longboat Award need to be promoted and introduced to elite teams and post-secondary institutions so as to encourage their continued athletic participation and educational pursuits.

In fact, Canadians, sport organizations, and all levels of government must create space and be truly inclusive in every way so that Indigenous athletes, officials, administrators, communities, and supporters have equal opportunities to develop in all aspects of sport and benefit fully. I believe that once this happens, everyone wins. Private industry too must increase or begin to contribute financial and other resources to build the infrastructure that is needed as well as to create the capacity at the community level. The positive returns from these initiatives for all in Canada are immeasurable. I sincerely believe—indeed, I *know*—that sport has the power to change and save lives of Indigenous people, in particular, the lives of children and youth. It also has the power to promote peaceful co-existence and advance reconciliation as we "work together" and "lift each other up." This is a glimpse of the future message you'll find in Janice Forsyth's history of the Tom Longboat Awards.

The Truth and Reconciliation Commission of Canada, with its court-ordered mandate to look into the Indian residential school history and legacy, was the most intensive consultation of Indigenous Peoples ever held from coast to coast to coast. During this oftentimes dark and sad process, we heard from student survivors horrific stories of abuses of children. But we also heard stories of Indigenous strength and resilience. What was it that helped some through this painful time? It was sports that provided a haven from the abuses: it was a time they could leave the school, eat better meals, meet other students in play or competition. The key message was "without sports, I would have never made it."

This was true for me too. As a former student over a span of fourteen years in three different Residential Schools, such was the role of sport in my life. I give tribute to sport for helping me run from the abuses and offering me a chance to learn to "win in life." Like some other athletes recorded in this book, sports saved my life. I used sport for motivation to pursue excellence everywhere, including in the classroom. It helped me find friends on teams who were much better athletes than I, as well as coaches who were great teachers for me. Combining all of this with the traditional teachings of my grandparents was a formula for success for me. Being named a Tom Longboat Award recipient helped me get on and stay on that path to success.

—J. Wilton "Willie" Littlechild
Ermineskin Cree First Nation
December 19, 2019

ACKNOWLEDGEMENTS

I came up with the idea for this book in 2000, when I was beginning my doctorate at Western University and working full-time as an interim program manager for the Aboriginal Sport Circle (ASC), the national non-profit organization responsible for Indigenous sport, physical activity, and recreation development in Canada. In addition to being the franchise holder for the North American Indigenous Games, hosting national championships in various sports, developing curriculum and workshops for coaching education, and designing federal-level policies to enhance Indigenous sports participation, the ASC also managed the Tom Longboat Awards. At meetings of its board of directors, members often talked about the need to document the history of the awards, including a list of all the winners going back to 1951, but the organization lacked the resources to produce such a record. I volunteered to carry out this work as part of my dissertation. Now, having turned that research into a book, I hope that it is an adequate response to what the ASC wanted back then and that it provides a new direction for thinking about the awards and their role in reimagining Indigenous involvement in Canadian sport.

I am especially indebted to Rick Brant, a former executive director and co-founder of the ASC, for hiring me in 2000, and to Alwyn Morris, a founder and past president, for inviting me to take a leadership role with the organization in 2013. Together, you have guided my thinking on Indigenous and Canadian sport in practical and productive ways, and provided me with ample opportunities to engage at the some of the highest levels of decision-making in the non-profit and government sectors. You will always remain an important part of my life. I also hope that I have adequately captured your involvement with the awards, as recipients and stewards. I admit to feeling a bit uncomfortable writing a history that we continue to live.

Similar to much Indigenous research carried out nowadays, this history of the Tom Longboat Awards is built upon the stories that people shared with me. I wish to offer a heartfelt thank you to all of the award recipients whom I have had the pleasure of interviewing since 2004 and to the family members who sometimes took part in those interviews. You let me into your homes and your communities and trusted me with your words. I hope that I have done them justice. Although only a small portion of the interviews are included here, all of the stories that people shared with me helped to inform the project's overall trajectory.

A number of colleagues deserve special mention for keeping me afloat through the years, and especially during the painful process of turning a dissertation into a book. Kevin Wamsley, my PhD supervisor, took a chance on this project many years ago when I started working for the ASC, giving me the room that I needed to explore its possibilities. Vicky Paraschak, my mentor and friend from the University of Windsor, helped me to lay the groundwork for this project and guided me through much of the complex thinking and storytelling that it required. She remains a key source of support for me and for the Tom Longboat Awards by completing biographical entries for recipients on Wikipedia and by serving on the awards' national adjudication committee. My dear friend Audrey Giles, whose contributions extend well beyond this book, has always responded to last-minute calls for academic and editing help via Facebook Messenger. She has also done her best to wean me from the passive voice, which I think is part of my genetic code. From McMaster University, Nancy Bouchier provided the gentle encouragement that I needed to publish my work as a monograph. This book would likely be a series of journal articles if not for her careful prodding. And Michael Heine deepened my appreciation of the Tom Longboat Awards as a cultural text and provided me with the conceptual tool kit to render the awards' history into the multi-layered conversation that it is. Our time together, first at the University of Manitoba and then at Western University, has been both productive and fun. Among other projects, Michael and I co-authored a paper on Jan Eisenhardt that sharpened my thinking about the role of the awards as a tool for cultural assimilation. Jan was the man who developed and implemented the Tom Longboat Awards while working at Indian Affairs in the early 1950s. I developed a dear friendship with him and his daughter, Lisa Spillane, who remains a constant ray of light in my life.

My conversations and interactions with many other friends and colleagues have also inspired this work. In particular, I would like to acknowledge Carly Adams, Chris Andersen, Ann Hall, Colin Howell, Bruce Kidd, Ken Kirkwood, Robert Kossuth, Robert Lake, Gord MacDonald, Malcolm MacLean, Pirrko Markula, Fred Mason, Alan Metcalfe, J.R. Miller, Don Morrow, Christine O'Bonsawin, Murray Phillips, Charlene Weaving, and the many people who have worked or volunteered for the ASC and Sport Canada. You have all played an important role in shaping various elements of this book.

Willie Littlechild, one of the three commissioners for the Truth and Reconciliation Commission of Canada and four-time Tom Longboat Award recipient, deserves special mention for something he told me in the late 1990s when I was interviewing him in his law office in Maskwacis, Alberta. I was a master's student at the time, writing about his involvement in the development of the North American Indigenous Games, a multi-sport and cultural festival for Indigenous people in Canada and the United States. When I turned the recorder off, he asked me that dreaded question: What do you want to do with your education? With no particular job in mind, I said that I wanted to be a decision-maker in sport. His response was simple: "Then you need one of three things: a law degree, a business degree, or a PhD." His words led me to pursue a doctorate. I now offer that guidance to students whenever it feels right. Since our meeting in Maskwacis, Willie has been particularly generous with his support for my academic work in Indigenous sport; I am grateful that even with his busy schedule he found the time to write the foreword to this book.

The staff at Library and Archives Canada, Weldon Library at Western University, Indian Affairs (which has undergone several names changes in recent years), the Woodland Cultural Centre, and the National Indian Brotherhood/Assembly of First Nations were instrumental in helping me find documents and related materials that few other researchers have ever requested. My favourite discovery is still the 13 mm film strip that Eisenhardt created in 1951 and released in 1952 with help from the National Film Board of Canada and that Walter Zimmerman, an archivist at Western University, located and retrieved from a friend at the University of Saskatchewan. As well, Vanessa Lodge Gagne spent several weeks retrieving valuable information from various repositories in the Maritimes, including the Provincial Archives of New Brunswick. She also conducted interviews with recipients from that region for her master's thesis on the Tom Longboat Awards. Some of that information was instrumental here, especially with the discussion on the Native Sport and Recreation Program. The ASC and Jan Eisenhardt also graciously granted me access to their records and collections. Information about all of these archives is available in the "Notes on Archival Sources" found at the back of this book.

The production team at University of Regina Press deserves the credit for any success that this book achieves. Karen Clark, the press's scholarly acquisitions editor, and Kelly Laycock, the managing editor, shepherded me through the intricacies of publishing a monograph, and freelance editor Dallas Harrison and copy editor Ryan Perks pulled the narrative threads together and cleaned the text up to make the story more appealing to a wider audience. I would like to thank James Daschuk for directing me to University of Regina Press and for letting me know about Dallas, in addition to supporting my work all of these years. I also want to extend my thanks to the two reviewers who provided helpful commentary, especially to the reviewer who offered extensive feedback and provided line-by-line edits on the manuscript. Any shortcomings that remain are mine alone.

Two different sources of funding helped me to carry out the research for this book. A Standard Research Grant from the Social Sciences and Humanities Research Council of Canada (SSHRC

410-2008-2608) was used to support a portion of this project. The other source was the Fisher River Cree Nation Board of Education, which funded my entire university education, from my undergraduate degree in history to the completion of my PhD. I am not sure that I would have gone to university, and I definitely would not have continued on to graduate school, without their generous support. Thank you for having the vision to see the value of education for our people: *hay-hay*.

Thank you to my family for giving me the freedom and encouragement to carry out this project. Guy Schultz, my Gentle Warrior, was there every step of the way. He nominated me for a Tom Longboat Award for my performances in track and field at the 2002 North American Indigenous Games in Winnipeg, Manitoba. The nomination went in and the months passed by until one day I received a package in the mail. The letter said I had won the 2002 award for Ontario. It was accompanied by a bronze medallion with a likeness of Tom Longboat engraved on one side and a description of the award on the other. The letter and medallion are framed together in museum glass, hanging in my home office. Winning the award set me on an emotional journey into my own family history and life experiences that inspired my thinking about this project and what it was like for others to be named a recipient. Guy also helped me with much of the data collection and produced several extremely valuable tables of information, including the list of recipients that is now on Wikipedia (thanks to Vicky Paraschak).

Finally, I would like to express my gratitude to my parents, Sara Forsyth and Tom Edwards, who I know would have read this book and given it centre stage on their plastic two-tiered TV stand in their cozy two-bedroom apartment in Sault Ste. Marie, Ontario. Their love for me never wavered and never grew old. They gave me everything worth having: a life filled with love, laughter, and a sense of purpose. My mother passed away in September 2015, a few days shy of her seventy-fifth birthday, and my father, who missed her dearly, followed her in February 2018. They are forever in my heart.

REMEMBERING TOM LONGBOAT

THE MAN

Tom Longboat was an Onondaga runner from Six Nations of the Grand River, Ontario, who reached a level of success that most athletes only dream of attaining. Born Cogwagee in 1887, he competed in foot races of various distances at the turn of the twentieth century, but he was best known for his success in long-distance running. For nearly six years, from 1906 to 1912, he won almost every major race in Canada, the United States, and Europe, and he set a number of world records, ranging from the fifteen- to the thirty-two-mile event. In 1908, Longboat competed for Canada in the marathon at the Olympic Games in London, England. Although he was favoured to win, he collapsed late in the race from possible heat stroke. The stifling temperature had not a stitch of breeze to cool the labouring athletes, and more than half of the runners, including Longboat, failed to cross the finish line that day.[1]

To say that Longboat was a prominent figure during his lifetime is an understatement. In the early 1900s, foot racing was a wildly popular sport. Hundreds and even thousands of people would gather to watch him race. Newspapers around the world printed stories about his achievements and his life. Readers learned that he was a dispatch runner for Canada in the First World War; that he held a job with the City of Toronto during the Depression in the late 1920s; and that he built a house for his mother on the Six Nations reserve, where he eventually retired with his wife and family. No matter where Longboat went, journalists followed him, paparazzi-like, digging into all aspects of his life and selling these tidbits as news for public entertainment. Longboat was not just an athlete; he was a superstar.

Such fame came with a challenge that few of his contemporaries had to face: unrelenting media attention that distorted his image to such a degree that it must have been hard for Longboat to recognize himself in the press. Journalists fostered his celebrity by adding

Tom Longboat (centre) at a marathon race in the United States, with Johnny Hayes (left) and Henri St. Ives (right), May 8, 1909. Source: Detroit Public Library, National Automotive History Collection, Lazarnick Collection, na018204. Creator: Spooner & Wells, Inc., New York.

racialized commentary to their reports and frequently drawing on stereotypes to describe his character, knowing that such commentary would make their stories more compelling for readers. On any given day, they would frame Longboat as a hero who had conquered the world; as a lazy Indian who would not train; as a gifted athlete admired by all; as a drunken Indian who squandered his prize money; as a cultured man with expensive tastes; as an uncivilized Indian who needed white men to help him find his place in mainstream society; as a role model to admire and emulate; or as a wayward Indian who needed to be steered away from his "natural" inclinations and vices. Longboat's status as a tragic hero thus hinged to a large degree on the desires and prejudices of writers who fused together ideas about nation, race, masculinity, and class to create a composite picture that barely resembled the man.

After Longboat passed away in January 1949, the public remained captivated by his story, upholding the narrative of the tragic hero. If anything, that motif had become more firmly entrenched in the public imaginary, buoyed as it was by such men such as Fergus Cronin, who wrote an extensive article for *Maclean's* in 1956 on the famed Onondaga with the title "The Rise and Fall of Tom Longboat." The article retold a well-worn tale: "He hated to train, and he was a fool with his money. But for half a dozen dazzling years this Canadian Indian could run farther, faster than any man alive. His downfall was just as swift."[2] Back then *Maclean's* was Canada's leading business and political journal. Many in the educated class would have read the six-page spread, absorbing the cultural assumptions that underpinned it.

The tragic hero narrative remained intact for another thirty years until historian Bruce Kidd published two seminal works that changed how many people came to see and understand Longboat. One was a book meant for a general audience, released in 1980 under the simple title *Tom Longboat*.[3] The other, a scholarly article titled "In Defense of Tom Longboat," was published in 1984. In it, Kidd confronted the racist media depictions of Longboat throughout and after his life, arguing that his "reputation fell because he did not embody the qualities the sports leaders and opinion-makers believed he should. He made his own decisions about training, racing and the conduct of his life: the criticism he received was a measure of his independence and self-determination," not an objective assessment of his efforts.[4] With these two publications, Kidd helped to redirect the national conversation about Longboat away from a racist discourse that emphasized individual failings to one that confronted the overt and systemic racism that influenced his life and career.

Of course, the new narrative did not emerge in a vacuum. Kidd was researching and writing about Longboat at a time when Indigenous people throughout Canada were pushing for social, economic, and political changes that would provide them with more control over their daily lives and more opportunities for the kind of growth that they needed and wanted. Their efforts had generated enough national and international attention through the 1960s and '70s that, by the time Kidd published his work on Longboat in the 1980s, his views already resonated with the public.[5] In this context Kidd's version became what William Brown, in his thoughtful historiography of Longboat, called "the new paradigm."[6] A new perspective about Longboat, one that emphasized the overcoming of obstacles and maintaining one's courage in the face of adversity, was thus put in play.

Yet many people were still unwilling to acknowledge—let alone address—their prejudices, especially when it came to sport. Writers of popular histories, whether in books or magazines, often focused on Longboat's tremendous athletic abilities and repeatedly identified him as one of the greatest athletes in Canadian history, sometimes taking into account the context in which he lived. Most often, however, they glossed over the racism and its profound effects, producing an easily digestible narrative asserting that Longboat succeeded in spite of the many challenges he faced and that sport, the great leveller, helped him to do that.[7] This narrative was appealing because it suggested that sport was somehow immune from the discrimination that structured everyday life and that evidence of bias, even when it was obvious, could be interpreted as a one-off incident that affected only a few people.

Tom Longboat standing beside trophies, April 22, 1907. Source: Charles A. Aylett, Library and Archives Canada, C-014090.

Longboat's passing in 1949 also began an outpouring of commemoration that continues to this day. In 1952, Indian Affairs sponsored the creation of a film strip titled *Tom Longboat: Canadian Indian World Champion*, to be circulated among Indian residential schools in Canada.[8] Jan Eisenhardt, the originator of the Tom Longboat Awards, created the film strip while working at the

Tom Longboat Stamp, issued February 17, 2000. Source: © Canada Post Corporation 2000. Reproduced with Permission.

department. Forty years later, renewed interest in Longboat's life and athletic career was evident with the release of two video productions: *Wildfire: The Tom Longboat Story*, a made-for-television film produced by the CBC,[9] for which Kidd served as script consultant, technical adviser, and actor, and the documentary *Longboat*.[10]

As well, Longboat was inducted posthumously into Canada's Sports Hall of Fame in 1955, the Canadian Olympic Hall of Fame in 1960, the Canadian Indian Hall of Fame in 1967, and the Canadian Road Running Hall of Fame in 1991. In 1998, *Maclean's* named him the top "star" of the twentieth century.[11] In 2000, Canada Post memorialized Longboat by creating a commemorative stamp for its Millennium Collection. And, in 2008, Bill 120 was passed by the Legislative Assembly of Ontario and given royal assent declaring that June 4 of each year be named Tom Longboat Day.[12] Few athletes have been remembered in so many ways.

THE AWARDS

The inauguration of the Tom Longboat Awards in 1951 was part of this larger trend. They were established by the federal government, through Indian Affairs, in collaboration with the Amateur Athletic Union of Canada (AAUC), the national governing body for amateur sport at the time, to commemorate Longboat's outstanding achievements in athletics and to acknowledge the ongoing contributions that Indigenous athletes were making to Canadian sport. The awards have been given out nearly every year since their inception, making them the longest-running and one of the most prestigious awards for Indigenous athletes in the country.

The Tom Longboat Awards are also an anomaly in Canadian history. Although by mid-century the practice of naming awards after athletes was not new, it was rarely done. One had to be exceptional, as Longboat was, to be recognized in this way. But being an exceptional athlete was not enough. The groups involved in creating sport awards used this form of recognition to promote ideas and behaviours that were important to them, such as demonstrating the proper conduct of men and women in public, the role of middle-class virtues in creating a vibrant nation, and the place and importance of racialized others in the growing body politic. In other words, for outstanding athletes to have awards named after them, they had to symbolize something important to Canadians. For the Tom Longboat Awards, this meant proper and progressive reform.

The earliest sport awards fused complex ideas about gender, race, class, and nation. In 1928, the AAUC established the Norton H. Crow Award to recognize the top male amateur athlete of the year in Canada. Crow, a baseball player in the summer and a speed skater in the winter, went on to become one of Canada's leading sport administrators by the early 1900s.[13] Historians have documented his fierce commitment to amateur sport and his deeply ingrained views about female frailty, which influenced the types of sporting opportunities available to men and women through his long working relationship with the AAUC.[14] The Norton H. Crow Award, though understood differently today, remains an emblem of a past that valorized masculinity through a lens of middle-class male domination, physical and emotional discipline, and citizenship.

Several years later, in 1932, the Women's Amateur Athletic Federation launched the Velma Springstead Award to recognize the top female amateur athlete in Canada. Springstead, who excelled at track and field, had passed away from pneumonia in 1926 at the age of nineteen.[15] Similar to the Crow award, ideas about gender, race, class, and nation were constructed and reinforced through the Springstead award, which assessed the "performance, sportsmanship, and behaviour" of female athletes, ensuring that recipients conformed to the social expectations for femininity that the Women's Amateur Athletic Federation espoused.[16]

In 1936, Canada's leading sports writers created the Lou Marsh Award to recognize the best athlete in any sport—amateur or professional, male or female. Marsh, who passed away suddenly in 1936, had dedicated his life to sport. Not only was he an athlete and a referee of the highest calibre, he was also a pioneer in Canadian sports journalism as a writer and editor for the *Toronto Star*—a job that he began at age fourteen and held for forty-three years.[17] Marsh knew

Longboat and had even coached the runner in 1907 and 1908, the two years in which Longboat was catapulted to worldwide fame. Marsh frequently used his newspaper column, the "Pick and Shovel," to write about Longboat, whom he praised for being an outstanding runner but upbraided for being too lazy and dimwitted to manage his own training and career.[18] Marsh was not alone in expressing such racism. Many if not most of his contemporaries believed that Indigenous athletes, including Longboat, could excel only by moving to urban areas where "proper" coaching and training facilities could be found, by adopting white middle-class habits, and by heeding the advice of white trainers and managers.[19] His views were made more potent because of his ability to reach a massive audience through the "Pick and Shovel." As one of the most widely read sports columns in Canada, it influenced how readers came to understand Longboat, and indeed many other Indigenous athletes who struggled for recognition while trying to make a living for themselves and their families through sport.[20]

The establishment of the Tom Longboat Awards in 1951 signalled a different type of recognition, one based primarily on race. The awards were given only to athletes defined as "Indian" (the common term back then) by the federal government through the *Indian Act*, a powerful piece of legislation that regulates nearly every aspect of Indigenous life, from property ownership to child welfare. It is still enforced today. Furthermore, unlike the other awards established by the AAUC, the Women's Amateur Athletic Federation, or journalists, the Tom Longboat Awards were initiated by Indian Affairs—at that time a branch of the federal government—making them the first and only government-derived national sport award in Canada, perhaps in the Commonwealth.

NOT JUST ANY SPORTS AWARD

Writing a history about a sport award is not much different from writing any other history that addresses the intersection of race and ethnic relations, class formation, sex and gender ideology, and national identity construction. In fact, this history falls in the same vein as critical analyses of commemoration projects, especially those that aim to capture the sentiment of a nation. The main problem, in the case of this study of the Tom Longboat Awards, was the absence of an established path set down by previous scholars who had already made forays into this area of research. Often in the course of my work I wondered: Who else has written a history of a sport award? The answer was no one. This meant using secondary sources creatively for context and arguments, along with asking myself a series of important questions. Would I find enough useful primary source material? What story would I be able to create from those sources? Did I have enough time and money to do a comprehensive search? What contribution would such a project make to the literature and to the wider society? Finding answers to these questions was in many ways a scholarly gamble.

I began in 2000 by constructing an administrative outline of the Tom Longboat Awards based upon what the ASC board members remembered. Many of them had been involved in Indigenous sport for decades, some having helped to manage the awards or were even past winners. Together we produced a skeleton framework. Between 1951 and 1972, Indian Affairs and the AAUC shared responsibility for the awards, with Indian Affairs managing the program at the local and regional levels and the AAUC directing activities at the national level. Through the years, responsibility for the awards shifted two more times. From 1973 to 1987, the National Indian Brotherhood (NIB) and then the Assembly of First Nations (AFN), the national political organizations representing First Nations interests in Canada, and the Sports Federation of Canada (SFC), a lobby group for national sport governing bodies, oversaw the ongoing development of the awards. The SFC would withdraw its support in 1987, leaving the AFN to manage the awards independently. Then, in 1998, responsibility for the awards was transferred to the ASC, where they remain a vital part of the organization's program.

In addition to the administrative outline, the ASC had a partial list of national award winners going back to 1951. I was told that some names had been taken from the plates fastened to the large

Tom Longboat Trophy, which was in disrepair and stored somewhere at the Canadian National Exhibition in Toronto. It was a surprisingly unceremonious fate for a national icon, referring to both the man and the award. Nonetheless, the names provided useful entry points for further research.

The logistics of collecting all of that information were not as simple as it initially appeared. Public and private archives—from London, Ontario, to Dorval, Quebec—had to be consulted, and interviews with key persons needed to be completed. For the interviews, foremost in my mind were Jan Eisenhardt (the originator of the awards), select members of the ASC, and the award recipients. The interview process was made more complicated by the need to construct a list of potential interviewees from the archival data without knowing who might be interested and available to talk to me. I needed names; any other identifying information—home addresses, for example—was a bonus. Since the awards were two-tiered, with recipients being selected at the provincial and territorial level first and the national winners then being chosen from that pool, I had to find the names and as much information as possible for approximately five hundred and fifty people. More than once the needle in a haystack analogy came to mind during my hunt in the archives.

Soon after I embarked on these tasks, it became clear to me that what began as a project of reclamation was in fact a complex and far more interesting story about sport, commemoration, assimilation, and Indigenous self-determination in Canada. I started looking into the history of sport and games at Indian Affairs, wondering why the federal government established the Tom Longboat Awards in 1951. What purpose did they serve for the government? It was a highly unusual initiative since the federal government would not take an active interest in developing sport for the masses for at least another ten years, with the passing of the *Fitness and Amateur Sport Act* in 1961. Never mind that it would take another ten years for the government to provide funding for Indigenous people to develop sport programs on and between reserves through the Native Sport and Recreation Program. The involvement of the AAUC seemed to be more straightforward, since it was a sports organization. So what happened in 1951 that encouraged the government to become involved in Indigenous sport by establishing the Tom Longboat Awards?

These initial thoughts raised more questions, especially since the NIB and AFN were powerful political entities, not sports organizations. If their primary objectives were more broadly political—negotiating Indigenous rights, advancing the treaties and land agreements, securing educational reforms—then why did the NIB and AFN want control of the Tom Longboat Awards in the 1970s? What value did they see in the awards and in sport more generally? Similar questions arose for the ASC. It made sense to me that it sought control of the awards from the AFN in the late 1990s, since the ASC was a national sports organization, established and run by Indigenous people, and perfectly positioned to manage the awards. Still, I wondered what effect the transfer had on the meanings attached to the awards. How would the political value established in previous eras change under ASC control, and to what effect? No less important were questions about the recipients. Did the awards mean the same things to them as they did to the organizers? Did the winners even know about Tom Longboat or his eponymous prize when they won the award? What value did being a recipient hold for them? These were the larger questions that set me on the path to writing this story.

This book is a cultural history of the Tom Longboat Awards. In it, I investigate why the awards were established, what purposes they served for the organizations responsible for their oversight, what they symbolized through the years (as responsibility for the awards shifted from one group to the next), and what they meant to the recipients, the athletes who continued Longboat's tradition of sporting excellence. Although we will never know what Longboat thought of his own experiences rubbing up against the stereotypes and discriminations that he faced, it is possible to know how others felt in similar situations.

I begin this cultural history with the premise that the Tom Longboat Awards are much more than a celebration of athletic excellence. Rather, they are an important part of Canada's cultural heritage that goes well beyond the realm of sport and into the politics of being Indigenous in a settler state. To understand the awards as an uncritical and celebratory aspect of sport devalues what they mean symbolically to the nation, and especially to Indigenous people. It is more productive, and definitely more interesting, to understand them in the context of Canadian colonialism, where sport was (and remains) a complex space in which individuals and groups struggled with and against settler domination. At its core, then, the history of the awards is a history of assimilation and self-determination told through the lens of sport.

The years 1951 to 2001 form the major bookends of this story. The time frame is limited to this fifty-year period because it encompasses all of the organizations responsible for the awards since their inauguration and provides sufficient evidence of continuity and change to make strong statements about what was happening over time. My focus throughout is on national-level activities, specifically the interactions among the administrative organizations: Indian Affairs and the AAUC, the NIB/AFN and the SFC, and the ASC.

What will become obvious in the chapters ahead is that the creation of the Tom Longboat Awards was no mere accident of history. Nor were they the consequence of serendipity, of the right people coming together at the right time without political intent to remember Longboat two years after his death. The opposite is true, in fact, for the awards were a coveted tool for organizations that wanted to advance their social and political agendas. As such, this book is not about Longboat or how he has been represented to the public, though parts of those discussions will surface again in various chapters and especially the conclusion. Instead, I focus on the meanings that have been attached to the awards by different groups of people who struggled for power and control over other people's lives while coming to terms with their own positions in society. In a sense, these two icons—Tom Longboat and the Tom Longboat Awards—share a peculiar history in that the awards, much like the man, have been used as a vehicle to construct, reinforce, and promote messages about what it means to be Indigenous in Canada and what it means to be Canadian.

THE MUTABLE NATURE OF SIGNS

"There are three ways to look at Tom Longboat," explained Malcolm Kelly for the CBC in 2017: "biographical, statistical and cultural." For Kelly, the first two ways were easy enough because they dealt with the facts of history: Longboat was Onondaga, he held a number of world records in running, he competed in the 1908 Olympics, and so on. No interpretation was needed. The third way was more intricate because it meant understanding the cultural context in which Longboat lived and competed, and then appreciating how society had changed, or hadn't, since that time: "Today the soft racism of low expectations is becoming familiar, but more than 100 years ago it was the hard racism of high expectations met but still not good enough because it wasn't somehow done the 'correct' way."[21]

The paradigm shift that Bruce Kidd initiated, and that others such as Kelly picked up and broadcast to a wider audience, highlight how someone or something can be turned into a sign—something that has been given meaning—and how the meanings attached to that sign can change over time. Longboat, once the tragic hero, was later remade into a self-determined man, his story recast at the same time that Canadians were forced to reassess their relationship with Indigenous people. Given the mutable nature of signs, and the broader reforms that Indigenous people and Canadians are still working toward—inspired by the Truth and Reconciliation Commission of Canada (TRC)—it is possible that the meanings attached to Longboat now will change again in the future.

We can use the three ways of looking at Longboat—administrative, statistical, and cultural—to look at the Tom Longboat Awards. This book incorporates all three ways and layers them on top of each other to offer a detailed and compelling account of Indigenous-state relations as told through the history of a sports award.

The first layer of analysis brings together the administrative and statistical history of the awards. It is the record of the development, implementation, and management of the awards, as well as the list of recipients, covering the time frame 1951 to 2001. These are the "facts" of history stitched carefully together from documents

and interviews. I introduce key figures involved in the organization and management of the awards where necessary and only if
enough information exists to warrant their inclusion. For instance,
I had the good fortune to meet and become good friends with Jan
Eisenhardt, the originator of the awards. I did not know what to
expect from the person who created an award for a branch of the
federal government that had always been fixated on systematically erasing Indigenous culture in Canada, but I soon came to
realize that he was a renaissance man who was way ahead of the
moral and philosophical curve at Indian Affairs: the job was a bad
fit for him. He began working there as the supervisor of physical
education and recreation in February 1950 and quit in December
1951 because of the lack of support for programs that First Nations
people wanted. Jan moved on to a better-paying position as the
fitness director for Canadair, but this position was short-lived. In
January 1952, the federal government blacklisted him for alleged
communist sympathies. Although he and his family survived the
indignity, confusion, and emotional turmoil stemming from years
of surveillance by the Royal Canadian Mounted Police and the
hardship of lost wages, the experience took its toll on him, his wife,
and his children. His story is featured in a documentary titled *The
Un-Canadians*, which can be found online.[22] It is worth watching.
When I met Jan in 2002, he was still trying to figure out how to
clear his name from the blacklist. He passed away in December
2004. His experience complicates stories about assimilation. He
was a libertarian who got caught in a system that absorbed his progressive views, turned them into something that worked for the
system, and then spit him out. Jan once told me that he thought
someone at Indian Affairs had put his name on the blacklist. He
deserved so much better.

The second layer of analysis is cultural. It looks at the meanings
that have been attached to the Tom Longboat Awards through each
administrative era: from 1951 to 1972, from 1973 to 1998, and from
1999 to 2001. I show that government and sport officials originally
designed the awards as a tool for Indigenous assimilation but that
Indigenous people appropriated the awards and transformed them

into a means of cultural expression and self-determination. This transformation came at a price, however, since Indigenous leaders had no choice but to negotiate their vision for sport within a context in which government and sport officials controlled the rules and resources for participation. Working within these restricted boundaries, Indigenous people successfully transformed the awards into a symbol of cultural pride, but they did so while simultaneously reproducing some of the ethnocentric assumptions about sport, and the role of Indigenous people in Canadian society, that the awards were meant to challenge.

The third layer of analysis, which builds upon the second layer, is also cultural. It is an analysis of selected oral interviews that I conducted with award winners from Ontario. In this layer, I explore what being a Tom Longboat Award winner has meant for individual recipients and examine the meanings that they have attached to the awards. I contrast their personal experiences with the meanings that the organizers constructed to highlight the extent to which the official goals were accepted, resisted, or subverted by the recipients. By offering an interpretation of their stories, I also shed much-needed light on the sporting opportunities available to Indigenous boys and girls, and men and women, from the mid-twentieth century onward and expand our understanding of how organized sport has shaped Indigenous identities along axes of nation, race, ethnicity, class, and gender.[23]

One thing is certain: the Tom Longboat Awards are far from a simple celebration of Indigenous excellence in sport. They cut to the heart of what it means to be Indigenous in Canada and to the heart of what it means to be Canadian. Clearly, the awards have meant a great deal to a great many people, or they would have passed by the wayside long ago.

CHAPTER OUTLINE

Chapter 1 provides the historical backdrop and helps readers understand the role of sport in the efforts to assimilate Indigenous people in Canada and how Indigenous people responded to these efforts. This chapter focuses on Indigenous life on the land before European settlement, formal cultural regulation from the late 1800s to the early 1900s, sports and games at Indian residential schools from the late 1800s to the mid-1900s, and the marginalization of Indigenous people from the organized sport system in Canada.

Chapter 2 begins with a look at the changes in the federal government after the Second World War that led to the creation of the position of supervisor of physical education and recreation within Indian Affairs. I focus on the story of Jan Eisenhardt, hired as the first supervisor, who created the Tom Longboat Awards in 1951. I then describe the history of the awards from 1951 to 1972, when they were co-managed by Indian Affairs and the AAUC. During this era, Indian Affairs and the AAUC used the awards to promote their social and political agendas. The official prescriptions established by these national entities are weighed against the local interpretations of Indian agents, missionaries, teachers, and school administrators responsible for nominating "worthy" candidates. This chapter is written from the perspective of Indian Affairs and the AAUC.

Chapter 3 considers the Tom Longboat Awards under the shared leadership of the NIB, the AFN, and the SFC from 1973 to 1998. The continuity and change in both the structure of the awards and the meanings attached to them are of particular interest here. This discussion takes into account the wider social context that influenced how the NIB and the AFN managed the awards, including their political interests in sport, as well as the termination of federal funding for the Native Sport and Recreation Program, which brought to a crashing halt the attempts of Indigenous leaders to use sport as a vehicle for social development, especially at the community level. These factors are examined in relation to the decline of the awards through the 1980s and '90s, culminating in their transfer to the ASC in 1998. This chapter is written from the perspective of Indigenous leaders at the NIB and the AFN and the sport sector via the SFC.

I follow a similar line of analysis in chapter 4 but focus on the transfer of the Tom Longboat Awards from the AFN to the ASC. I emphasize the implications of this shift—from a political body to a sports organization—on the structure and the meanings of the awards. Although they were an important point of discussion for Indigenous sports leaders throughout the country during this era, the awards' full immersion into a sport environment had the effect of depoliticizing them, at least at the level of official discourse. I use the broader context of Indigenous sport development in Canada to frame this depoliticization.

Chapter 5 examines what being a Tom Longboat Award winner has meant to individual recipients from Ontario, whose stories I collected in the 2000s. This was the first set of interviews I carried out for this project, which means the interviewees' voices have been waiting to be heard for a long time. Their stories are therefore privileged in this book. I focus on the extent to which they incorporated, resisted, challenged, or subverted the official meanings produced by government and sports officials, thereby making the awards their own.

In the conclusion, I bring readers back to the main question: What do the Tom Longboat Awards celebrate? I expand on why they are an important part of Canadian cultural history and what they tell us about the relationship between Canada and Indigenous people today. I also discuss the awards and Indigenous sport more generally within the context of the TRC. I offer what I hope is a strong rationale for why we all need to pay more attention to the experiences of Indigenous athletes in Canadian sport, as well as insights into the necessity of listening to them.

---

* This chapter draws on previously published material from "Make the Indian Understand His Place," 2015.

CULTIVATING
CIVILIZED HABITS:
SPORT AND ASSIMILATION

Tom Longboat came of age as an athlete at the turn of the twentieth century, when life for most Indigenous people was being radically transformed by racist legislation that aimed to "help" them by forcing them to assimilate into broader society. In recent years, much of this history has been made public thanks largely to efforts of Indigenous leaders and their allies who pushed for special commissions and inquiries into the lasting effects of these policies. The Royal Commission on Aboriginal Peoples (RCAP), which published its five-volume report in 1996, and the Truth and Reconciliation Commission of Canada (TRC), which released its suite of reports in 2015, are two prominent examples. Both address the long-lasting consequences of policy actions that removed Indigenous people from their traditional territories, split kinship groups and families apart, actively suppressed Indigenous cultural practices and traditions, and kept Indigenous people in a state of poverty and poor health that would otherwise be considered criminal.

Significantly, the RCAP and the TRC also drew public attention to the role of sport in the process of Indigenous assimilation, thus challenging the positive assumptions that often underpin sports and sport development initiatives for Indigenous people. To take the RCAP and the TRC seriously means one also needs to take sport seriously. To do this we must switch mental gears, moving away from a focus on sports scores, sporting greats, and our positive associations with sport, to talking about sport (and all physical culture) as a "kind of education of the body" that has significant implications for Indigenous identity and well-being, as well as Indigenous-settler relations in Canada.[1] Seeing sport in this light, as a "kind of education of the body," opens up new possibilities for understanding the various discourses that have made sport an important part of our everyday lives and that shape our understanding of what is appropriate physical movement (with some movements being discouraged while others are privileged and supported with resources), what health looks like (which influences what types of activities people will engage in, or not, for reasons of health), and what is socially and culturally rewarding (with implications for what people will spend time watching and supporting as spectators, making them feel connected to a larger community of people).[2] This is the "serious" side of sport addressed in this chapter.

What follows are three case studies that illustrate this serious side. They focus on the era from the 1800s to the 1950s and include the history of Indigenous cultural repression, residential schooling, and integration into organized sports. While each case focuses on a distinct aspect of Indigenous life in Canada, they should be understood as an interconnected whole. Importantly, this interconnected whole also forms the backdrop to understanding the broader context in which the Tom Longboat Awards were introduced in 1951 and their significance to Canadian and Indigenous history.

CULTURAL REPRESSION

In his treatise on Indigenous self-government, *Peace, Power, Righteousness: An Indigenous Manifesto*, Mohawk scholar Taiaiake Alfred critiques the Western notion of power that aims to regulate, dominate, and control. Drawing on the work of French theorist Michel Foucault, Alfred contends that state power is extended through constitutional frameworks that claim to define the relationship between the state and its citizens even when those citizens are not part of the decision-making process. Alfred sees this extension of state power through legislative means as evidence of a coercive relationship. For Indigenous people, this coercion is even more pronounced because the federal government, supported by a majority of voters, has claimed the power to define how Indigenous people should participate in Canadian society. As Alfred explains,

> a critique of state power that sees oppression as an inevitable function of the state, even when it is constrained by a constitutionally defined social-political contract, should have special resonance for indigenous people, since their nations were never party to any contract and yet have been forced to operate within a framework that presupposes the legitimacy of state sovereignty over them. Arguing for rights within that framework only reinforces the state's anti-historic claim to sovereignty by contract.[3]

Alfred's critique has merit. In 1876, the Government of Canada created the *Indian Act* to protect First Nations lands from the encroachment of white settlers and to establish autonomy for First Nations from the developing society, but soon the act came to be interpreted by policy-makers as an instrument to control almost every aspect of life for Indigenous people, whose leaders did not formally approve this piece of legislation (unlike the so-called Numbered Treaties).[4] No agreements were signed. No verbal promises were made. In short, the act was drafted in Ottawa by federal bureaucrats who took responsibility for defining the relationship between the Canadian state and Indigenous people, who were positioned as wards of the state. With this type of bureaucratic power, federal officials asserted the right to regulate Indigenous people and restrict their access to resources that could be used to develop their human and financial potential.[5] The result was a complex federal policy framework that took responsibility for certain segments of the Indigenous population. People who lived in remote or isolated regions—such as those in the interior of British Columbia, east of Ontario, or the Far North—were excluded from the treaty-making process and left to continue with their traditional lifestyles as much as possible until settler encroachment on their lands forced changes on them in the twentieth century.[6]

In addition, the federal government reserved the right to identify who would qualify as Indian under the *Indian Act* so as to reduce its financial responsibilities for treaty rights and to expedite its takeover of Indigenous lands. In some instances, the bureaucratic method for selecting who would be covered under the *Indian Act* was arbitrary. Author Maria Campbell describes how her family was absent when government officials were making treaty with her people, resulting in some community members being called "Indian" and others being designated Non-Status or Métis depending on the heritage of the family (Inuit and Métis people are not subject to the act).[7] More than a hundred and forty years later, the act continues to regulate First Nations lives from "the cradle to the grave," in spite of efforts for self-determination.[8]

For many people, the *Indian Act* has come to symbolize the paternalism embedded in government policy-making. In the past, Indigenous people were rarely consulted on how to improve their lives through government policies. When their opinions were sought, their recommendations were almost never taken seriously. In her study of the development of the 1969 White Paper, Sally Weaver shows how this paternalism continued well into the twentieth century.[9] Although Indian Affairs hosted a series of consultations with Indigenous leaders throughout the country to gather their input on how to revise the act, when the White Paper was released it was obvious these concerns had been ignored in favour of federal objectives. Rather than revise the act, the federal government proposed abolishing its historical relationship with Indigenous people by transferring responsibility to provincial governments. Although the *Indian Act* remains a controversial piece of legislation, Indigenous political leaders—notably through the AFN, the national organization representing First Nations interests in Canada—have often pointed out that the solution is not to abolish it but to revise it, with input from Indigenous people leading the way. Understandably, many First Nations, along with Inuit and Métis people, have expressed their dismay at the federal government's actions. This was summed up memorably in 1996, when the RCAP described the relationship between Indigenous people and the settler state as a "dialogue of the deaf" characterized by "vast differences in philosophy, perspective and aspirations."[10]

Indigenous authors, too, have criticized the enormous power wielded by the federal government through the *Indian Act*. Thomas King, for example, calls attention to the irony of a Canadian nationalism that boasts of "fair" treatment of Indigenous people by contrasting its history of bureaucratic management with American efforts to exterminate Indigenous people.[11] To be sure, south of the border it was far more common for militiamen to shoot or imprison Indigenous people if they impeded American settlement in any way. However, the Government of Canada has also endorsed physical violence, particularly when Indigenous people have asserted their rights or attempted to protect their lands from corporate takeovers. Indeed, the connection between Canadian and American practices has not escaped critique by Indigenous authors; as King wryly notes, "no need to send in the cavalry with guns blazing. Legislation will do just as nicely."[12] The process of colonization, whether through legislation or brute force, has always been violent and, in spite of Indigenous resistance, persists in Canada.[13]

Yet the state could not achieve its goals without the assistance of religious denominations, whose missionaries came in the seventeenth century with their Bibles and their beliefs in competition for new souls. Assumptions about Western cultural and religious superiority influenced how they saw and understood Indigenous ways of life and helped to legitimate colonial authority over Indigenous affairs. To the missionaries, Indigenous people were uncivilized heathens in need of moral and spiritual guidance. Opposition to their authority was interpreted as childish hedonism and reinforced religious beliefs that their work was an act of benevolence that Indigenous people would one day learn to appreciate. Missionaries did not generally question their own assumptions, seeing their ways as natural and right. They worked closely with government authorities to maintain their control over Indigenous people by influencing legal and bureaucratic channels and by promoting their views through everyday practices, whether they be articles written for journals and newspapers, the various societies they ran, or song and scripture.

Beginning in 1885, the federal government implemented a series of amendments to the *Indian Act* to put an end to Indigenous religious ceremonies because they were thought to be incompatible with Euro-Canadian Christian life. There was a widespread belief among government and church officials that if these ceremonies remained intact Indigenous people would never realize the spiritual benefits of Christianity or learn how to engage in productive labour. Armed with documents they produced to justify their actions, church and state officials attempted to replace traditional Indigenous practices, such as the Potlatch and Sundance ceremonies, with secular activities, relying on Euro-Canadian sports and games to help them accomplish this task.[14] Superintendent General of Indian Affairs David Laird clearly articulated the goal of civilization in his 1876 report to the Department of the Interior:

> Our Indian Legislation generally rests on the principle that the aboriginies are to be kept in a condition of tutelage and treated as wards or children of the State. The soundness of the principle I cannot admit. On the contrary, I am firmly persuaded that true interests of the aboriginies and of the State alike require that every effort should be made to aid the Red man in lifting himself out of his condition of tutelage and dependence, and that is clearly our wisdom and our duty, through education and every other means, to prepare him for a higher civilization by encouraging him to assume the privileges and responsibilities of full citizenship.[15]

For the process of cultural regulation to work, there had to be a reference point for assessing the difference between "savage" and "civilized" behaviours. Without such a point to mediate this understanding, attempts to civilize Indigenous people lacked meaning. Thus, Euro-Canadian sports and games provided a convenient standard with which to measure such behaviours.

At the local level, where missionaries and Indian agents attempted to carry out their directives, traditional Indigenous physical practices were discouraged as much as possible and replaced by secular sports and games. It was hoped that this process of cultural replacement and transformation would facilitate an understanding of Euro-Canadian sports and games as modern and appropriate and Indigenous physical practices as uncivilized and undesirable.[16] Within these repressive environments, sports days emerged as appropriate forms of social activities for Indigenous people and were often held in conjunction with national celebrations, such as Dominion Day, symbolically linking sports to Canadian citizenship and patriotism. Sports days also coincided

Inuit women's boot race on Sports Day, Wakeham Bay, NWT [Nunavut], c. June or July 1928. Source: Canada, Department of Transport, Library and Archives Canada, PA-127263.

with Euro-Canadian-style gatherings, such as stampedes, agricultural exhibitions and fairs, and government-approved community celebrations, suggesting that Euro-Canadian sports and games would help to usher Indigenous people into the twentieth century through hard work and patriotic play.

The extent to which these sports days replaced Indigenous ceremonies is not discussed extensively in the secondary source literature, though some evidence shows they took on more significance for Indigenous people after 1914, when off-reserve dancing was punishable by fine or imprisonment. As sports days offered a chance for Indigenous people to gather without raising the suspicions of local missionaries or Indian agents, they served a dual purpose. On the one hand, they were opportunities for Indigenous people to engage in friendly competition, a practice already well established among Indigenous people throughout the country. On the other hand, they were opportunities to host traditional religious ceremonies, as some people took advantage of these hectic and boisterous meetings to engage in their old-time practices. Daniel Kennedy, a Nakoda chief from Saskatchewan, recalls how his Elders used him as a spokesperson to convince government officials to host sports days and other Euro-Canadian celebrations so they could gather and engage in their own dances.[17] Many Indigenous people integrated Western sports and games into their everyday lives, and some did so to divert attention from continuing their traditional ceremonies.[18]

Rewards for participation were a prominent feature of sports days. Through this system of symbolic signification, government and religious authorities deliberately encouraged involvement in Euro-Canadian activities by publicly rewarding individuals who "adopted the dominant society's value system and lifestyle" while simultaneously repressing and thereby discouraging traditional physical practices.[19] For example, in 1917, the Indian agent for the Kainai reserve in southern Alberta recommended that a departmental grant be allocated for the purchase of prizes for fairs and sports meets—but for Euro-Canadian activities only.[20] Awards, whether cash prizes or medals, thus played a key role in recognizing and encouraging conformity with the dominant culture.

SCHOOLING BODIES

The most aggressive attempt to Christianize and civilize Indigenous people occurred through the Indian residential school system. In his detailed study of residential schools in Canada, J.R. Miller discusses the difference between education and schooling, noting how the two concepts are often mistaken as one and the same. According to Miller, education is a process that all cultures of the world possess, but not all cultures engage in schooling to educate their young.[21] The difference between these two practices is more than a matter of degree; it has to do with practices fundamental to creating and maintaining cultural stability.

Before Europeans settled in North America, Indigenous people received their education by learning how to survive on the land, and physical games and contests were central to this training. For example, the Dene and Athapaskan participated in a variety of games to develop strength, speed, flexibility, and endurance. Both men and women joined in activities that emphasized the gendered nature of their roles, which entailed different strenuous tasks. As one fur trader noted at Fort Resolution around 1800, "it is true the men have to undergo the fatigue of the chase, but still the women must carry the meat home."[22] The Inuit, whose traditional territory spans the most northerly reaches of the continent, competed in events— such as the knuckle hop, mouth pull, and ear lift—that developed the same skills as the Dene but with an emphasis on pain tolerance. This was meant to prepare them mentally and physically for the harsh realities of life on the land in an extreme climate.[23]

Traditional sports and games were also key sites for reinforcing social, political, economic, and spiritual aspects of life. For the Haudenosaunee, whose home extended along both sides of the St. Lawrence River and Lake Ontario, lacrosse was a means by which to cement social ties, physically prepare men for war, engage in economic relations, connect with the spiritual world, and have fun.[24] Although some activities, such as lacrosse, were connected to religious traditions, others, such as the Inuit ear lift, were not. Yet all physical activities were crucial for maintaining their practitioners' unique cultural identities and connection to the land while ensuring basic survival.

Changes came with the formal establishment of the Indian residential school system in the late nineteenth century. Missionaries had tried to establish schools in Eastern Canada as early as the seventeenth century, but their initiatives failed; there was little incentive for Indigenous people to alter their traditional ways since their knowledge of the land and its resources was still vital to their survival and provided a viable means for living. Religious authorities would have to wait another two hundred years before their visions for schooling were implemented, and this was achieved only after many Indigenous people, weakened by disease and starvation, acquiesced to federal demands to settle on reserves.[25] In some cases, Indigenous leaders asked for schooling so that their young would be adequately prepared for the massive changes taking place around them.[26] What they did not ask for was for their children to be taken far away and assimilated.

In 1860, responsibility for Indigenous-settler relations was transferred from the British Crown to the Province of Canada, and a new bureau focusing on Indian administration was established. In 1867, the new federal government, under the Department of Secretary of State, was given legislative responsibility for managing its relationship with Indigenous nations. Soon, an administrative team was charged with creating a national policy on Indigenous education and it drew on the services of the Roman Catholic, Anglican, Methodist, and Presbyterian Churches to implement its program. It was in this fashion that the two major institutions in Canada—the church and the state— came to dominate Indigenous life, pooling their human and financial resources to Christianize and civilize Indigenous children. For more than a hundred and fifteen years, beginning in 1880, when the Department of Indian Affairs was established and drafted the first policy on Indigenous education, to 1996, when the last government-run residential school closed its doors, more than 150,000 Indigenous youth received their education away from home and off the land.[27]

For the schooling to be effective, it had to be a lived experience.[28] Euro-Canadian sports and games were integral to the department's program of assimilation, a reality well understood by Indigenous people today. The 1996 *Report of the Royal Commission on Aboriginal Peoples* notes how the department used popular Euro-Canadian sports and games to help bring about fundamental changes in the values and behaviours of Indigenous students. It was thought that participation in Euro-Canadian activities would contribute to the breakdown of communal values by fostering a competitive spirit among pupils and that, hopefully, through regulated instruction, the skills that they learned would translate into a desire for individual achievement and wealth.[29] Canada was not alone in its focus on regulating student bodies.[30] In the United States, government policies influenced the development of physical education programs and competitive opportunities at Indian boarding schools, even though the rhetoric of assimilation contained contradictions, for sports and games helped to reinforce a collective sense of identity among Indigenous people throughout the country.[31]

Generally speaking, in Canada, federal priorities for Indigenous education shaped the sport and recreation activities offered at government-run schools. Two broad phases, differentiated by amendments made in 1951 to the *Indian Act*, characterized the federal approach to Indigenous education. The policy approach taken during each phase shaped the sport and recreation opportunities available at residential schools—from which many of the Tom Longboat Award winners came—especially between 1951 and 1972, the first administrative era of the awards. As federal policy on Indigenous education shifted, so did its emphasis on sports and games.

In the pre-1951 era, the primary responsibility for schooling of Indigenous youth fell to the churches. Left largely to their own devices, religious officials implemented curricula geared to their own practical and moral objectives. Financial support was provided by the federal government through a grant based upon the number of students enrolled in each school. The more students identified on the registry, the greater the amount of funding from Indian Affairs. The per capita grant system might have been a financially prudent decision in the eyes of bureaucrats in Ottawa, but in practice it led to fierce denominational rivalry among the different sects competing for students.[32] This rivalry, combined with the lack of a standard curriculum and the means to enforce it, meant that residential schools throughout this period were chronically underfunded, almost always in disrepair, poorly staffed, and lacking in qualified teachers.

During this era, physical activity programs were linked directly to biological health, in addition to concerns about assimilation. From the late 1800s to the late 1940s, waves of communicable diseases circulated through the schools, wreaking havoc on the bodies of Indigenous pupils, who were generally overworked, underfed, and emotionally exhausted, leaving them vulnerable to viruses and infections. This vulnerability was exacerbated by the terrible living conditions inside the schools, which had overcrowded rooms and poor air circulation. According to historian Mary-Ellen Kelm, the department's failure to improve the health of the pupils in the early half of the twentieth century contributed to the abolishment of the residential school system in later years.[33] As parents increasingly spoke out against the atrocities of residential schooling, the department had little choice but to address the high morbidity and mortality rates among students. The number of dead or ill was simply too high. A national survey completed in 1902 revealed that one-third of residential school graduates in Canada were known to be dead, while an additional one-third were unaccounted for, in poor health, or had "turned out badly."[34] One report from the Prairies, filed in 1907, found that at least one-quarter of the students had died of disease while on school rolls or shortly thereafter. Another study, completed at a residential school in British Columbia, found that 34 percent of the students admitted since 1892 were dead by 1909. Some families are reported to have lost all of their children at school during this era.[35] The introduction of physical activities was thus an efficient and cost-effective way to deal with the recurrent health issues in the schools.

Initially, calisthenic programs were used widely as part of the health curriculum. The Department of Indian Affairs introduced these exercises in 1910 in an effort to reduce the spread of pulmonary diseases among Indigenous pupils.[36] These exercises could be performed indoors when the weather was poor because they required relatively little space and no equipment, but instructors were encouraged to move outdoors whenever possible to capitalize on the fresh air. Indigenous bodies, once a symbol of strength and virility, were repositioned within the growing discourse on physical education as weak and diseased, justifying the need for proper and orderly instruction on how to regain vitality.

The introduction of calisthenic programs coincided with the use of military drills, also a common feature of the public school system because of funding through the Strathcona Trust.[37] The link between

Open air exercises at Mission Indian School (also known as St. Mary's Indian Residential School) under direction of provincial recreation instructors, Mission, British Columbia, December 1945. Source: Jack Long, National Film Board of Canada, Library and Archives Canada, PA-160943.

military training and nationalism was unmistakable since the drills were designed to replace tribal allegiance with a sense of patriotic duty.[38] Though military drills focused on the boys, both boys and girls were effected as military techniques were incorporated into their daily routines. For example, standing at soldier-like attention was the primary starting position for all calisthenic exercises advocated by Indian Affairs.[39] As well, pupils marched everywhere and lived according to bells and whistles that operated from morning to night. Even in the Far North, at the Hay River Mission School—located at the southern tip of Great Slave Lake in the Northwest Territories—Indigenous pupils, male and female, were trained in the military style.[40]

Popular recreational activities, such as baseball, basketball, hockey, and lacrosse, rounded out the regimen and provided students with some respite from the monotony of everyday life. These opportunities were few and far between and available mainly to boys. For the most part, students played among themselves, though from

Calisthenics at St. Eugene Mission (also known as Kootenay Indian Residential School), Cranbrook, British Columbia, c. 1950. Source: Western Archives and Special Collections, Western University, AFC 451, Jan Eisenhardt Fonds / Folder: AFC 451-S5-F14, [Photographs, Tours of Inspection] AFC 451-3/14 / File: Tour of Inspection.

time to time activities were organized with students from nearby residential schools or, less frequently, with non-Indigenous students from nearby towns and cities. These meetings usually occurred only on special occasions and were normally limited to sports days or national celebrations. Although most students seemed to enjoy these activities, it is clear that school instructors augmented their power by awarding or withholding recreational time. Sports and games were thus collateral for teaching obedience and adherence to school rules and educational objectives, as much as they were about training Indigenous students to adopt new values and behaviours. They were not a right but a reward for "good" behaviour. Pupils who disobeyed the rules or who fell into disfavour with instructors could have their recreational privileges taken away.[41]

The point about students enjoying sports and finding respite in these activities must be clarified since it is too easy to conclude that sports were positive elements of the schooling system, suggesting that the system and these institutions were not as bad as contemporary understandings make them out to be. As sociologist Andrew Woolford explains in his examination of the assimilative techniques used in the Indian residential school system, "visions of order—such as attempts to fit the Indigenous child within European society—are pursued and achieved by methods other than strict discipline."[42] In other words, repression alone is not enough to bring about fundamental change in a population; it must be coupled with enabling techniques that lure members of that population into managing their self-transformation. Woolford goes on to highlight the importance of "regulated desire" in this process: "Pleasure and excitement were deployed, and operated in conjunction with discipline, as techniques to co-facilitate Indigenous assimilation."[43] Therefore, attempts to understand the way in which Indigenous physical culture was being controlled, especially in the residential school system, should also consider the role of desire, as one augmented the other, forming a powerful effect that seduced students into embracing their metamorphosis. This helps to explain sport's complex role as the enabling agent in the residential school system, where "students were able to enjoy certain pleasures within a broader logic that nonetheless sought to re-make their identities."[44] This effect might also help to explain the ambivalence that former residential school students have expressed about their sporting experiences at these institutions and to illustrate why we should think of sports in residential schools not as simply a "good" or "bad" feature of the system, but as a "kind of education of the body" with profound consequences extending well beyond the playing fields.[45]

A poignant example of how "regulated desire" functioned in one residential school, as well as student responses to what was offered, is found in Basil Johnston's semi-autobiographical novel *Indian School Days*. Johnston recalls his youth at the Spanish Indian Residential School (later renamed Garnier), an all-male institution in northern Ontario. He describes how, in the late 1940s and early 1950s, the students were divided into four groups named after professional hockey teams—the Montreal Canadiens, the Toronto Maple Leafs, the New York Rangers, and the Chicago Black Hawks—and competed against each other in loosely organized events. The primary objective was to foster a competitive spirit among the students in the discharge of

Boys playing football with "Black Hawks" written on the ball. Spanish Indian Residential School, Spanish, Ontario, c. 1940s. Source: Shingwauk Residential Schools Centre, Algoma University.

their regular chores. If one member failed to live up to the expectations of the Jesuit instructors, then the entire team suffered for his negligence; the team that finished first was usually given a bit of free time. Interscholastic competition served a more dubious purpose at Spanish, since it was meant to exhaust the students, thus ensuring that any remaining energy would be spent on the playing fields rather than in an attempt to run away.[46]

Mass displays and sporting competitions also provided church and state representatives with opportunities to promote assimilation and to attract new students to the residential schools. In areas where there was more than one school, parents had some measure of control over where their children would be educated. Perhaps physical activity programs helped to sway their opinions. Images of young students moving in formation could evoke ideas about health and well-being and lend visible support to the ideological contention that the children were being mentally and physically prepared to meet the demands of the industrial labour force. Many families, however, had little or no input regarding where their children would be schooled, nor did they have much contact with their children during the school year. Thus, it is more likely that the military drills, mass gymnastic displays, and sports competitions were contrived to win public support for the federal government's agenda rather than to gain parental backing.

Euro-Canadian sports and games also reinforced dominant assumptions about appropriate male and female sporting behaviour. As was the case in the public school system, Indigenous boys and girls were channelled into gender-appropriate activities.[47] Male students were provided with opportunities to participate in vigorous activities that were thought to develop manly character, while female students were encouraged to participate in gentle, healthful exercises deemed appropriate for young women, even though they were required to demonstrate incredible strength and stamina as the housekeepers of entire institutions. Opportunities for female students to engage in competitions or to participate in traditionally male-dominated sports were rare. For instance, in the early 1900s at the Mohawk Institute in Brantford, Ontario, female students played ice hockey in their recreational time. According to Martha Hill, a former student of the school, the girls were "a little clumsy" in getting the puck to "go right" on the ice.[48] Generally, however, memories of this aspect of residential school life are not as vivid among female students compared with male students, and in many cases they were not recorded at all. One arid description reads: "Boring, that's what play time was. Some play. We couldn't do nothing. Dolls, knitting, things like that, but not playing, not like the boys. They had balls, bats, hockey sticks, everything. Sundays were the worst. I hated Sundays. We couldn't even work on Sundays. Just sat in the playroom or went out on those awful walks."[49] Such gendered distinctions were also built into the use of space, with boys and girls segregated during leisure and recreation time, including on school grounds. Rarely were boys and girls allowed to interact; this separation was bridged only on special occasions, such as sports days or national celebrations, which always took place under the surveillance of their instructors.

The post-1951 era saw a shift in the balance of power between church and state, with Indian Affairs taking on more responsibility for government-run residential schools. Three key factors precipitated this move. First, the churches were interested more in converting Indigenous youth than in providing them with vocational training, such that government intervention was deemed necessary if the youth were ever to become productive members of society. Second, increasing public awareness of the deplorable conditions in the schools gave credence to Indigenous demands for better care and education. Third, the schools were to follow provincial curricula, which, in 1951, included training in physical education. These factors led Indian Affairs to take over the hiring of teachers and replace unqualified missionary instructors with professionally trained instructors who could implement provincial curricula, and to substitute the per capita grant with a global funding structure, though strict criteria prevented many school administrators from accessing those funds.[50] In spite of these improvements, the government was still unwilling to make serious investments in Indigenous education and increasingly looked toward the public school system to achieve integration.

Girls at Kenora Indian Residential School, Kenora, Ontario, c. 1950. Source: Western Archives and Special Collections, Western University, AFC 451, Jan Eisenhardt Fonds / Folder: AFC 451-S5-F35, Kenora, R.S. (RC), AFC 451-3/31 / File: AFC 451-S5-F35.

Sports teams at Brandon Indian Residential School, Brandon, Manitoba, c. 1936 (front row: football team; second row: girl's softball team; back row: winners in the National Athletic Meet, 1935). Source: The United Church of Canada Archives, Prairie to Pine Region, Indian Residential Schools Collection, 1936 Brandon Indian Residential School Yearbook.

Athletic competitions became a more pronounced feature of residential schools during this era as federal officials believed that athletic contests would help to facilitate integration, and they encouraged school staff to promote participation, especially in team sports. The in-house league at Spanish that Johnston describes in *Indian School Days* was expanded in the 1950s to include competitions against local white teams in a range of sports, including softball, baseball, touch football, boxing, basketball, and hockey.[51] In Alberta, Blue Quills held its first all-Indigenous track and field meet in 1961, presenting the first opportunity for its students to develop contacts with students at other residential schools.[52] Some institutions developed outstanding athletic programs, and a number of students who honed their athletic skills in the residential school system later moved on to professional sports careers or competed successfully in elite-level amateur sports. Yet, even when the global funding system replaced the per capita grant system, funding for sport and recreation remained scarce, and normally only those institutions situated a reasonable distance from other residential schools or urban centres, and managed by sports-minded teachers and administrators, engaged in regular competitive play.

During this era, competitive sporting events replaced the mass displays and military drills as the best way to promote the schools and their students and to facilitate integration. This competitive ethos furnished these meetings with signifying power so that contests between Indigenous and non-Indigenous teams were more than just fun and games—they were highly racialized events.[53] In the words of historian John Bloom, "not only did winning teams spread a school's name but they also provided an easily interpreted set of representations that fit well with the boarding-school agenda."[54]

With the development of a competitive ethos in the school system, winning took on an increased significance as athletic competitions became the arena in which ideas about race, ethnicity, class, and gender were contested on a regular basis. Students as well as their instructors placed a high premium on successful teams and athletes, especially when competing in explicitly racialized contests of "Indians" versus "whites." For many Indigenous youth, athletic competitions were also one of the few areas of life in which they could derive some pleasure and foster a sense of pride. Sometimes the contests were one-sided affairs. Male athletes at Spanish, for example, repeatedly had their clothes and bodies "patched up" and sent back onto the playing field to finish matches against older and stronger white teams. In *Indian School Days*, Johnston recalls one particularly memorable game of touch football played against a group of senior high school students from the nearby town of Espanola, Ontario. His remembrance not only highlights the importance of winning but also suggests the heightened sense of masculinity and racial identification that students might have felt in a competitive atmosphere: "If we were expected to risk cuts, gashes, lacerations, bruises, welts and maybe even broken bones while clinging to Jack Major or oversized backs, we preferred to maintain some style and respectability while doing so."[55] If Johnston and his teammates could not win against the white teams, then losing with their dignity intact was the next best thing.

In the logic of competitive sports and games, medals and awards became an important means through which to articulate and reinforce a narrative of progress among Indigenous people. Winning athletes came to symbolize the best that the race had to offer, with male athletes emerging as the symbolic leaders of the residential school era.[56] Female athletes, in contrast, were generally relegated to non-competitive events or participated in contests in which the social aspect outweighed the value of competition. Although most references to athletes do not specify whether they are male or female, it is clear from the mention of boisterous and competitive sports in government documents and newspaper reports that the term "athlete" almost always refers to a male student. The contrast in treatment resulting from this differential status could be dramatic. As Tsianina Lomawaima points out in her study of the Chilocco Indian School in northeast Oklahoma, "athletes" stood as a signifier for males who were "universally respected" by their peers and administrators.[57] In contrast, female students had to earn respect through other means since they were not considered to be proper athletes deserving of widespread admiration.

The overwhelming emphasis on competitive sports meant that male athletes received the majority of the limited financial support for equipment, coaching, and travel provided by Indian Affairs. For boys, being on a sports team meant other privileges as well. The most significant advantage was time away from school, but fringe benefits could also entail better food and accommodation. Yet students understood at some level the limits of these benefits of being an athlete. Time away and better food were one thing; changing the culture of schooling was another—a point clearly articulated by a female student at Kamloops Indian Residential School: "You won prizes and wondered why the hell you even bothered to go because when you got back it was still the same way."[58]

INTEGRATION INTO ORGANIZED SPORT

The mainstream sport system in Canada developed in tandem with the emergence of the modern state. Ideas about the nation— who belonged and under what conditions—were thus linked with sport. As a product of white upper- and middle-class interests, organized sport was structured by and reinforced colonial understandings of Indigenous-settler relations in Canada. While some Indigenous athletes, such as Tom Longboat, achieved remarkable success in sports, their success was nevertheless enveloped in a system that stereotyped, devalued, and marginalized their involvement and accomplishments, sending strong messages about the role of Indigenous people in both sport and Canadian society writ large.

For instance, in the nineteenth century, organizers of sporting events often restricted Indigenous involvement or joined media in ridiculing Indigenous participants. Sports leaders, assuming that Indigenous athletes possessed natural athletic abilities, channelled participants into segregated "Indian" events in order to preserve and protect their ideas about white social, cultural, and athletic superiority. This was evident in early nineteenth-century Montreal, where it was generally understood among local snowshoeing clubs that Indigenous athletes were not allowed to compete in organized events against white athletes. The prestigious Montreal Snow Shoe Club later challenged this informal ruling by allowing Indigenous people to compete under its name; however, as historian Don Morrow points out, the club made this unprecedented move only because its members wanted to reclaim their elite racing status.[59] Even though Indigenous athletes were subsequently allowed to compete against white athletes in club-sponsored events, the fact remained that "no Indian was ever allowed or even considered for membership" during the years when snowshoe clubs dominated the local sporting landscape.[60]

In the latter half of the nineteenth century, sport organizers in Central and Eastern Canada attempted to restrict their competitions to participants of gentlemanly status by codifying the concept of an "amateur" athlete. Originally, an amateur was a gentleman of the leisured class who had the time and money to travel and compete. With the emergence of a strong middle-class presence in sport, the concept of amateurism took on explicitly classist and racist dimensions as organizers sought to define their distinctiveness from what they believed were less desirable elements of society. Manual labourers and "Indians" were the primary targets of these restrictions since their physicality was thought to provide them with an unfair advantage in competition. When Indigenous athletes were allowed to compete alongside their white counterparts, measures were taken to ensure that their difference was publicly known. In foot racing, for instance, organizers often wrote the word "Indian" beside the anglicized name in the posted entries to warn white athletes of an unfair advantage in the race.[61] The fact that many Indigenous athletes also played for pay was thought to degrade the character-building qualities that amateur sport supposedly provided, and mainstream organizations took steps to restrict their participation. This move was typified by organizations like the Montreal Pedestrian Club, whose 1873 bylaws and constitution formally excluded "labourers" and "Indians" from its competitions.[62] In 1880, the National Amateur Lacrosse Association implemented similar restrictions in an effort to ensure that the sport—itself appropriated from the Haudenosaunee—remained a closed space in which middle- and upper-class men could engage in their gentlemanly pursuits without having to engage with the Haudenosaunee or any other Indigenous people.[63]

The emergence of a competitive ethos at the turn of the twentieth century provided some incentive for the owners of sports clubs to hire Indigenous players as ringers to help build winning teams. However, sports leaders held the power to decide how and when to involve them, usually basing their decision on the need for gate receipts to fund travel and competitions. This meant that Indigenous athletes were allowed to participate at the discretion of organizers because of their exotic appeal, the latter knowing full well that spectators would pay to see Indian and "white" athletes compete against one another. Even the sporting experiences of well-known Indigenous athletes, including the superstar Longboat, were understood and framed differently from those of mainstream athletes. The former were never allowed to forget that they were Indigenous and therefore different from and subordinate to the people against whom they were competing.

Contrasting images of "savagery" and "civilization" were a regular feature of the early Canadian sports landscape. Often, when opportunities to participate in white-sponsored events arose, Indigenous athletes were relegated to events in which they were cast as spectacles for white crowds. Returning to snowshoeing, for example, Indigenous athletes often competed for cash prizes in novelty events, such as toboggan and what were oddly called "potato" races, that emphasized white assumptions about Indigenous social and cultural inferiority.[64] This process of "inclusion by derogation" also occurred during the Klondike Gold Rush at Dawson City, Yukon, where the Gwitch'in and Han were completely excluded from the field of sport except for special events in which they were allowed to enter sometimes as clowns but more often as participants in pie- and bun-eating contests.[65] As in nineteenth-century Montreal, these special Klondike events were for Indigenous participants only.

Over time, these contrasting images and the messages they conveyed became naturalized as the standard by which "civilized" individuals were measured, with far-reaching implications for Indigenous and settler identities.[66] In nineteenth-century Montreal, for instance, this contrasting ideology was codified and standardized through the rules for play in lacrosse. The leaders of the Montreal Lacrosse Club, led by George Beers, not only constructed rules that privileged their preferred playing habits but also restricted Indigenous styles of play, thus formalizing their advantage by endorsing what was civilized and proper and attacking what they believed was dishonest and unruly.[67] Additionally, they had the human and financial capital to support and enforce their vision for sport, thus transforming one way of playing—their way of playing—into the most legitimate way of playing. Indigenous people were largely absent from these decision-making processes.

Sport—and more broadly ideas about appropriate physical culture—have always been wrapped up in efforts to conquer new lands, whether in Canada or elsewhere. European missionaries, government agents, and settlers, particularly those from the British Empire, have a long track record of attempting to bring Indigenous people under control by constraining and regulating their physical movements.[68] These newcomers were intrigued by Indigenous people's strength, speed, agility, and endurance as much as they were appalled and even threatened by what Indigenous physicality signified: independence, sovereignty, difference—all of which had to be repressed if the British were to succeed at establishing their authority in the colonies.

Conversion strategies included the development of small parcels of land called "reserves" that Indigenous people were to live on; the pass system, which was a form of surveillance that restricted who could leave the reserve and for what reasons; legislation that prohibited Indigenous people from practising their traditional spiritual ceremonies, some of which were extremely physically demanding; and residential schools, where students were taught new ways of moving their bodies, rendering their physicality more familiar and less intimidating to settlers. The history of sport and physical activity in Canada, therefore, is not a history of empowerment or inclusion, or even of opportunity, accommodation, or amalgamation. Rather, it is a history of containment, control, and elimination.

Indigenous people did not passively accept these physical interventions. As Malcolm MacLean explains in his thoughtful analysis of the cultural politics of sports and physical activities, adoption is the not the same as adaptation, especially in colonial contexts where there is a growing recognition among scholars of the fascinating ways Indigenous people have exerted and continue to exert their agency in sport to carve out meaningful spaces for themselves.[69] The growing number of articles, chapters, and books that look at sports and physical activities from Indigenous points of view is an example of this trend.[70] Generally, these authors try to tease out examples of Indigenous resistance to colonizing body practices using existing historical materials (e.g., archival documents), or to construct examples through new data collection and analysis (as with oral histories), to show how Indigenous people have taken up the colonizer's games to reinforce, rather than break down, Indigenous ways of life. MacLean's creative application of Homi K. Bhabha's term "sly civility" is useful here since it refers to "the intentional modification or distortion of the colonizers' rules and practices in a form of parody to subvert and destabilize the power/knowledge relations of colonialism."[71] In other words, many Indigenous people purposefully integrated these new practices into their rapidly changing lives (and continue to do so), adapting them as best as they can to meet their aspirations and needs. The challenge for researchers is to interpret their evidence properly so as not to mistake adaptation for adoption. Not unlike the colonizers who, when they see Indigenous people engaged in colonial activities, only ever see "imitation and an aspiration to be or be like the British, or French, or German, or Chinese, or Muscovite/of Rus, or whatever group the dominant may be," authors who approach their work through a lens of Indigenous resistance are equally at risk of misinterpreting what they see, read, and hear.[72]

For the colonizers, getting Indigenous people to imitate British physical movements provided them with a sense of comfort since it not only rendered Indigenous movements knowable but also presented an opportunity to realign Indigenous values with their own, which in their estimation would make Indigenous people easier to govern.[73] Importantly, it also presented colonizers with an opportunity to evaluate their sense of moral, cultural, and physical superiority relative to Indigenous people, whose own histories of progress (or perceived lack thereof) could be recorded, tracked, measured, displayed, and discussed in ways that buttressed the colonial imagination. In short, physical culture was a crucial element of regulating Indigenous populations and of constructing and maintaining the unequal power relations that underpinned the nation-state.

---

* This chapter draws on previously published material from "The Indian Act and the (Re)Shaping of Canadian Aboriginal Sport Practices," 2007; "Bodies of Meaning," 2013; and "Make the Indian Understand His Place," 2015.

CHAPTER 2

ESTABLISHING THE
TOM LONGBOAT AWARDS,
1951–72

y the late 1940s, a number of factors led Indian Affairs to think
seriously about the role of sports and games in its broader plan
for Indigenous assimilation. Among them was the passing of
the *National Physical Fitness Act* in 1943, which aimed to spur
the nation to greater health. Then, in 1945, the Department of
National Health and Welfare was created in order to improve the
health of all Canadians; physical fitness was seen as a cornerstone
of that goal. The new department was given responsibility for the
Indian Health Services Directorate, as well, with the result that
physical fitness also became a prominent talking point at Indian
Affairs.

Along with these changes came another discussion at Indian
Affairs in the mid-1940s: how to channel Indigenous political organizing into socially appropriate pursuits, the aim being to fracture
the Indigenous rights movement in Canada.[1] In 1946, in a rare
effort to consult with front-line workers, the minister in charge
of Indian Affairs invited Indian agents to comment "directly

and confidentially" to him on how to diffuse the growing tide of Indigenous activism throughout the country.[2] The top three recommendations that field agents put forward were for more education, the development of sports and sports clubs, especially in the day and residential schools, and increased contact with whites—in that order, though all were considered intertwined and were discussed that way.[3] Such was the response from Gifford Swartman, Indian agent for the Sioux Lookout region: "Athletic and other forms of recreation should also be encouraged—this should be stressed more in the Schools than it has been, in order that young people could carry the ideas back to their respective reserves."[4] This would reinforce the already popular assumption about the ameliorative and civilizing effects of organized sports and games, especially the amateur kind.[5]

Finally, between 1948 and 1950, responsibility for Indian Affairs was transferred to the Department of Citizenship and Immigration, which prepared people for settlement by teaching them the values and behaviours desired in Canadians. The assimilationist goals pursued by Indian Affairs dovetailed nicely with Citizen and Immigration's mandate to educate, train, and integrate newcomers into the broader fabric of national life.

Here was a perfect policy storm waiting to centre its attention on Indigenous sport and recreation: Euro-Canadian physical activities would be used to address the government's concern about physical fitness and health among Indigenous people while simultaneously facilitating their assimilation into mainstream society. Taking these broader factors into account, in 1949 Indian Affairs created a new position, that of supervisor of physical education and recreation. Within this larger context, the Tom Longboat Awards came to play a small but important role in achieving federal objectives.

JAN EISENHARDT AND INDIAN AFFAIRS, 1950–1

Putting into practice a national program of physical education and recreation required another staff person at Indian Affairs, someone sensitive to Indigenous political issues.[6] This delicate matter was

THE PUBLIC SERVICE OF CANADA

FOR THE
INDIAN AFFAIRS BRANCH
DEPARTMENT OF MINES AND RESOURCES
AT OTTAWA

A SUPERVISOR OF PHYSICAL EDUCATION AND RECREATION
(Administrative Officer, Grade 2)

$3,360 - $4,080

Application forms should be filed with the
CIVIL SERVICE COMMISSION, OTTAWA not later than ⟩ **April 16, 1949**

DUTIES

Under direction, to be responsible for carrying out a program of physical education and recreation on Indian Reserves and in Indian Day and Residential Schools throughout ° Canada; to conduct courses in physical education and recreation for field officials of the Indian Affairs Branch and teachers of Indian Schools; to co-operate with provincial authorities in joint programs of physical education and recreation; to deal with correspondence and to prepare reports; to make recommendations leading to improvement in the efficiency of existing physical education and recreation activities among the Indian population; and to perform other related duties as required.

QUALIFICATIONS

Graduation from a university of recognized standing with a Bachelor's degree in Health and Physical Education; knowledge of modern teaching methods and physical education and at least five years' experience in physical education and allied fields; knowledge of and experience in corrective physical education; ability to instruct and supervise the work of others; ability to prepare reports and recommendations and to deal with official correspondence; personal suitability; satisfactory physical condition.

NOTE

Except in the case of persons entitled to the preference for war service, preference in appointment will be given to qualified candidates who are not over forty years of age on the closing date for the receipt of applications.

Competition number - 49-4669 - should be quoted.

Ottawa, March 23, 1949   List 1679

READ CAREFULLY THE POSTER "INFORMATION ESSENTIAL FOR APPLICANTS"
NOTE WHICH I… …ED WHEREVER THIS ANNOUNCEMENT IS DISPLAYED…

1949 job advertisement for Supervisor of Physical Education and Recreation, Indian Affairs. Source: Library and Archives Canada, J. Eisenhardt, (gr. 2), Education Division, Resigned CCI-IAH-3059 / RG 32, Vol. 1408.

tied to the long-term relationship between Indian Affairs and the various religious orders whose job it was to carry out the day-to-day operations of the schools. In the 1940s, the churches still maintained a significant amount of control over the education pupils received, though their influence dwindled through the 1950s as the federal government assumed greater control of the schools, especially with the hiring of university-trained teachers who could implement provincial curricula. Indian Affairs was aware of the need to consider its relationship with the churches and proceeded with caution. In 1949, Superintendent of Education Bernard Neary described the situation in the following terms:

> This newly created position in our Branch will require a man of considerable tact and diplomacy. While our Indian day schools are operated directly by the Department, the residential schools are operated for the Department by various religious denominations. Therefore, in introducing a program of physical education and recreation, we require a supervisor who can bring in new ideas without creating resentment and ill feeling.[7]

Neary's heavy emphasis on the schools was an early indication that the primary target group was Indigenous youth. Under the watchful eyes of their instructors, students would be taught new ways of moving their bodies and behaving in public without parental interference. Furthermore, because health conditions in the schools continued to be a key issue for the government, there was a heavy emphasis on remedial physical training and health education.[8]

In February 1950, Jan Eisenhardt was hired as the supervisor of physical education and recreation.[9] This was the first position of its kind at Indian Affairs, and it marked the formal beginning of direct federal involvement in Indigenous sport and recreation development in Canada.[10] Eisenhardt, accustomed to taking on pioneering roles, applied for the position because he was, in his words, "attracted by the challenge of the work."[11] With almost twenty years of administrative experience in physical fitness, he played a strategic role in shaping the new curriculum at Indian Affairs.

Eisenhardt had gained much of his experience as a physical educator during the Depression, when he worked as the director of parks in Vancouver, and later, from 1934 to 1941, as the director of a province-wide physical activity program in British Columbia called Pro-Rec, where he helped raise the morale of thousands of

Jan Eisenhardt, Supervisor of Physical Education and Recreation, Indian Affairs, c. 1950. Source: Western Archives and Special Collections, Western University, AFC 451, Jan Eisenhardt Fonds / Folder: AFC 451-S5-F4, Photos, Indian Affairs, AFC 451-3/4 / File: Pro-Rec, Tour of Inspections.

unemployed and working-class men and women by organizing publicly run sport and recreation programs.[12] In the early 1940s, some of these services were extended to residential schools throughout British Columbia; this included the program established in 1941 at St. Mary's Indian Residential School at Mission City and the program initiated at the Squamish Indian Residential School in North Vancouver.[13] It was through these outreach programs that Eisenhardt was introduced to the residential school system and developed his ideas about the problems and possibilities of establishing a broad program of physical education and recreation for Indigenous youth in Canada.

Owing to the lack of information on the relationship between Pro-Rec and residential schools, it is impossible to adequately address the range of issues that undoubtedly arose from this type of intercultural contact. Even Barbara Schrodt, in her meticulous history of Pro-Rec, overlooks residential schools as a critical site for analysis. This omission is significant given that Schrodt describes the schools as "special" outreach projects, a label that places them on the periphery of the public recreation movement in British Columbia. Nor does she make clear why Pro-Rec services were extended to special populations in the early 1940s, almost six years after the program was founded. One possible motive might have been to increase enrolment in Pro-Rec to maintain government funding since the war effort had drastically reduced its membership, especially among young men.[14] If Pro-Rec extended its services to residential schools in the 1940s to keep its funding, then Indigenous youth were hardly marginal to the program, even though their status as special populations might have resulted in such an understanding. Nevertheless, it is clear from the field reports filed by Eisenhardt that Pro-Rec was still providing services to various residential schools throughout British Columbia in the 1950s and that a wide range of school staff embraced these initiatives. At the Squamish Indian Residential School, for example, even the female members of the order celebrated student victories in the manly sport of boxing, a popular Pro-Rec activity encouraged among boys.[15]

The mass displays used by Pro-Rec to sell its programs to the public were also used at residential schools. The subtexts of these displays were unmistakable, as strong Christian ideals about race, civility, and citizenship were meshed together in a living tableaux. In June 1951, after watching a mass display hosted by Indigenous pupils from the Kamloops Indian Residential School, one male spectator, George Beete, was so moved that he wrote to the head-master of the school, Reverend O'Grady, to congratulate him for the good work that he was doing with the students:

> I was down at the park and viewed the whole of the display from the standpoint of a long experience in watching and enjoying any spectacle where the results of training are put before the critical eye of the public and I assure you that of all the people I have interviewed not one but has agreed with me that if all our young people were trained by the same method where learn-ing walks side by side with decorum and good behavior, where Christian precepts are imparted, we would have no more of hoodlums and gangs....I am not speaking of that physical training so necessary to develop the body, I am only referring to the minds you are so painstak-ingly molding and shaping so that they can take their place in society as real men and women trained in all those branches of learning which will form the neces-sary attributes to that future welfare.[16]

For many spectators, young Indigenous bodies moving in for-mation reinforced the widespread belief that religious instruction combined with schooling would instill in Canada's youth respect for discipline and deference to authority.[17] To attain self-improvement, Indigenous students were subjected to regimented physical train-ing programs that were quite distinct from their own cultural traditions, as they were intended to inculcate patriotic values and to instruct male and female students in Euro-Canadian under-standings of masculine and feminine behaviours. Furthermore, when prevailing attitudes toward Indigenous people are considered, the idea of self-improvement is linked directly to notions of racial uplift. A successful curriculum would help Indigenous students rise above their race and assume positions in the labour force, as well as entice them to give up their Indian Status, thus whittling away the Indigenous population in Canada by instilling a deep appreciation for dominant mainstream cultural practices and values. For Indigenous boys at least, these lessons could be imparted through an organized structure of competitive sports and games.

In 1941, Eisenhardt left his position at Pro-Rec to take the position of officer of the Canadian Army Sports Program, and he was soon seconded to the Department of National Health and Welfare to become Canada's first national director of physical fitness. He then worked briefly with UNESCO in Paris before applying for the position of supervisor of physical education and recreation at Indian Affairs. Thus, by the late 1940s, Eisenhardt had a tremendous wealth of knowledge and experience as a physical educator and was well acquainted with government bureaucracy. He brought this familiarity and knowledge to Indian Affairs in 1950.

Eisenhardt's principal duties as supervisor included developing and implementing a comprehensive program of physical education and recreation for students in day and residential schools and for people on reserves, conducting courses in physical education and recreation for field agents and teachers of the schools, and co-operating with provincial authorities in joint programs of physical education and recreation.[18] Within his first few weeks on the job, Eisenhardt became responsible for consulting people in the day and residential schools and on reserves about the establishment of the program.[19] This consultation took the form of a detailed survey that he conducted from April to October 1950.

In March, prior to engaging in his consultative fieldwork, the *Brantford Expositor* ran a story on the outcomes that Eisenhardt envisioned for the program; it quoted him as saying that "the Indian himself will be encouraged to run his own show and it is our intention to allow as far as possible...the Indian to personally direct his own activities."[20] A similar and much lengthier story titled "Inaugurate New Deal for Canadian Indians" was printed in Ottawa's *Evening Citizen*. With eight pictures spanning the top of the page, it opened with a promising statement: "Canada's new deal for her Indian Canadians has begun. And the Indians are receiving the plan with acclaim."[21]

Although Indigenous people might have been looking forward to the changes, Eisenhardt's superiors at Indian Affairs were not. In a personal memorandum to Eisenhardt, Superintendent Neary explained the dilemma using direct language:

> You can understand that both this [the *Brantford Expositor*] release and the *Citizen* release leave the impression that major changes are being planned in Indian education under your supervision. Considerable misunderstanding is likely to arise from such releases and objections are likely to be registered by our field officials, teachers and the religious denominations concerned in this work. Many people have devoted valuable years of their lives to educating the Indians and they will naturally not be too pleased with the tone of these press stories.[22]

Neary's point was that school and church leaders would be upset with the "new deal" because it suggested a massive influx of new dollars for sports and games when other policy and program areas, such as education, would not receive the same attention. It also suggested that the new program of physical education was going to empower Indigenous people to regain control of their lives and free themselves from tutelage, thereby undoing decades of work led by the government and churches. From then on, Eisenhardt was directed to submit all press releases in writing and could publish them only with prior approval from the director's office.[23] He was off to an inauspicious start.

For his fieldwork, Eisenhardt visited thirty-two residential schools, twenty-one day schools, and twenty reserves in Quebec, Ontario, Saskatchewan, Alberta, and British Columbia. He surveyed the types of sport and recreation available and for whom, and he documented the facilities and equipment used in each area. In addition to creating an inventory of activities and facilities, Eisenhardt reported on the general health, hygiene, clothing, and sanitation in each school, emphasizing the remedial elements of official intentions, a common concern in the public school system as well.

His reports show that neither the religious denominations nor Indian Affairs devoted much attention to this aspect of Indigenous administration prior to 1950. In terms of outdoor amenities, most schools lacked basic playground equipment such as swings and teeter-totters. Space and equipment for relatively inexpensive sports such as softball, volleyball, and basketball, and jumping pits for track and field, were also almost non-existent. One exception was outdoor hockey, which emerged as one of the most popular activities among Indigenous boys in the early twentieth century. Still, most schools lacked the necessary hockey equipment for students to engage in competitive play.

Boys hockey at Fort Frances (also known as St. Margaret's) Indian Residential School, Fort Frances, Ontario, c. 1950. Source: Western Archives and Special Collections, Western University, AFC 451, Jan Eisenhardt Fonds / Folder: AFC 451-S5-F14 [Photographs, Tours of Inspection]. AFC 451-3/14 / File: Wikwemikong, Shingwauk, Caughaugaga, Fort Frances, Kootenay.

Indoor facilities at the schools were not much better. Where gym space existed, it was often too small to accommodate team sports. Some schools used basement halls for recreation. Others made use of dining rooms. Even then most institutions were poorly equipped for indoor games, a problem compounded by the fact that most teachers either lacked the training, experience, and imagination to implement a physical education program or were not interested in leading one at all. To make matters worse, poor air circulation inside most schools detracted from the health benefits that physical activities were expected to provide. In his final assessment of both residential and day schools, Eisenhardt identified only three as having "good" indoor facilities: Kamloops (British Columbia), Lebret (Saskatchewan), and Spanish (Ontario). Nine schools were given a "fair" rating: St. Mary's Mission, Alberni, and Squamish (British Columbia); Blood, Grouard, and Joussard (Alberta); Shingwauk and Fort Francis (Ontario); and Brandon (Manitoba).[24]

In spite of these limitations, some schools excelled at competitive sports and games. For example, in 1949 a team from Duck Lake Indian Residential School won the Saskatchewan Midget Hockey Championship. Father Roussel, who served as director of sports for the school, coached the Duck Lake team.[25] Also that year a team from Spanish Indian Residential School won the Algoma-Manitoulin-area hockey championship, one of the stronger regional divisions belonging to the Ontario Secondary Schools Hockey Association.[26] Although these victories demonstrate that a few institutions offered active programs with good coaching—at least in the sport of hockey—most schools lacked the facilities, equipment, and leadership to provide competitive opportunities. In Eisenhardt's estimation, however, the lack of competitive opportunities was not the main problem since it constituted only one small part of his overall strategy. Although he agreed that competitive sports undoubtedly benefitted participants, "they only affected a small number of children, one or two teams (we find exceptions in schools where house leagues are conducted) and in almost all cases, the girls are neglected."[27] A broad program that encompassed appropriate physical training for Indigenous boys and girls was needed.

The situation on reserves was similar to the environment in the schools. Opportunities varied widely and were shaped by proximity to major urban centres as well as existing knowledge, experience, and dedication in the community for developing and implementing sport and recreation programs. In Wikwemikong, Ontario, for example, where there was much enthusiasm for hockey, community members accessed $30,000 in band funds and relied on volunteer labour to build an indoor arena. (It was one of the few indoor arenas known to exist on a reserve in 1950.) The local press in Sudbury, Ontario, nearly two hundred kilometres away, reported on this infrastructure: "The people of Wikwemikong Indian reserve have demonstrated to their 'progressive' white brethren that a united volunteer effort is still the best way to get things accomplished in a community."[28] Even in remote areas such as Kitamaat, British Columbia, located about 110 kilometres southeast of Prince Rupert, community members built a $40,000 recreation centre with the main facility reserved for basketball. Periodically, trained coaches were brought in from cities to prepare teams for inter-reserve competitions, which had been taking place annually among Kitamaat, Bella Coola, Nass River, and other small communities for some years. The athletic competitions fostered a spirited battle in facility construction among Indigenous people on the West Coast; as Eisenhardt noted, "other communities also have community centres varying in size but there is quite a rivalry in regard to the building of a centre better than the one in the next village."[29] The examples at Wikwemikong and Kitamaat demonstrate that some communities had incorporated mainstream sports and games into their cultural frameworks and devoted significant financial resources to the development of modern recreation facilities.

In terms of organized activities on reserves, for most communities the annual sports day was the social highlight of the year. It was generally a one- or two-day event that attracted hundreds of participants and spectators from the host reserve and neighbouring areas. In Cowichan, British Columbia, for example, nearly eight hundred people attended the field day competitions in 1950. The festivities included races for all ages, ranging from the seventy-five-yard dash to the mile-long run, softball and soccer games, "comical" contests, and a bone game.[30]

For many Indigenous people, annual sports days were strictly social affairs, a focus that precluded the need for physical training throughout the year. But the poor performances that inevitably resulted concerned Eisenhardt and reinforced his belief in the need for a systematic approach to sports and games that would involve the whole community. His standard response was to recommend that a recreation leader be hired to coordinate activities on a reserve so that its residents would be involved in physical training throughout the year. Such was the advice given to the residents of Alert Bay, British Columbia, where it was proposed that a recreation director would "give this community a real uplift as the Indians here are not alone interested in better living but can contribute themselves towards the cost of a recreational program."[31]

Just below the surface of these discussions was an idea of racial progress that linked the development of modern facilities, the provision of recreation services, and athletic achievement to ideas about civilization. Indian Affairs interpreted Indigenous interest in organized sports and games and facility construction as evidence of a

Soccer at Alert Bay, British Columbia, c. 1950. Source: Western Archives and Special Collections, Western University, AFC 451, Jan Eisenhardt Fonds / Folder: AFC 451-S5-F9, Reports on Schools and Reserves, April 16-May 25, AFC 451-3/9 / File: 6.

progressive attitude. That Indian Affairs provided less than adequate funding through its per-capita grant system to support the development of sport and recreation programs on reserves was beside the point.[32] The $30,000 facility at Wikwemikong, for example, demonstrated to Eisenhardt that it was one of the most "advanced and progressive" Indigenous communities that he had seen to date.[33]

Successful sports teams were another way for Indian Affairs to measure Indigenous progress. The outcomes of competitive sports events were often mentioned together with the working conditions, building projects, and school enrolment in each region in the annual reports for Indian Affairs. For example, in the early 1950s, government agents in Eastern Canada showed a particular enthusiasm for Indigenous achievements in baseball and hockey. The 1953 report for Nova Scotia gives a sombre description of the employment opportunities for Indigenous people on reserves, which is followed immediately by an upbeat and detailed account of a local hockey tournament:

> For a reserve so small, Lennox Island does well athletically. Their baseball team is among the best locally and in hockey they reached the intermediate finals for Prince County. By outscoring Eskasoni 10-6 in a two-game total goal series held at North Sydney, N.S., they clinched the Indian hockey championship of Nova Scotia, Prince Edward Island region. This series was watched by more than 1,500 people.[34]

Perhaps living conditions in the East were so poor that Indian agents felt compelled to record any evidence of positive development.

The problem with the notion of progress was that it led to a false dichotomy that positioned schools and reserves with successful sports teams and mainstream recreational facilities as proof of assimilation and those without them as backward and in need of further encouragement to adopt mainstream ways. In 1951, the year the prohibition on traditional cultural practices was removed from the *Indian Act*, the superintendent for the Kwawkelth Agency in

British Columbia looked forward to the day when organized sports and games would replace the Potlatch on Gilford Island, where this traditional religious ceremony was still practised. Upon concluding his inspection, Eisenhardt was certain that, with a program of organized sports and games, "improvements could be brought about almost immediately" since it would teach the residents how to use their leisure time properly and foster respect for the individual accumulation of wealth.[35]

Eisenhardt's detailed plan included a brief recommendation that Indian Affairs supply prizes and trophies to encourage participation in physical education, sports, and games.[36] In his report, Eisenhardt briefly referred to the Tom Longboat Awards:

> I feel that throughout the years that our children go to school we could conduct many self-testing activities of benefit to child growth and development which finally would culminate in certain tests and certificates and medals to be given [to] those who pass them before leaving school. Encouragement would then be given to continue these activities on the reserves and eventually we might arrive at recognition being given to outstanding Indian athletes. Possibly someday a Tom Longboat medal for outstanding runners might be created.[37]

Eisenhardt originally envisioned the Tom Longboat Awards as a series of foot races among Indigenous male athletes. The winners from each region would then compete for top honours at an all-Indigenous national championship. In this way, the awards would further celebrate the memory of Longboat by keeping his running tradition alive. As a tool for assimilation, it was also to entice participants to better themselves through organized sport and recreation by providing them with something to work toward—a prize. This strategy was not unique to sport. Indian Affairs often used awards and prizes in priority areas, such as agriculture, animal farming, crafts, and woodworking, to entice Indigenous people to adopt Canadian industrial practices, which would, as historian Brian Titley points out, eliminate the need for meticulous government oversight since Indigenous people would have developed "a willingness and ability to transform themselves in the image of the colonizers."[38]

To Eisenhardt, the awarding of prizes was not enough to foster permanent change. In his estimation, Indigenous people also needed an Indigenous role model, a sports hero to emulate.[39] He found that inspiration in Longboat, who had only recently passed away. Eisenhardt, who had always been an avid sports fan, grew up knowing about Longboat and often wondered why there were so few Indigenous athletes of the same calibre in Canada. When he started his job at Indian Affairs in February 1950, he immediately began researching Longboat's history, eventually amassing a collection of published accounts, duplicate photographs, and some historically important documents about his life. In effect, Eisenhardt had become a de facto historian, availing himself of the resources that he could access at work and through his professional contacts to learn everything that he could about the acclaimed runner.[40]

At about the same time that Eisenhardt proposed the idea for the Tom Longboat Awards, another idea sparked his attention: he wanted to create a film strip about Longboat that would be shown alongside the awarding of the Tom Longboat prizes to reinforce the underlying objective of the awards. In typical fashion, Eisenhardt poured himself into the project, becoming the driving force behind the 1952 film strip sponsored by the Department of Citizenship and Immigration. The film was divided into forty-one individual picture clips and accompanied by a script written by Eisenhardt.

Set within the context of Indian Affairs, *Tom Longboat: Canadian Indian World Champion* is best understood as a morality play, one that emphasized the health-and-welfare benefits of participating in organized sports. Such messages were woven throughout the script, as indicated in frame nineteen:

Tom's participation in big-league sport inspired other Indian runners. Fred Simpson from Peterborough and Joshua Nichols from Oneida scored several victories in Canadian track meets. Boys of all nations felt the urge

Hand sketch of frame for Tom Longboat filmstrip, depicting Tom with his father, c. 1951. Source: Western Archives and Special Collections, Western University, AFC 451, Jan Eisenhardt Fonds / Folder: AFC 451-S5-FI9/F23/F41.

to excel as long-distance runners. Their effort brought prizes to some, while bringing improved health and strength to all who followed the example of clean living which good sportsmanship requires.[41]

Given that students in the day and residential schools were the intended audience of the film, the storyline depicted Longboat as the prototypical child that Indian Affairs was trying to create—that is, someone who would leave the traditions of his people behind, go to day or residential school, learn to compete in the white man's world, and win the respect and admiration of his fellow citizens by making a contribution to broader Canadian culture.

Early on, the film strip attempted to create a sense of familiarity with the students. Frame five described the time that Longboat spent at a residential school in an easy and uplifting light: "He grew up like any other boy in the tribe. He attended the Mohawk Institute, an Indian school [in Brantford] which includes among its former pupils leaders such as Professor Jamieson, Magistrate Martin, and Principal Joseph Hill."[42] Such propaganda helped to normalize and glamorize the act of going to school, suggesting to students that, if they worked hard enough and abided by their lessons and school rules, they, too, could be successful like Longboat and other former pupils. The fact that Longboat ran away from the Mohawk Institute after his first year there was never mentioned in the script.

Upon completing his fieldwork, Eisenhardt summarized his findings and outlined his plans in the *Journal of the American Association for Health, Physical Education, and Recreation*, in an article published in June 1951.[43] In it, he described the impoverished state of physical education, sport, and recreation for Indigenous people throughout the country and stated that both day and residential schools and reserves required immediate government intervention. Eisenhardt explained that, while there were small pockets of activity in each area, they were "not general"; he therefore called on Indian Affairs to aim for "a higher degree of social organization" in health and recreation by fostering an appreciation among Indigenous people for sports and games as well as "music, dancing, theatre, moving pictures, plastic arts, and literature."[44] To achieve that end, he proposed a six-pronged approach that focused on improving physical education programs in schools; providing leadership training to teachers involved in Indigenous education; encouraging participation in competitive sports; supplying equipment; constructing playing fields, outdoor hockey rinks, and lacrosse boxes; and facilitating the development of community halls. According to Eisenhardt, the key to successful program implementation was greater supervision and financial support in all areas of physical education, sports, and recreation.

Eisenhardt, envisioning a better future for Indigenous people, also made sweeping statements about the social benefits that they would receive from regulated activities, stating it would "help the Indian to achieve the social and economic progress necessary to enable him to take his place in the modern world and will enlist his active participation in the shaping of the future of his people."[45] He further claimed that Indigenous people had a "natural inclination" toward physical activities and would adopt "worthwhile" programs if offered to them.[46] "Worthwhile" to Indian Affairs meant activities that were directed and purposeful so that they contributed to its broader goals for education and assimilation.

Even with all of his experience, Eisenhardt underestimated the bureaucratic inertia at Indian Affairs, where his plans were strongly contested. As soon as he completed his seven-month consultation, he returned to the head office in Ottawa to find his portfolio rendered inactive. All activity was put on hold until the revised *Indian Act* was passed in 1951. For the time being, Indian Affairs would act only on reports regarding the medical inspection of schools.[47] Little effort was devoted to physical education, sports, and games, and the grand plan that Eisenhardt had worked so hard to create failed to materialize while he was employed in the government. The "new deal" did not constitute a fundamental shift in Indian Affairs policy, as Neary had indicated. Although the emphasis on physical education and recreation was somewhat novel, the goal was still assimilative, and the program was under-resourced. The sting of defeat stayed with Eisenhardt for life. In 1964, in response to a personal letter from Mohawk (Kanien'keha:ka) activist Kahn-Tineta Horn asking him about his opinion on whether Indian Affairs would be interested in developing an ambitious research plan to study Indigenous issues in Canada, Eisenhardt wrote that, "from my knowledge of the Indian Affairs Department policy, I can assure you that nothing will be started in a bold imaginative manner."[48]

However, one aspect of Eisenhardt's plan that did receive some attention was team sports. It was widely believed that team sports would aid in the development of leadership skills, teach co-operation, and facilitate integration, especially into the public school system.[49] To this end, in 1951 Indian Affairs began providing one-time grants to schools that already had well-established sports programs and whose students were competing successfully against other Indigenous or white teams.[50]

Such was the case for the Black Hawks hockey team from Sioux Lookout Indian Residential School, an Anglican-run institution located in northwestern Ontario.[51] In April 1951, the Department of Citizenship and Immigration and the Department of Health and Welfare co-sponsored a friendly competition between the bantam-aged Black Hawks and the top bantam-aged teams in Ottawa and Toronto. The primary purpose of the trip was to reward the Black Hawks for their "ability, behavior and sportsmanship" on the ice.[52] The secondary rationale was to call attention to the national purposes of sport. It was through the availability of such grants that the government hoped "to encourage hockey among Canada's Indians."[53] In addition to these objectives were the intangible benefits that the students would supposedly accrue from this excursion, as their coach, Bruce McCulley, explained to the *Ottawa Journal*: "These three days in Ottawa will be worth three years' schooling for the boys."[54] The trip was simultaneously an educational project to introduce the youth to the nation's cultural centre—a visit that included, among other things, a tour of the national archives, the

Sioux Lookout Black Hawks hockey team attend a luncheon in the east private dining room, Parliament Buildings, Ottawa, Ontario, April 1951. Source: G. Lunney, National Film Board of Canada, Library and Archives Canada, PA-196481.

national museum, and the Parliament buildings—and a govern-ment-generated spectacle to promote the good work being done at Sioux Lookout. The tour was thus an ideological campaign that encouraged Indigenous assimilation by accentuating settler cul-ture and promoting Indian Affairs as a benevolent institution that indulged the youth in its care.

School leaders, hoping to secure government funding, wrote to Indian Affairs extolling the educational benefits of sporting com-petitions that introduced Indigenous students to cities and towns where they could intermingle with non-Indigenous youth. Reverend Eric Cole, the principal of Old Sun Residential School, an Anglican institution in southern Alberta, described how his bantam-aged team (composed of students from two residential schools) won the Central and Southern Hockey Championships in its class, stating that the games would have "far reaching effects as the boys from both schools travelled a lot and they mixed well with the white boys."[55] But in spite of the enthusiasm for sport at schools across the country, the budget at Indian Affairs was insufficient to meet com-petitive needs, prompting Reverend O.N. Rushman of Holy Cross Mission on Manitoulin Island, Ontario, to write to Eisenhardt stat-ing, "I just can't let the enthusiasm of the schools be killed for want of support from Ottawa."[56]

A similar focus and approach was undertaken on reserves, where the assimilation agenda was coupled with austerity measures. Through the strict allocation of resources, Indian Affairs shaped the facilities and activities available throughout Canada. Residents were required to engage in fundraising for the development of rec-reation facilities and to access sporting equipment through charity organizations. Only when Indian Affairs thought that a reserve had adequately demonstrated community initiative would it provide leadership training in recreation.[57] It was hoped that, with a properly trained recreation director guiding activities on reserves, residents would form their own athletic associations in sports such as hockey and baseball and compete against nearby cities and towns, thereby facilitating interactions with white people so as "to integrate the Indians in the white man's life."[58] The challenges of raising funds in impoverished, rural, and remote areas were apparently not considered stumbling blocks to development. As explained in the *Indian School Bulletin*, a newsletter published by Indian Affairs that communicated its educational imperatives to residential school workers, "It has been proved though that where enough enthusiasm has been aroused in an Indian community the people themselves have been able to get the necessary funds to build community halls, skating rinks or other facilities."[59]

In some cases, nearby cities and towns contributed to the efforts of Indian Affairs. For instance, in 1951, the *Sault Daily Star* in Ontario reported that Eisenhardt had successfully negotiated with city council to have one of their recreation directors spend two days per week during the summer at the Garden River reserve, located a few kilometres east of the city. To Eisenhardt, the arrangement would benefit people from both the Garden River reserve and Sault Ste. Marie. "The Indian people's contact was with the wrong type of white man," he explained. "From contact with city children in an organized recreation scheme, the reserve children would learn a great deal of good. The city would benefit by getting better future citizens."[60] The incentive was made more attractive for the city in that Indian Affairs would cover the costs of the additional programming. In response, alderman Peter King emphasized the economic benefits of the deal, stating that such a simple plan "would make the children better citizens at no cost to the city."[61] Here the "right" kind of "white man" was someone who could show Indigenous youth how to behave in order to gain the respect of white people.

INDIAN AFFAIRS AND THE AMATEUR ATHLETIC UNION OF CANADA

In the fall of 1950, as he was completing his survey, Eisenhardt contacted Colonel George Machum, a prominent Montreal businessman and an influential member of the Amateur Athletic Union of Canada (AAUC), to request his assistance with the development and implementation of the Tom Longboat Awards. There were two principal reasons for seeking this partnership. First, the lack of financial support from Indian Affairs meant that Eisenhardt would have to rely on the goodwill of non-governmental organizations and private businesses to establish the awards. Second, the AAUC possessed the knowledge and experience to oversee such a program.[62] This was not Eisenhardt's first encounter with the amateur sport body. As the director of Pro-Rec, he had convinced the AAUC to eliminate membership fees for its Pro-Rec members since they were unemployed and could not afford the expense.[63]

In December 1950, Eisenhardt presented his idea for the awards to the AAUC. He requested the union's assistance in developing the awards, indicating that it was one way it could help to revive Indigenous interest in amateur sports.[64] The AAUC agreed that Indigenous athletes would benefit from amateur sports and should be encouraged to take part in its competitions. A motion was then passed for Machum to assist Eisenhardt on this project. More importantly, the members also specified that "full credit" for this work be given to the union.[65] When the AAUC formally announced its involvement in the Tom Longboat Awards to Indian Affairs, it claimed full responsibility for the idea, stating that "this is to advise you officially that the Amateur Athletic Union of Canada is prepared to initiate a Tom Longboat Trophy to be awarded annually to the most outstanding native Indian athlete in Canada, with the objective of increasing the interest of the Indian population, especially the children, in amateur sport and recreation from the competitive angle."[66] Eisenhardt later described this relationship as a "raw deal" for himself and Indian Affairs because it saw the AAUC claim ownership of the awards and reap the benefits of gratitude that should have been due to him and, by extension, Indian Affairs.[67] Yet Eisenhardt, with no money and little encouragement from his employer, had little choice but to acquiesce to AAUC demands and relinquish recognition and control of the awards.

The AAUC was interested in the awards for several reasons. In the late 1940s and early 1950s, the union was slowly losing its status as the arbiter of amateur sports in Canada. The most revealing sign that its power base was being eroded came in the 1940s, when the Canadian Olympic Association usurped the right to select teams for major international games, specifically the Olympic Games.[68] Its power was further challenged when the Canadian Sports Advisory Council, comprised of various sports governing bodies, was established in 1951 to coordinate amateur sports in Canada.[69] Despite its loss of status, the AAUC still retained a great deal of influence in amateur sport through its control of seven national championships—fencing, gymnastics, handball, track and field, weightlifting, boxing, and wrestling—as well as arbitrating amateur sport issues.[70] The AAUC's involvement in the Tom Longboat Awards expanded its sphere of influence to day and residential schools, as well as reserves. This involvement bolstered the union's image as the governing body for amateur sports in Canada and provided an opportunity for its members to promote their middle-class values to Indigenous people.[71] It was an ironic situation given that the AAUC, throughout much of its history, had actively marginalized Indigenous participants; now the union was reaching out to them hoping to produce new adherents to its brand of amateur sport.

Machum and Eisenhardt worked through the opening months of 1951 to bring the awards to fruition. Eisenhardt drew up the governing rules, while Machum ensured that they conformed to AAUC standards.[72] Initially, Machum wanted the "head of a Chief" on the regional medallions,[73] but his wish never materialized, and an image of Tom Longboat was used instead.[74] The AAUC had arranged for a corporate sponsor, the Dominion Bridge Company, to pay for the Longboat trophy and the initial cost for the medals, with the result that the program could be implemented immediately and without financial assistance from the federal government. The Dominion Bridge Company was a major employer of Indigenous people— primarily ironworkers from Kahnawake, Quebec—and because of this working relationship it was interested in increasing Indigenous participation in sport.[75] Its total contribution amounted to approximately $500.[76]

In addition to the activities of the national organizers, the structure of the awards revealed who was involved in selecting and celebrating Indigenous athletic accomplishments. At the community level, Indian agents, superintendents, missionaries, and residential school authorities were responsible for identifying appropriate candidates. Each of the regional directors for Indian Affairs was instructed to establish a selection committee to determine the most outstanding athlete in the region.[77] The committees were almost identical in terms of their representation, consisting primarily of officials from Indian Affairs and AAUC leaders.[78]

The situation was different at the national level, where all of the decision-making power rested with the union's Honours and Awards Committee, which generally met in private during the AAUC's annual general assembly in November. The committee then reported its results to the assembly. Not surprisingly, this chain of command excluded Indigenous involvement, thus ensuring that the vast majority of perspectives on Indigenous participation in sport were in line with the objectives of Indian Affairs and the AAUC (see Illustration 1).

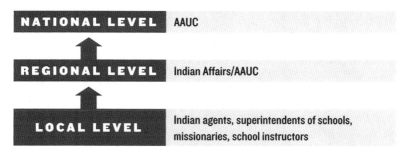

ILLUSTRATION I. Structure of the Tom Longboat Awards, 1951–72.

In December 1951, after serving less than two years in the government, Eisenhardt resigned from Indian Affairs, citing a lack of funding for the physical education and recreation program as his chief concern and a "very low salary" as a significant contributing factor.[79] In a letter sent almost fifty years later to Phil Fontaine, national chief of the Assembly of First Nations (AFN), Eisenhardt explained his rationale for leaving: "But it was all done Mickey Mouse style. When I asked for 12 gross of lacrosse sticks, I was lucky to get one, and the same for the array of sporting goods in general. My demands were never met, which left me stranded."[80] The budget for the 1950–1 fiscal year for the physical education and recreation program substantiates Eisenhardt's claim that Indian Affairs neglected to allocate resources specifically for physical education and recreation development. Instead, small pockets of money were redirected from other accounts to purchase lumber for playground equipment and sporting goods; cover the costs for two part-time and one full-time recreation director; cover travel expenses in connection with Indian Affairs–sponsored teams; develop the Tom Longboat film strip; and purchase projectors, films, and radio phonographs.[81] No funding was made available for the following fiscal year, indicating that the program would operate in the same ad hoc manner, borrowing from different sections of the branch. Clearly, the focus at Indian Affairs was not on physical education, sport, and recreation.

THE TOM LONGBOAT AWARDS, 1951–72

In the spring of 1951, the AAUC inaugurated the Tom Longboat Awards with a ceremony at the Montreal Amateur Athletic Association, the AAUC's founding member and a staunch defender of gentlemanly amateur sport. It was a gathering of self-declared "earnest sportsmen" interested in honouring the late Tom Longboat by establishing the awards.[82] Invitations were extended to members of the AAUC, the Dominion Bridge Company, and Indian Affairs. Two members of the Mohawk community of Kahnawake, Quebec, were also on hand to observe the launch, but their involvement was peripheral to the main show—a celebration of the combined beneficence of business, sport, and government. Some of the dignitaries were there strictly for ceremonial purposes since none of the invited guests had been involved in either the development or the implementation of the awards in any significant way.

The call for nominations was circulated through the regional superintendents and educational staff of Indian Affairs. The stated purpose of the awards was to recognize Indigenous athletes who had made outstanding contributions to Canadian amateur sport. Respondents were directed to outline how the nominee demonstrated leadership in three areas: character, sportsmanship, and athletic achievement. Aside from the obvious influence of muscular Christianity, which linked sport to character development, were several unstated assumptions. For instance, nowhere on the nomination form was it specified which type of sport would be considered for the awards, whether Status or Non-Status Indians were eligible to participate in them, or if they were open to male and female athletes. However, when the awards were handed out, it was clear that the organizers were referring to male athletes with Indian Status competing in mainstream amateur sports. Thus, what appeared at first glance to be an open description of the Tom Longboat Awards was a politically charged system of rewards that constructed and reinforced ideas about how Indigenous men and women should participate in competitive amateur sports. In short, the awards were not simply a celebration of Indigenous athleticism. Rather, they were part of a much larger project that equated Indigenous participation in competitive amateur sports with their integration into a modernized, mainstream Canada.

From the start, the Tom Longboat Awards were intended for residential school students who were thought to be "the most promising athletes" among the Indigenous population.[83] The AAUC fully supported this emphasis, for here was a source of untapped physical potential and a group that could be taught to appreciate the middle-class virtues of competitive amateur sports. There had been some discussion between Indian Affairs and the AAUC about implementing an age restriction, but it was never carried out. Indeed, there was no need for such a rule since the call for participation was directed at Indian agents, religious officials, and school administrators actively involved in the lives of Indigenous youth on a daily basis. From 1951 up to the late 1960s, the greater part of the award winners were students aged fourteen to nineteen who attended day and residential schools that offered opportunities for organized sports and recreation. Recipients aged twenty or older were often former residential school students.

Ideas about integration were understood within a racialized context in which white middle-class standards of achievement served as benchmarks by which Indigenous achievements would be measured.

Soon after the awards were launched, Superintendent of Education Philip Phelan wrote to George Machum thanking him for his leadership and the AAUC's contribution. In his letter, Phelan emphasized the importance of the awards' combined social agenda:

> As you know yourself the Canadian Indian is very interested in sports and games and has in many fields showed tremendous prowess, but the general participation of Indians in White men's competition is not as frequent as could be. The establishment of the Longboat Awards will bring to the fore Indians who probably would be able to compete on a par with the Whites.[84]

These sentiments were sometimes shared with the recipients. In a letter of congratulations to Frederick Baker, the first national award winner, Eisenhardt heaped on the eighteen-year-old athlete from Squamish, British Columbia, the pressures of living up to imposed expectations: "It is my hope that you in your particular field of sports and games will endeavor to go even further than you have done so that possibly the Canadian Indian someday will be on par with the Canadian Whites in any sport that will be practiced in this country."[85] Baker won the award for his achievements in boxing, basketball, gymnastics, lacrosse, and track and field.

Where the trophy was put on display also conveyed messages about racial progress. In 1957, six years after Baker was named the national recipient, Andrew Paull, president of the North American Indian Brotherhood—which would eventually evolve into the National Indian Brotherhood—wrote a letter to Indian Affairs on behalf of Baker asking about the whereabouts of the Tom Longboat Trophy. Paull was under the impression that the trophy had been sent to the national recipient, who would keep it for one year. Throughout the 1950s, however, it was branch policy to keep the trophy at the Indian Affairs office in Ottawa; it did not normally circulate through the communities. This practice was altered in the early 1960s so that the trophy went to the regional office of the winner for six months and then to the agency office for another six months.[86] The trophy was put on display at both regional and agency offices for community members to see and to inspire them to become active agents in their own self-improvement.

Although Paull might have misunderstood the procedures regarding the trophy, he wrote to Indian Affairs criticizing it for creating another program that engendered mistrust: "Now, is this

Andy Paull with Tom Longboat Trophy, 1957. Source: *The Province* (Vancouver, British Columbia), February 5, 1957, p. 14. Material republished with the express permission of: Vancouver Province, a division of Postmedia Network Inc.

a myth originated by the white people or is it only another way of deceiving the Indians?"[87] Paull wanted the trophy in hand within two weeks, in time for its presentation to Edward Vernon Campbell, a boxer from the Musqueam Band in British Columbia and the national recipient for 1956.[88] The trophy, always given out in the following calendar year, arrived on time, and the presentation was made to Campbell.

The ideological connection between racial progress and sport was also evident in the nomination forms and letters of support for the awards. When Reverend D. Hannin of the Holy Cross Mission on Manitoulin Island, Ontario, nominated Henry Wibokamigad for the 1951 award, he emphasized the integrationist aspects of Wibokamigad's behaviour. As captain of the senior men's hockey team for Wikwemikong and shortstop for the Manitowaning base-ball team, Wibokamigad was "popular with Indians and whites" and "interested in all progressive movements on the Reserve."[89] Similarly, in 1958, Reverend Harry Miller from the Old Sun Anglican Indian Residential School in southern Alberta described the qualities that made Randy Youngman—an accomplished athlete in rugby, hockey, and track and field—an excellent candidate for the award, writing, "His competitive spirit and good sportsmanship have helped him make many friends amongst the white people, and to place his people [the Blackfeet]...in a highly favorable light throughout the Province of Alberta" as well as in various sports circles throughout Canada.[90]

Although most views about Indigenous athletes expressed by school officials and the public were generally sympathetic to the broader goals of Indian Affairs and the AAUC, there is evidence that these views were far from unanimous. The detailed nomina-tion letter for Doug Skead, the 1971 national recipient, is a case in point. Peter Kelly wrote the nomination on behalf of the Grand Council Treaty No. 3, the political organization representing Treaty 3 interests, spanning northwestern Ontario and eastern Manitoba. In it, Kelly challenged the colonial notions underpinning the administration of Indigenous people: "Doug Skead represents the Indian person who will always remain undefeated. Doug has come through the demoralizing era of residential schools, the tough life of a trapper, guide and wood cutter, and the destructive experiences of alcohol, to become the manager of his band's corporation and captain of the hockey team he co-founded twenty years before."[91] The letter describes how in 1947, at age six, Skead was sent to St. Mary's Residential School in northern Ontario, where he remained until he graduated from elementary school at age sixteen. Although he was interested in pursuing his education, the staff at St. Mary's told him that there was no room for him at the local Catholic high school, and because he was Catholic he was not allowed to attend public school. Like many young people in his position, he returned to his reserve. After a few years, Skead and several friends from school established a co-operative in pulpwood cutting that turned enough profit for them to earn a living. All of the extra proceeds went to a hockey team that they were building, the Co-Op Braves. They were able to purchase suitable equipment and pay for their travel to competitions in Dryden, Sioux Lookout, Red Lake, and Fort Francis. In the 1950s, local priests became active in the co-op, and, as their veto became stronger, they attempted to take over the hockey team. Skead and the other Indigenous players wanted to retain control of the team and thus withdrew from the co-op, renaming the team the Kenora Braves. When asked by a reporter what advice he would give to youth, Skead, now forty-one, replied, "get more schooling and take opportunities that are presented" and "hold on to their culture and speak their native language."[92] Such portraits, especially those that criticized church or government policy, were rare. Instead, most newspaper reports were brief athletic biographies that were produced from information that was provided by Indian Affairs or AAUC personnel. Furthermore, few recipients had an opportunity to express their thoughts publicly as Skead had. As with most facets of Indigenous life, even the newspaper coverage of Tom Longboat Award recipients was monitored and controlled.

In establishing the parameters of the awards, the AAUC made it clear that only athletes approved by the union could participate in the program, a restriction that eliminated a number of successful Indigenous athletes who, because they competed for cash prizes, were deemed professional and therefore ineligible. An underlying assumption was that only amateur sports could deliver the character-building qualities that physical activity promised. Indeed, amateur status was strictly enforced by the AAUC as well as by Indian Affairs. In 1954, the athletic union called into question the amateur status of nineteen-year-old Thomas Davey, a member of the Six Nations reserve and winner of the 1953 Tom Longboat Award for southern Ontario.[93] The problem began when Davey was presented with his award at the annual sports day on Six Nations. In addition to the Longboat medallion, he was handed a cheque for twenty-five dollars from the local band council.[94] Unfortunately for Davey and the council, a picture of the ceremony and a short write-up was printed in the *Brantford Expositor*.[95] This caught the attention of the superintendent of education, who promptly wrote

Presentation of the national Tom Longboat Trophy to Doug Skead, 1971 recipient, by Jean Chrétien, Minister of Indian Affairs and Northern Development, Winnipeg, Manitoba, April 19, 1972. Source: University of Manitoba Digital Collections, Archives and Special Collections, Winnipeg Tribune Fonds, PC 18, A.81-12, Winnipeg Tribune Personalities Collection.

to the superintendent of the Six Nations Agency, informing him that Davey's amateur status was in jeopardy unless a detailed explanation of the payment was given.[96] The Six Nations Band Council then had to pass a resolution at a meeting the next month stating that the money had been offered as a "scholarship" to Davey for his work at the Cadet Training School held in Banff earlier that year.[97] The newspaper reports do not specify whether Davey was allowed to keep the money. However, the renaming of the prize money likely satisfied the AAUC.

By promoting Indigenous participation in competitive amateur sports, Indian Affairs and the AAUC were reinforcing the idea that white, male, middle-class ways of engaging in sport were the most correct. This notion was highlighted by the absence of traditional Indigenous sports and games at most day and residential schools and public schools throughout Canada.[98] In addition, events such as rodeo, competitive powwows, dogsledding, snowshoe racing, canoeing, and orienteering, which typically offered prize money and were thus labelled professional events, were deemed to fall outside the realm of acceptable forms of sport. Not surprisingly, as the Davey case shows, some people found ways to circumvent the rules and to support their athletes financially.

Prevailing notions of gender-appropriate behaviour also shaped the types of programs that were available to students. Generally, girls were channelled into non-competitive, healthful activities to prepare them for domestic roles as mothers and wives, whereas boys were encouraged to participate in competitive, physically demanding activities. For example, in 1950 the annual sports day for students at Cecilia Jeffrey, a Presbyterian residential school in Kenora, Ontario, featured a full slate of track and field races, which included a "makeup race" for senior girls. This event required them to run twenty-five metres, apply makeup and bobby pins without the aid of a mirror, and return to the starting line.[99] These were not the types of activities that were rewarded with a Tom Longboat Award.

Conceptions about appropriate masculinity and femininity not only informed criteria for the awards, they also reinforced their logic. Since there was no point system to guide the decisions made by selection committees, all of the judgments were based upon subjective interpretations of the criteria. As a result, nominators stressed different characteristics depending on what they thought was important. Gender was always a key issue, though rarely was it made explicit. Male winners at either the regional level or the national level displayed competencies in all three areas, including character, sportsmanship, and athletic achievement. Meanwhile, it was not necessary for female candidates to be athletes. In 1959, nineteen-year-old Donna Laura Pine, from the Garden River reserve, was awarded the regional Tom Longboat medal for northern Ontario for her dedication to the playground movement in the area. According to her nominator, she did not possess any athletic experience worth noting. Indeed, under the category for athletic achievement was written the word "none."[100]

The criteria were biased in other ways as well. Like their contemporaries in mainstream sport, Indigenous girls and women played in an environment characterized by fewer competitive opportunities.[101] Thus, they had fewer chances to demonstrate their athletic prowess and, by extension, to compete for a Tom Longboat Award. The issue of gender was such an integral part of the structure of the awards that, when the program was launched in 1951, the call for nominees did not specify if the awards were open to both male and female athletes. Instead, nominees were to be "Indian athletes" who had made significant contributions to Canadian amateur sport.[102] Sometimes, however, this gendered interpretation came to the forefront. Such was the case for the regional supervisor for southern Ontario, J.E. Morris, who in 1956 directed his superintendents to nominate any "outstanding high school boy" whom they thought eligible.[103] Notwithstanding issues of interpretation, formal exclusion was not necessary since most Indigenous girls did not have access to organized competitive sports.

On the rare occasion that a female athlete did emerge with outstanding credentials, she still had to contend with a system designed to celebrate male athletic achievements. This issue surfaced in 1955 when Betty Goulais, a fourteen-year-old athlete from a day school in Sturgeon Falls, was named the regional recipient for northern

Ontario and her sixteen-year-old brother Paul was identified as the runner-up.[104] The AAUC's Honours and Awards Committee had originally selected a male athlete from British Columbia as the national winner, but later reversed its decision. The union had received notice from the superintendent of education for British Columbia that the athlete had been withdrawn from the national competition because of "unsportsmanlike" behaviour, demonstrating that Indian Affairs was policing the awards.[105] The committee agreed to meet again and this time identified Paul Goulais as the recipient of the Tom Longboat Trophy even though he was not an eligible candidate. Betty, who competed in softball, volleyball, basketball, track and field, and swimming, was able to keep the regional award since "she was the only girl nominated" for 1955.[106] When her nominator pointed out the discrepancy with Indian Affairs, the issue was ignored, and the awards stood as final.[107]

Even after the controversy in 1955, Indian Affairs and the AAUC did not clarify their positions on the issue of gender, and requests for "Indian athletes" were received with predictable results. From 1951 to 1972, a total of 149 Tom Longboat Awards were given to regional and national recipients. Of that number, only 13 young women (less than 10 percent) were named regional winners. Just one, Phyllis Bomberry, a softball player from Six Nations, was named the national recipient in that time frame.[108] Some regions with long histories of participation in the awards, such as Saskatchewan and Alberta, did not

Betty and Paul Goulais, 1955 Tom Longboat Award recipients. Source: Library and Archives Canada, *Indian News*, March 1957, p. 8, OCLC 39298349.

identify any female athletes during this era. Thus, it was not necessary to formally exclude young Indigenous women from the awards
since the structure of competitive sports and games on reserves and
in schools, combined with gendered notions about which athletes
were most deserving of public recognition and support, worked
against them anyway.[109]

NOMINATION FORM

TOM LONGBOAT AWARDS   FILE NO. __1/1-2-15-2__

NAME IN FULL _____ ADDRESS _____

AGE _____ REGION _____ AGENCY _____

BAND _____ BAND NO. _____

CHARACTER

LEADERSHIP

ATHLETIC ACHIEVEMENTS—(PROVIDE SPECIFIC AND FACTUAL INFORMATION)

SPORTSMANSHIP

I RECOMMEND THAT THE ABOVE INDIAN ATHLETE BE CONSIDERED BY THE AWARD COMMITTEE OF THE A.A.U.C. FOR A TOM LONGBOAT AWARD

DATE _____   SIGNATURE OF RECOMMENDING OFFICER _____

FILL OUT IN QUADRUPLICATE:

1972 Tom Longboat Award nomination form. Source: Library and Archives Canada, Medals &
Awards to Indians, Tom Longboat Award, Headquarters, 1974-1976, RG10-B-3-e-xiv, Volume
12712, File 1/1-2-15-2.

For nearly twenty years, the Tom Longboat Awards bolstered the racist, classist, and gendered dimensions of the growing Canadian sport system. They were conceived by white middle-class men (and sometimes women) who drew on dominant ideas about "Indians" and their role in Canadian society to furnish the awards with meaning. For the organizers, the athletes identified through the awards embodied the values and ideals that they endorsed. At the grassroots level, where Indian agents, religious officials, and school administrators worked closely with the youth, the awards reinforced their ideas about the good work they were doing in schools and on reserves, and they submitted names and letters of support for candidates whom they thought deserved official recognition. Indian agents and superintendents of schools often mentioned how helpful it would be if one of the students in their agency or school won a Tom Longboat medal, for it would raise the morale of the people. Thus, nominators also had personal and professional stakes in the awards since they came to represent public acknowledgement of their hard work and dedication to the civilizing mission. As the 1970s rolled around, and Indigenous political organizing strengthened at the national level, Indigenous leaders looked to the awards as a way to advance their own political aspirations, using the power of symbolism to broadcast messages about Indigenous resurgence and integration on their own terms.

---

* This chapter draws on previously published material from "Bodies of Meaning," 2013, and "Make the Indian Understand His Place," 2015.

CHAPTER 3

FROM ASSIMILATION TO SELF-DETERMINATION, 1973–98

I n 1973, responsibility for the Tom Longboat Awards was transferred from the Department of Indian Affairs and Northern Development and, by then, the defunct Amateur Athletic Union of Canada to two different organizations: the National Indian Brotherhood (NIB)—which in 1981 became the Assembly of First Nations, the national political organization representing Status Indians in Canada[1]—and the Sports Federation of Canada (SFC), a non-profit advocacy organization for national sport governing bodies.[2] The transfer of the awards was carried out quickly and decisively, in a simple bureaucratic process led by Indian Affairs and the AAUC. Even though responsibility for the awards was ultimately transferred to the NIB and, thus, symbolically to the First Nations, the politics surrounding the transfer underscored the unequal power relations that existed between First Nations leaders and government officials involved in amateur sport at the time.

Once the transfer was completed, the NIB—and later the AFN—embarked with the SFC on a professional relationship that lasted fourteen years, from 1973 to 1987, at which point the SFC withdrew its involvement, leaving the AFN to manage the awards on its own until 1998. The relationship between the NIB, the AFN, and the SFC was an uneasy one marked by struggles and compromises from all parties, but mostly First Nations political leaders. During this era, all three organizations replicated key patterns originally established by Indian Affairs and the AAUC, in addition to forging new ones based upon the mainstream competitive sport model. In terms of structure and focus, the Tom Longboat Awards still celebrated Indigenous contributions to amateur sport, thus lending credibility to the idea that the Canadian sport system was the best model for sport, that mainstream amateur sports were the activities most worthy of funding, and that athletes who competed in the mainstream were the most deserving of public recognition and financial support. At the same time, however, the awards underwent a subtle but significant change in terms of their meaning. As political organizations, the NIB and the AFN challenged popular ideas about integration, preferring to chart their own course for Indigenous involvement in Canadian society. First Nations leaders argued for integration on their own terms and not for the outright assimilation proposed by the federal government. With NIB and AFN involvement, the awards reinforced this political point of view.

SPORT FOR SOCIAL DEVELOPMENT, 1964–8

As Indigenous people began to organize themselves politically after the Second World War, the issue of self-determination became a serious point of contention. Even though many Indigenous people had provided dedicated service to the war effort, Indian Affairs was reluctant to relinquish its strict control of Indigenous lives. For instance, in 1963, Arthur Laing, then the minister in charge of Indian Affairs, conveyed this paternalism in a letter to the Privy Council Office in which he expressed his concerns about devolving responsibility for Indian Affairs to the provinces: "The prime condition in the progress of the Indian people must be the development by themselves of a desire for the goals which we think they should want."[3] Within the context of Indian Affairs, the opinions expressed by leaders such as Minister Laing were often interpreted as "progressive" thinking. Whereas Indigenous people argued for the right to define their own lives with federal support, the federal government sought to reassert its control through the strategic allocation of its human and financial resources.

Despite government assertions about the positive potential of sports and recreation, the federal government maintained strict control over the types of activities available to Indigenous people. Its control was difficult to detect because of a widespread belief in the apolitical nature of sport, always cast in positive and patriotic terms so that most Canadians did not see federal involvement in Indigenous sport as a form of control. These views tended to obscure the distinct purposes of programs established by those with administrative powers and particular political interests. For instance, though the ban on traditional religious cultural practices such as the Potlatch and Sundance had been quietly removed from the *Indian Act* in 1951, the thinking that underpinned that policy continued through informal measures that provided financial assistance to sport and recreation activities that fit government-approved criteria, thus ensuring that Indigenous energies would be channelled into appropriate physical behaviours.

Initially, the Tom Longboat Awards were situated in the physical education and recreation portfolio at Indian Affairs. However, by the late 1960s and early 1970s, many of the day and residential schools had been shut down and their students placed in the public school system. This move toward integration was made possible by the 1951 revisions to the *Indian Act*, which permitted Indian Affairs to enter into contractual agreements with provinces and territories to provide education to Indigenous students.[4] Once an agreement was signed, the local school board assumed day-to-day responsibility for educating the students, while Indian Affairs was to provide funding.[5] The process of integration was slow to start, but by 1960 the number of Indigenous students in non-Indigenous schools (9,479) began to outpace the number in residential schools (9,471).[6] By 1964, more than two hundred joint agreements were in place throughout Canada.[7]

The Sixties Scoop also contributed to the growing number of Indigenous children in the public school system. As McKenzie,

Varcoe, Browne, and Day explain, the "state-led apprehension of Indigenous children did not end" with the winding down of the residential school system; it merely shifted from educators to child welfare workers, whose job was to remove Indigenous children from their families if they were considered by the state to be unfit to raise them.[8] From the 1960s to the 1980s, tens of thousands of Indigenous children throughout Canada were placed into foster care with non-Indigenous families. Abuse, poverty, and neglect were said to be rampant among Indigenous families during this era, thus justifying the need for removal, though as McKenzie and colleagues argue, discourses that linked civility and whiteness to health and safety became a convenient way to declare a family unfit for raising children. The problem continues. In one alarming report, child welfare activist Cindy Blackstock and her co-authors estimated that there were three times as many Indigenous children in child welfare in 2004 as there were children in residential schools in the 1940s, when the system was at its highest operation.[9] The issue has since become a "humanitarian crisis" in Canada. In 2017, in Manitoba alone, there were reportedly 11,000 children in care, 10,000 of whom were Indigenous.[10]

Regardless of the benevolent rhetoric that Indian Affairs used to promote integration as being in the best interests of Indigenous people, it was a strategy motivated largely by economics: simply put, it was more efficient to send Indigenous children to integrated schools than to meet the demands for Indigenous education on and off reserves. Even the Hawthorn Report, in line with the views of the federal government, concluded that Indian Affairs was "putting all its hope" in integration through the public school system.[11] From an Indigenous perspective, the costs associated with this strategy extended well beyond financial considerations to include the human toll. Students coming from remote or isolated areas had no choice but to live in boarding homes in unfamiliar cities and towns for the school year. Faced with living in strange and often hostile and racist environments, many of the students dropped out of school and returned home.[12]

Indigenous leaders argued that, while the public school system was profiting from this method of integration, it was doing little to ensure that Indigenous students were receiving a quality education.

The agreements were such that each school board received an annual allotment of money based upon the number of Indigenous students enrolled at the time of the agreement. As government money was being diverted to local school boards to finance the construction of new facilities or to enhance old ones to accommodate the increased enrolment, funding for schooling on reserves dwindled. The fact that Indian Affairs delivered on its promise for funding to the school boards no matter the educational outcomes for Indigenous students was a source of serious contention for Indigenous parents and leaders throughout the country.[13]

In 1971, the issue of funding came to the fore when the Dene in northeastern Alberta led a school strike to oppose federal plans to close on-reserve schools and bus Indigenous children into nearby towns to attend provincial schools.[14] The strike provided the impetus for the NIB to write and publish *Indian Control of Indian Education*, a position paper on what Indigenous people were looking for in terms of schooling.[15] In it, Indigenous leaders drew on their principles and values to describe a collective philosophy of education, an exercise that demonstrated the importance that they attached to education. They began with a clear, simple statement: "We want education to give our children a strong sense of identity, with confidence in their personal worth and ability."[16] Describing its goals for physical activity, the NIB identified the need for recreation directors in each school; if that plan was not economically feasible, then it requested that local recreation programs offer the school's physical education curricula.[17] Indigenous leaders recognized organized physical activities, whether in the schools or on the playgrounds, as key ingredients of community well-being. Significantly, they also challenged the idea of educational integration as a unidirectional process whereby Indigenous students were expected to fit into the dominant culture of each school, arguing that Indigenous and white students should learn from each other.[18] Physical education, sport, and recreation were proposed as ways to facilitate this two-way learning process.

As increasing numbers of Indigenous youth were integrated into the public school system, Indian Affairs shifted its priority from supporting physical education and recreation programs in the residential school system to supporting sport and recreation programs that contributed to broader social development. Established in 1964, the Social Development Program at Indian Affairs was designed to provide Indigenous people living on reserves with leadership skills to enable them to contribute effectively to the betterment of their communities. However, the radical potential that Indigenous leaders saw in the fledgling program was short-lived. Peter McFarlane writes that in 1967 Minister Laing expressed his concern for the way First Nations people had embraced the program, with Laing stating that community development was not "a process of agitation and revolt" but a means to "arouse the people from sloth and apathy."[19] Additionally, the bureaucrats failed to consider that Indigenous self-determination was an objective that clashed with the role of the Indian agents, who realized that Indigenous independence would jeopardize their employment with the federal government. In 1969, Laing's realization that the Social Development Program had the opposite effect than what he, and by extension Indian Affairs, envisioned, combined with criticisms from field agents, led to a revised program focusing on leadership development for band council members, whose political orientation generally leaned toward the servicing of federal demands.[20]

In the Social Development Program's first four years, sport and recreation brought people together and politicized their activities. George Manuel, the first president of the NIB and a social development worker for Indian Affairs, believed sport and recreation could "rekindle their sense of community."[21] Meanwhile, in keeping with its status as a government-funded program, old patterns continued. The development discourse that equated mainstream sport with progress and traditional Indigenous practices with stagnation structured the range of possibilities for sport so that Indian Affairs subsidized mostly mainstream amateur activities. Other sports—and traditional pursuits specifically—were positioned as either quaint or regressive, or as commodified tourist attractions disconnected from modern Indigenous culture, resulting in what business scholar Dean Neu and activist Richard Therrien describe as a socially acceptable form of cultural genocide.[22]

Originally, the movement of the Tom Longboat Awards from the physical education and recreation portfolio to the Social Development Program signalled a shift in government priorities, from supporting residential schools to supporting community development on reserves. By 1966, however, sport and recreation activities were redefined in purely economic terms. Henceforth, the annual reports for Indian Affairs refer to sport and recreation exclusively as hunting and fishing activities that could be used to promote tourism on reserves, thus making Indigenous communities dependent on public interest in their resources and cultures.[23] Now sport and recreation were less a vital part of community well-being than important ways to stimulate economic growth. Accordingly, the awards no longer fit the mandate at Indian Affairs, with the result that federal administrators began looking to divest responsibility for them. In fact, the awards had already been deemed a peripheral program at the federal level for some time, and the final year that they were mentioned in the annual reports for Indian Affairs was 1960.[24]

SHIFTING RESPONSIBILITIES TO THE NIB, 1968–73

In 1968, the Department of Indian Affairs and Northern Development underwent a massive housecleaning exercise to rid itself of all extraneous programs and files. It was a tremendous effort intended to transform Indian Affairs into an efficient bureaucratic machine. No area was left untouched, including the Tom Longboat Awards, which underwent review that year—the first time since they were established in 1951 that they were subjected to such a process. That Indian Affairs did not terminate the program in 1968 demonstrates that the federal government saw some value in maintaining the awards, in particular since they supported its larger strategy for integration.

The review was a simple task performed by L.J. Hyslop, a social development officer for Indian Affairs. After examining the administrative procedures, selection processes, and criteria, he concluded that the Tom Longboat Awards had evolved into "a rigid Branch administrative exercise" with only token involvement of the AAUC and no Indigenous participation whatsoever.[25] The awards were organized in such a way that the Indian Affairs office in Ottawa received the majority of nominations from the agencies, with the regional headquarters acting essentially as post offices. Once all of the nominations had been gathered and reviewed, the national office forwarded its selections to the AAUC. In an attempt to make the awards more efficient, Indian Affairs looked to the AAUC for support, hoping that the amateur sports body would assume "practically all responsibility" for the program.[26] As part of the recommendations, Hyslop proposed that the AAUC select the regional as well as the national recipients and that Indigenous involvement be limited to nominating athletes at the local level. Indian Affairs was recast in an advisory role at both regional and national levels to ensure that the awards still corresponded to federal objectives.[27]

At the same time that Indian Affairs was looking to divest responsibility for the Tom Longboat Awards, Hyslop suggested further revisions to the prizes, even though he had no direct involvement in their day-to-day management. He made three recommendations. First, the awards should be revised to emphasize Indigenous contributions to the "betterment" of sports, games, and recreation in Canada. Greater emphasis on organizing and coaching was needed. Second, nominees should have contributed to Canadian sport over a "considerable number of years" in order to be named a regional or national award winner. This stipulation would help to ensure sustained involvement in the mainstream sport system. Third, better evidence of character and leadership was needed to counterbalance the emphasis on athletic achievements.[28] In the end, Indian Affairs supported only the first two recommendations. The third recommendation, made to offset the emphasis on performance outcomes, was ignored in favour of the rational pursuit of excellence, which would dominate amateur sport from the 1970s onwards.[29]

Acting on his recommendations, Hyslop wrote to the AAUC to negotiate with the amateur sport body on the proposed changes. He asked the union to clarify its position on the Tom Longboat Awards to ensure that its objectives were still philosophically aligned with those of the federal government. The purpose, Hyslop wrote, was to encourage Indigenous integration into mainstream society through amateur sports competitions. In response, Margaret Lord, chair of the Honours and Awards Committee, replied that the AAUC had "no intention to isolate them [Indigenous people]...but rather to invite them to join with us in all our activities."[30] Hyslop had also recommended in his report that, if the AAUC was going to assume nearly all responsibility for the awards, then it should also be responsible for the budget, which included a nominal fee of seventy-five dollars per year to maintain the trophy and medals.[31] The AAUC flat out refused this responsibility.[32] Lord explained that, though the union welcomed increased Indigenous input at the regional level, as the AAUC was "too far away from the scene" to make regional selections, it was "not able to absorb the costs" of the medals and trophy. Nevertheless, Lord stated, the union would be "happy to continue in its present role" as the provider of the national award.[33] Although the AAUC supported several prominent national sports awards at the time, including the Norton H. Crow Award and the Viscount Alexander Trophy (for top junior athlete in amateur sports), it refused to assume more responsibility for the Tom Longboat Awards, thus reinforcing the marginal status of Indigenous athletes within the mainstream sport system.[34]

Two years passed before Indian Affairs devolved its responsibility for the awards. That shift came in 1970 when the AAUC chose to disband, believing that it had outlived its usefulness as an amateur sport governing body.[35] Nevertheless, official correspondence demonstrates that the union, though no longer an official organization, remained involved in the Tom Longboat Awards for another two years, leaving the program only after the 1972 season. With the approval of Indian Affairs, the AAUC handed over responsibility for the awards to the Canadian Amateur Sports Federation, which, in 1973, transitioned into the SFC. Lord, who had chaired the Honours and Awards Committee for the AAUC, was named awards chair for the SFC. Once again, Indian Affairs attempted to separate itself from the Tom Longboat Awards, indicating that the SFC had the expertise needed to guide the awards and suggesting that it take complete ownership of the program. And for one year, 1973, the SFC selected the regional and national award winners on its own, while Indian Affairs supplied the medals for the regional recipients and a framed photograph of the trophy for the national recipient.[36]

At the same time that Indian Affairs was moving its resources away from sport and recreation, another division of the federal government, Fitness and Amateur Sport (FAS), was looking to increase the participation rates of "disadvantaged" Canadians in organized sports and identified Indigenous people as a group needing specific attention.[37] With this broad objective in mind, the federal government, through FAS, established the Native Sport and Recreation Program to increase sport and recreation opportunities for Indigenous people on and off reserves. From 1972 to 1981, the program flourished as Indigenous organizers throughout the country coordinated local, regional, and national activities in a wide range of events that addressed pressing community needs. Despite its success, the program was terminated in March 1981 when the federal government shifted its priorities from mass participation to elite sport development. Upon learning about the government's decision, Fred Sappier, acting chairman of the National Indian Sports Council, a committee that the NIB established in the late 1970s to advocate for more sport and recreation opportunities for First Nations people, wrote to the minister of justice, Jean Chrétien, requesting the federal cabinet reconsider its decision. He explained the dire need for such a program in the following way:

> The high representation in jails and juvenile courts also reflects the scarcity of preventative service programs. Sport and recreation is one program that must be considered to alleviate the alcoholism, drug, suicides, school-drop-outs and family problems, and our Band leaders realize the importance of a good sport and recreation program. This is where our program staff assist in developing recreation leaders and programs to counter act towards these problems.[38]

With the new focus on competitive outcomes, reviewers of the Native Sport and Recreation Program concluded that the range of pursuits fostered by Indigenous organizers was outside the scope of initiatives supported by FAS and that the programs developed by Indigenous organizers would not produce the high performance results desired by the federal government.[39]

The Native Sport and Recreation Program supported regional games throughout the country, such as the 1978 Indian Summer Games in Woodstock, New Brunswick. Source: Provincial Archives of New Brunswick, MC 1795, Box 25, Content ID 3692.

The NIB was involved in the Native Sport and Recreation Program through its regional political associations, which received funding from FAS. Thus, by the early 1970s, the shift away from sport and recreation at Indian Affairs was offset to some extent by the increasing involvement of the federal government through FAS. In 1973, in addition to transferring responsibility for the Tom Longboat Awards to the SFC, Indian Affairs approached the NIB to enlist its assistance in changing the scope and selection of the awards. The NIB had already expressed its interest in becoming more involved in the Tom Longboat Awards, making the political body the obvious and only choice for caretaker. In July 1972, George Manuel, president of the NIB, wrote to Jean Chrétien, who by this time was the minister in charge of Indian Affairs, supporting Hyslop's review. Not only did Manuel understand sport and recreation as an important aspect of community development, he also saw competitive sport as a means through which to promote Indigenous pride and to advance claims of Indigenous nationhood: "It has always been my personal feeling that one of the best vehicles that Indian People can use in their struggle for recognition are the fields of sport and athletics."[40]

In his letter to Chrétien, Manuel outlined several ways in which the Tom Longboat Awards could be improved. First, he explained, the Indigenous associations linked to the NIB should make the regional selections, not the SFC. Second, the awards should be divided into junior and senior divisions, with the junior winner receiving a special trophy. Third, the senior division should be broken down into two categories, one to recognize the most outstanding Indigenous athlete in Canada, the other to recognize Indigenous coaches and organizers for their contributions to the Canadian amateur sport system. The winner of the most outstanding athlete category would automatically be named the Tom Longboat Award winner. Fourth, Manuel recommended that a banquet for the award winner be held in a different part of the country each year and that the occasion be used as much as possible for public relations. Fifth, he recommended that Indian Affairs pay for the costs of the revised program until other sponsors could be found. In closing, Manuel expressed his confidence that, "with these recommendations completed and with the full commitment of the Indian associations...it would be possible for the Award to not only become indicative of Indian athletic excellence but [also] of Canadian athletic excellence."[41]

These recommendations were significant in that they challenged the idea of integration that Indian Affairs was still endorsing, even with the revisions to the awards. In contrast to outright assimilation, the NIB took the view that Indigenous people had the right to define which roles they would occupy in mainstream Canadian society. In terms of participation in sports, the NIB viewed Indigenous athletic achievement as both a distinct feature of the dominant sport system and an integral part of organized sport in Canada. To the NIB, this fostered Indigenous pride and brought honour to the Canadian sport system. Whereas Indian Affairs and the AAUC sought to replace Indigenous cultural values with a mainstream Canadian identity through the Tom Longboat Awards, the NIB sought to reassert Indigenous values by deciding which aspects of the awards to keep, which to change, and which to discard entirely.

A critical point to consider here is the power of the NIB, relative to that of Indian Affairs, to determine its priorities and to access the resources to work toward those goals. When Indian Affairs transferred responsibility for the Tom Longboat Awards to the NIB, First Nations leaders had little choice but to operate within the boundaries constructed by the federal government. In short, the NIB was given responsibility for administering another Indian Affairs program. Indigenous leaders were attentive to this idea of control, having learned from their struggles in education the difference between the appearance of control and actual decision-making responsibility for policies and programs.[42] NIB involvement in the awards did not signify an increase in political power relative to that of Indian Affairs; this was not an opportunity for the NIB to reshape the awards. Rather, the federal request for input was an exercise in futility, designed as it was to engage the NIB in a process of consultation that would help to make the awards more efficient from a government point of view.

In October 1973, the NIB met and discussed the proposed changes to the Tom Longboat Awards, giving its full support to the recommendations made by Manuel.[43] Indian Affairs understood this support to mean that the regional associations would henceforth take responsibility for the selection of the regional recipients. The structure of the awards was altered accordingly.[44] The regional associations would now forward their nominees to Margaret Lord at the SFC in consideration for the national trophy. The NIB was allowed one representative on the National Selection Committee. Indian Affairs shelved all of the other recommendations forwarded by Manuel for consideration in the following year.[45] Despite repeated requests by the NIB to revise the awards, neither Indian Affairs nor the SFC made a serious attempt to communicate with the NIB on this issue; Indian Affairs was still "considering" the matter in September 1974.[46]

Despite efforts to remove itself completely from the administration of the Tom Longboat Awards, Indian Affairs remained involved until 1974 to help the NIB coordinate the regional selection processes.[47] Indian Affairs subsequently removed itself from the administration of the awards but continued its arm's-length involvement through funding the program.[48]

THE NIB AND THE AFN TAKE CONTROL, 1974–98

When responsibility for the Tom Longboat Awards was transferred to the NIB in 1974, First Nations political leaders, in spite of resistance from Indian Affairs, made a series of minor adjustments to the awards so that they more closely aligned with the goals of Indigenous political organizers in Canada. The most visible change was the restructuring of the awards. They were updated to correspond to the twelve administrative regions: Yukon, the Northwest Territories, British Columbia, Alberta, Saskatchewan, Manitoba, Ontario, Quebec, New Brunswick, Nova Scotia, Prince Edward Island, and Newfoundland and Labrador (which formed one administrative region). Most provincial and territorial representatives were amenable to the arrangement since most had representation at the NIB, though some expressed frustration with the new design. For example, Ontario had three political organizations struggling for legitimacy within the province, while Newfoundland and Labrador had no political representation at the NIB at all. Indian Affairs recognized these dilemmas and recommended that Newfoundland and Labrador combine with Nova Scotia and New Brunswick to form a "Maritime Region"—as was done in earlier years—to participate in the awards.[49] Similarly, the associations in Ontario were encouraged to "co-operate" with each other, even though the province had been divided into two regions, north and south, in the previous era of the awards.[50]

The issue of political representation was important symbolically since regional representation through the Tom Longboat Awards signified both political representation at the NIB and a relationship with the federal government. The Ontario leaders could not come to an agreement, and the NIB refused to accept any application from that region for 1974 since it might have been misconstrued as political representation at the national level of the NIB.[51] This was the first year since 1951 that Ontario did not participate in the awards. To make matters worse, in 1976 Indian Affairs unilaterally withdrew Prince Edward Island, as well as Newfoundland and Labrador, from the competition on the ground that neither region had an Indigenous association supporting nominations for the awards.[52] The NIB later worked around this issue by having participating bands and reserves not represented by a provincial or territorial organization forward their nominations directly to the NIB for consideration.[53]

As a national political lobby group for Status Indians in Canada, the NIB was concerned primarily with issues on reserves, where the majority of Status Indians lived at the time. NIB involvement in the Tom Longboat Awards ensured that nominations would come from band councils and Indigenous sports associations, thus linking candidates directly to their home communities. The nominations were then forwarded to the appropriate political organization for the selection of the regional recipient, or, where none existed, were forwarded directly to the NIB, which would make a determination. The names of the regional recipients were then forwarded to the SFC for the selection of the national award winner (see Illustration 2).[54] The power to decide which athlete was the most suitable for the national award was left primarily to sfc members and federal sports officials, as they outnumbered nib representatives. For example, the National Selection Committee for the 1976 awards was composed of four members: Jo-Ann Lawson, executive director, sfc; Joyce Coffin, chairperson of the Honours and Awards Committee, sfc; Tom Bedecki, director, fas; and Ron Albert, executive director, nib.[55] This balance of power shifted over the years to include more Indigenous input. In 1986, for example, the committee was composed of one federal official, one sfc member, two representatives of the afn, and, significantly, one member of the Longboat family.[56]

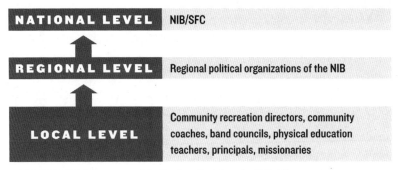

NATIONAL LEVEL NIB/SFC

REGIONAL LEVEL Regional political organizations of the NIB

LOCAL LEVEL Community recreation directors, community coaches, band councils, physical education teachers, principals, missionaries

ILLUSTRATION 2. Structure of the Tom Longboat Awards, 1973–98.

Including a member of Tom Longboat's family on the National Selection Committee was meaningful in that it helped to promote the awards as a program operated by and for Indigenous people and an homage to the famed Onondaga. Since 1951, high-ranking government officials and sports leaders had been celebrating the athletic achievements of Longboat while paying little heed to descendants of the man whom they professed to honour. When Jan Eisenhardt conceived the awards in 1951, he was not aware that members of the Longboat family were still living on the Six Nations reserve. Thinking only about Longboat the athlete, Eisenhardt did not try to locate and involve the family in the development or management of the awards.[57] The formal inclusion of a Longboat family member on the National Selection Committee—a tradition that began in the early 1980s and was continued by the Aboriginal Sport Circle (ASC)—added a historical dimension to the awards that extended well beyond their 1951 origins to the early twentieth century, when Longboat was at the peak of his career.

With NIB involvement in the program, the meanings attached to the awards reinforced Indigenous political aspirations for self-determination, especially at the community level. The rhetoric of self-help, so obvious under Indian Affairs and AAUC control, was also used by the NIB but with a significant shift in terms of final objectives. The aim was not to elevate Indigenous people to the standards imposed by others but rather to generate a movement toward Indigenous self-determination through competitive amateur sports and games. This was an important symbolic shift demonstrating the significance that Indigenous leaders attached to sport as a vehicle for instilling cultural pride. As Clive Linklater, NIB vice-president, explained to the executive directors of each provincial and territorial member organization, "these awards, it is hoped, will not only preserve the memory of one of the greatest marathon runners Canada has had but will also serve to encourage Indians to participate with other Canadians in amateur sports."[58] Therefore, the views espoused by the NIB were not totally incompatible with amateurism; rather, the Indigenous leaders were attempting to augment the dominant belief system by telling their own stories about how to fit into that system.

Under NIB and SFC control, the criteria for participating in the Tom Longboat Awards were clarified. The revised deed of gift, finalized in 1974, specified that the awards were open to both male and female athletes and to athletes with Indian Status as defined by the *Indian Act*.[59] Of the two criteria, the latter was the most contentious. The issue first surfaced in 1964 when the AAUC found itself embroiled in a minor controversy regarding the nomination of Non-Status athletes for the awards. The union deferred the matter to Indian Affairs, whose officials determined that the awards were open to Status Indians only.

Ten years later, in 1974, the issue surfaced again, this time within the NIB. The Indian Brotherhood of the Northwest Territories, a regional association, voiced its concerns regarding the Status-only criterion and questioned the power and authority of the federal government to decide on this matter. The issue was raised in a telex sent by the association to Tim Steward, a social development worker at Indian Affairs, protesting the awards on the basis that they were open to Status Indians only. The association argued that Indian Affairs had no business tying the awards to the *Indian Act* and that to limit them in this fashion was "another process by which the federal government tends to lend itself to the rendering asunder of all natives in Canada" and as such was in direct conflict with "the principles of the Dene" in the region.[60] It believed that federal involvement in the awards was another process by which the government attempted to pit Indigenous people against each other through divide-and-conquer tactics.

The Indian Brotherhood of the Northwest Territories also protested the individual nature of the awards on the ground that they contributed to the breakdown of communal values. "To work as a team is to work as one," the association stated, making the case for the nomination of the Northwest Territories Cross-Country Ski Team, which was composed of Sharon and Shirley Firth, Herbert Bullock, and Ernie Lennie. In response, a representative from Indian Affairs explained to the association that, since the government was no longer involved in either the nominations or the conditions that applied to the awards, and since its only involvement was to pay for the regional medals, the association needed to take the matter up with the SFC.[61] Nothing came of this team nomination, as the awards were meant for individual athletes. Nor did the Firth sisters, each of whom competed in four consecutive Winter Olympics, ever receive a regional or national Tom Longboat Award on account of their not meeting the Status criteria.[62]

The number of female recipients of the Tom Longboat Awards, especially at the national level, increased dramatically between 1974 and 1998. Although the records for these years are incomplete,[63] it is clear that female athletes were finally being recognized for their contributions to sport. Of the fifty-five male and female recipients known to have won an award during this era, twelve (21.8 percent) were female. Six of the twelve females (50 percent) won the national award.[64] However, no female recipient was identified in the records during this period for Yukon, the Northwest Territories, Saskatchewan, Manitoba, Nova Scotia, Prince Edward Island, and Newfoundland and Labrador. The first young woman to be named a national recipient during this time—and only the second in the history of the awards—was Beverly Stranger, a thirteen-year-old athlete from the Temiskaming Band of Notre Dame du Nord, Quebec. Stranger, a blind athlete, won the 1976 award for her outstanding performances in track and field. In that year, she was a member of the Canadian team at the Olympics for the Physically Disabled held in Toronto, where she won a gold medal in high jump and a silver medal in the pentathlon and the javelin throw. She later went on to win one gold and four silver medals in various track and field events at the 1977 Ontario Games for the Physically Disabled in Brantford.[65]

Stranger was also the first Indigenous recipient in a "disabled" sport, though not the first recipient to deal with a physical barrier. For example, George Colin Wasacase, a grade 7 student at Portage Indian Residential School, was awarded the regional medal for Manitoba in 1952 for his exploits in baseball and hockey. Wasacase had lost his left arm at the age of seven.[66] Identifying Stranger as a recipient of the prestigious national award indicates that the Tom Longboat Awards were beholden to different standards than the Canadian Sport Awards, for which disabled athletes were not yet recognized. Nor was Stranger the only person to be named a national recipient for 1976. She shared that honour with Reginald Underwood, a member of the Tsawout Band in British Columbia. Underwood, who was a talented basketball player, also excelled in baseball. Playing with the Victoria Bates, he won the 1976 World Fastball Championship title. It was the first time in the history of the awards that two athletes shared the national honour.

Judging by the minutes of the National Selection Committee, the decision to name Stranger a national recipient appears to have been controversial. The committee debated at length the value of having someone as young as Stranger, even with her outstanding athletic resumé, compete for an award designed to celebrate contributions to Canadian sport over a number of years.[67] Her disability was never an issue for them. At the time, there was no provision in the deed of gift for identifying two athletes to share the national award (that rule was implemented when the awards were transferred to the ASC). Neither was there an assessment tool to identify which accomplishments were valued most, which meant the final decision was based wholly on the social orientation of the committee members.

Couple share coveted Tom Longboat awards

WINNIPEG (CP) — A 14-year-old Quebec girl who overcame her blindness to win a host of medals in national and international games for the handicapped joined a British Columbia fastballer Thursday in receiving the Indian people's highest award for sport.

Pretty Beverly Stanger of the Timiscamingue Reserve and Reginald Underwood of the Tisawout Reserve near Victoria were presented with the Tom Longboat awards in a National Indian Brotherhood ceremony.

It was the first time the brotherhood has named two winners for the award it has been presenting since 1951 to commemorate the marathon running feats of Indian Tom Longboat in the early years of the century.

Beverly has acquired a host of awards in handicapped sports in the last couple of years. She won gold medals in javelin, long jump, high jump and swimming at the handicapped olympics in Toronto this year. She also won two silver medals.

Later she went to the Canadian championships in Edmonton and won seven more medals. She and Underwood received standing ovations when they went to collect their awards at the annual banquet of the brotherhood.

Underwood was a member of the world champion Victoria Bates fastball team this year. He has been named most valuable player in fastball and basketball and has participated in other sports.

Speakers at · the ceremony said he provided leadership in sport as well as excelling as a player.

It was announced Thursday that the Longboat Trophy and all its winners will become part of the Canadian Sports Hall of Fame.

Newspaper reporting on Beverly Stranger and Reginald Underwood sharing 1976 national Tom Longboat Award. Source: *Red Deer Advocate*, September 16, 1977, p. 7. The Canadian Press.

Perhaps due to the debate surrounding Stranger's nomination, in 1977, the National Selection Committee developed a scoring system to help guide its decisions (see Illustration 3).[68] It aimed to create a "fair" process for selecting the national recipients and to suppress charges of favouritism, especially toward male athletes, by providing an unbiased method for assessing nominees.[69] It was also intended to make the decision-making process more efficient by systematically eliminating nomination packages that did not provide the appropriate information. In 1977 the National Selection Committee was instructed by the SFC to follow the rules strictly; this included eliminating incomplete packages from the competition, even if it was the only nomination from a region.[70]

A. ATHLETIC ACHIEVEMENT (Max. 50 points)

International:	20 points
National:	15 points
Provincial:	10 points
Local:	5 points

B. LEADERSHIP AND ORGANIZATION (Max. 30 points)

National:	15 points
Provincial:	10 points
Local:	5 points

C. PERSONAL CHARACTER AND SPORTSMANSHIP (Max. 20 points)

ILLUSTRATION 3. Scoring system for the national Tom Longboat Award, 1977.

By creating a scoring system based upon performance outcomes, with greater values attached to higher levels of athletic achievement, the rankings served to reproduce and rationalize the mainstream sport model, which emphasized elite athletic development and participation in major international games. Unfortunately, the available documents do not make it clear whether the subcategories (local, provincial, national, international) refer to participation in the mainstream sport system or the Indigenous sport system; however, given the limited range of opportunities in Indigenous sports at the time, and the fact that the national award winners were highly successful athletes in the mainstream sport system, it is likely the subcategories were developed in reference to the latter rather than the former.[71] The scoring system clearly favoured Indigenous athletes who competed in elite-level mainstream sports—a long-standing tradition that had become part of the Tom Longboat Awards—and systematically marginalized those who spent countless hours participating in and developing the Indigenous sport system.

Sometimes people who sought to recognize other forms of Indigenous sporting contributions beyond athletic achievement called the emphasis on performance into question. This happened in 1974 when Mrs. Olga Stusick, a field nurse working on the Cote reserve in Saskatchewan, submitted a detailed, four-page nomination for Chief Antoine Cote, aged forty. The letter described how Chief Cote was helping to restore community pride by creating jobs for men and women on-reserve and, where possible, encouraging them to work off-reserve, as was the case for women trained in nursing. Stusick also linked the increased employment opportunities and surge in community spirit resulting from the building of a sports complex that included a fifteen-hundred-person indoor ice rink to a decrease in the number of "juvenile delinquents" in the community. She maintained that clubs for boxing, hockey, fastball, volleyball, basketball, track and field, and figure skating were keeping the young people healthy and productively engaged. Stusick, who had been working on the reserve since 1967, also argued that sport and recreation promoted good relations between Indigenous people and non-Indigenous people in nearby towns and cities:

> Community spirit among the native people is now at a high level. This is noticed by the success of the events on the reserve. Team work is very much in evidence, as the last community project was the Wrestling Card brought to the reserve. This was a success, not only, financially but the morale of the people is now at a high peak. The racial barrier is now fading and the white society now

is beginning to see that the native people are able to do things by themselves and they are very capable.[72]

As evidence of loosening racial barriers, Stusick stated that the Cote reserve had lent its bleachers to the town of Kamsack for a rodeo and stampede, and, when it sponsored a "gigantic" bingo, the Elks organization of Kamsack lent the Cote reserve its bingo cards.[73]

In its support for Chief Cote, the Federation of Saskatchewan Indians identified his efforts to spearhead the first Indian Summer Games in Saskatchewan. The games, intended for children aged fourteen and younger, were hosted on the Cote reserve in celebration of the Treaty 4 centennial. This echoed the earlier sports days that provided Indigenous people with a reason to gather, discuss politics, and engage in recreation without federal sanctions. At the opening ceremonies for the games, the chief of the Federation of Saskatchewan Indians, David Ahenakew, announced that Chief Cote had won a regional Tom Longboat Award. Ahenakew had these words to say about him: "I feel it very fitting that the man behind the Games, the man who worked seemingly endless hours, and the man who never gave up, should be recognized as the individual who made the greatest contribution to Indian sports in the province this year."[74] Clearly, some people at the local level had very

---

By Dave Senick
Tribune Sports Writer

Many years later, Courchene is honored

John C. Courchene received the Tom Longboat provincial nominee medal Friday night during a banquet sponsored by the Manitoba Indian Brotherhood (MIB).

It was one of the few times the 61-year-old gentleman has been honored, but that doesn't really matter. He is content to see his efforts reflected among the people he associates with rather than in a trophy case.

J. C., as he is called by all those who have come in contact with him, will travel to Montreal Jan. 16 where the final award winner will be announced.

The Tom Longboat Trophy, named after the famous long-distance runner, is presented each year to a native Canadian who has made an outstanding contribution or achievement in the field of sport.

Courchene hasn't very many medals or trophies to support his bid for the national honors but his reputation should be more than sufficient.

The life-long resident of the Fort Alexander Reserve has been involved in sports since 1937, when he organized the first Indian hockey team in the area.

Courchene has seen a big change since the days when the 12 members of the local squad would hike 11 miles across Lake Winnipeg to Victoria Beach to participate in a game.

He instigated and participated in the planning, fund raising for and construction of the first arena to be built on a Manitoba Reserve. That dream became a reality in 1967.

The modest sportsman has also been a strong promoter of baseball among the Fort Alexander residents.

Members of the reserve, who gathered to pay tribute to Courchene last night, all agreed that he has played a major role organizing the local people in the field of sports.

They also presented him with the John C. Courchene Trophy, which will be awarded each year to the most deserving native athlete in the province.

That momento should preserve J. C.'s reputation for a long time.

Courchene wasn't the only one to bask in the limelight. Gerald Sinclair of the Peguis Reserve; Ralph Wilson, Winnipeg; Sam Myran, Long Plains; Vernon Jebb, The Pas; Doug Garrick, Cross Lake and Swanson Highway, Brochet were also recognized by the MIB as Tom Longboat nominee runners-up.

Milton Courchene, John's grandson, Derrick Fontaine and Warren Mousseau were presented awards by Earl Dawson, Fitness and Amateur Sport regional representative, for their achievements in minor hockey.

Detailed reporting on John Courchene, 1975 national Tom Longboat Award recipient. Source: *The Tribune* (Winnipeg, Manitoba), December 20, 1975, p. 74. University of Manitoba Digital Collections.

different perspectives about which activities represented contributions to Canadian amateur sport.

Other nominations were rich in detail and shed much-needed light on Indigenous efforts to create sport and recreation opportunities on and off reserves—work that required a high level of volunteer commitment, as the example of Chief Cote shows. In 1975, the nomination letter submitted by Neeghani-Binehse, grand chief of Manitoba, for John C. Courchene of the Fort Alexander reserve in Manitoba stated:

> Awards and trophies and national publicity may be given to, and are no doubt deserved by, athletes who make spectacular individual achievements. Yet how often the real contribution to our people and our communities is made by those who work far less spectacularly, but with unrelenting determination, to contribute to our lives at home. I have known John C. Courchene all my life. I am one of hundreds of people from three generations who have benefited from his work at the community level.[75]

Courchene won the national Tom Longboat Award in 1975 for his unwavering commitment to providing sport and recreation opportunities for young people on reserves throughout the province. The nomination from Neeghani-Binehse described the enormous contributions that Courchene made to his community through his volunteer efforts.[76] His long-term commitment to sport and recreation also depicts some of the obstacles with which members of rural communities had to contend in order to participate in sport:

> Since an early age, John has been extremely active in the field of Recreation. In 1937, he organized the first Indian Hockey Team, which went into competition against Pine Falls and Victoria Beach. The Fort Alexander Indians, comprising of 12 teammates, went into this competition wholeheartedly, for travel in these days

was mainly by horse-drawn sled, or by foot. This team walked eleven miles across Lake Winnipeg to Victoria Beach for a game. The team arrived home after the game by the same route at five the following morning. John has been active in organizing the sports and recreation activities of Fort Alexander reserve ever since.[77]

Throughout his involvement, Courchene often performed several roles simultaneously. In the 1949–50 season, he was both manager and coach for the local hockey team. In the summer of 1951, he was both coach and umpire for a baseball competition against a neighbouring community, a situation that frustrated the opposing team but was a source of amusement for Fort Alexander residents.[78]

The nominations forwarded from local people and organizations and supported by regional associations demonstrate that volunteer efforts were sometimes more valued than athletic accolades. Efforts to build sport and recreation opportunities for Indigenous people at the local and regional level thus clashed with the perspective of the National Selection Committee, which favoured high performance outcomes.

In 1981, the National Indian Brotherhood changed its name to the Assembly of First Nations to signify its political objective of attaining nationhood.[79] That same year, it encountered a setback with the cancellation of the Native Sport and Recreation Program, which meant fewer opportunities for Indigenous athletes to participate in sports. The program's demise left the Indigenous organizations and participants confused and frustrated. Many people had devoted years to providing competitive opportunities for the people they served. Furthermore, without the program there was now a much smaller pool of candidates from which to select Tom Longboat Award winners, though this challenge must have seemed inconsequential next to the task of rebuilding the nascent Indigenous sport system.

These changes disrupted the Tom Longboat Awards program. The AFN postponed the awards for 1981; they did not resume until 1983, when it had determined that there were enough applicants to run a national awards program. Thus, in 1983, the AFN presented the awards retroactively for 1981, bringing to an end a quirky, convoluted process. For example, when Gordon Lee Crowchild from Alberta was nominated for an award in 1981, the AFN responded to his nominator in 1983 with a request that his athletic accomplishments be updated so that Crowchild could compete for the 1982 award as well.[80] Moreover, the committee automatically considered candidates nominated for the 1982 awards for the 1981 competition since their applications already had the necessary details for that year. It must have been a puzzling situation for the nominators and nominees anxiously awaiting news from the AFN. The decision to wait for the nominations to accumulate made it appear as though the awards were running smoothly from year to year, a prerequisite for maintaining government funding. Thus, in the early 1980s, the AFN found itself in a precarious position, striving to keep the awards afloat in the face of the cancellation of the Native Sport and Recreation Program, which was a serious blow to Indigenous sports enthusiasts throughout the country. Finally, in 1983, two years after being nominated, Crowchild was named the national recipient for 1981.[81] Tyler Sunday from the St. Regis reserve in Quebec, an accomplished athlete in boxing, field and box lacrosse, as well as hockey, was named the 1982 national recipient.[82] Both athletes received their awards at the annual meeting of the AFN in Winnipeg in May 1983.

The national Tom Longboat Awards ceremony emerged as an important event for the NIB and AFN. According to the AFN, the awards inspired Indigenous people to participate in sport and recreation while providing athletic role models for Indigenous youth throughout the country.[83] The recognition given to a few individuals, it believed, would translate into a mass social movement among Indigenous people who aimed to better their lives through sport and recreation. This argument echoed the one forwarded by Indian Affairs and the AAUC years earlier, only now the awards were meant to provide images of Indigenous people competing in the mainstream sport system as athletes with distinct histories and cultures, and not as assimilated outsiders. The national awards ceremony thus gave Indigenous leaders a platform from which to strengthen Indigenous identities by instilling pride in the accomplishments of highly successful athletes. It also provided Indigenous leaders with an opportunity to broadcast messages about the significance of self-determination. On these matters, the AFN wrote that the Tom Longboat Awards, in particular the ceremonies, "represent to First Nations the strength and awareness of their culture and identity by having their own people acknowledge the individual's athletic achievements."[84] Fittingly, the AFN also changed where the Tom Longboat Trophy would be displayed. Provisions were made in the deed of gift to allow national recipients to decide where they wanted the trophy shown, whether in their homes, their communities, or with other trophies managed by the SFC. The AFN, like Indian Affairs and the AAUC before it, capitalized on the symbolic value of sport.

As in the previous era, the decision to host banquets for the regional recipients was left to the discretion of the provincial and territorial associations, which allowed the NIB and the AFN to focus on the national ceremony. Between 1973 and 1975, the national Tom Longboat Award had been presented at the Canadian Sport Awards banquet, inaugurated in 1972. However, in 1976 the SFC stopped presenting the national award at its banquet while retaining its role on the National Selection Committee. This meant the NIB was responsible for all facets of the celebrations, including costs. Thus, between 1976 and 1987, Indigenous leaders hosted their own special banquets and awards luncheons during their annual assembly, where the national recipients were assured a large gathering of Indigenous delegates who would understand the purpose of the awards.

The anomalies were 1984 and 1985, two exceptional years for Indigenous athletes the SFC did not mind celebrating. Both events were elaborate and expensive affairs. In 1984, the AFN got almost $17,000 from the SFC to host an awards dinner for the national recipient, Alwyn Morris, with a guest list estimated at three hundred people.[85] Morris had just won gold and silver medals in kayaking at the 1984 Olympic Summer Games. His ceremony took place at the SFC banquet in Toronto, where he received the Tom Longboat Trophy and was given a small replica to keep.[86] Morris would later go on to co-found the ASC. The 1985 national recipient,

Tom Erasmus, also received his trophy at the annual SFC awards banquet.[87] Erasmus was an outstanding baseball player whose career culminated in 1979 when he helped the Barrhead Blue Jays win a silver medal at the Canadian Championships and played for Team Canada at the Pan-American Games in Puerto Rico.[88] Morris and Erasmus had made outstanding contributions to the mainstream Canadian sport system.

Throughout the 1980s and '90s, the AFN experienced a number of setbacks that ultimately led to the transfer of the Tom Longboat Awards to the ASC. First, owing to a lack of federal funding, the awards were suspended in 1983.[89] This was the first time in the history of the awards that there was a break in the program. While funding was restored for 1984 and 1985, it was soon withdrawn again for 1986, due to a lack of nominees. Worse still, by 1987, the SFC had lost interest in the program and chose not to renew its sponsorship, bringing an end to mainstream involvement in the AFN-controlled Tom Longboat Awards. This left the AFN to cover the costs of the 1987 national award on its own.[90] The 1987 ceremony for national track and field team member Rick Brant, who would go on to co-found the ASC with Alwyn Morris, took place but lacked the splendour of years past.[91] The ceremonies hosted from 1976 to 1982 inclusive were the last great celebrations arranged by Indigenous political leaders (see Table 1).

In 1988, the AFN introduced a new program called the Heroes of Our Times Awards to recognize accomplishments in the fields of law, politics, community service, and athletics. The awards consisted of six scholarships given annually to Indigenous students enrolled in college or university programs who demonstrated a high level of academic achievement. They included the Omer Peters Award, the Robert Smallboy Award, the James Gosnell Award, the Tommy Prince Award, and the Walter Dieter Award, in addition to the Tom Longboat Award. AFN organizers provided no clear distinguishing criteria in the application form for any award, suggesting that nominators and applicants knew enough about each "hero" to select the proper category; otherwise they simply guessed where someone might fit best.[92] The one criterion common to all of the awards was educational achievement: all recipients were expected to demonstrate good academic standing in a post-secondary institution to be eligible for an award.

TABLE I. National Tom Longboat Award Ceremonies, 1973–88

1973	SFC, annual awards dinner, Ottawa, Ontario, March 1974
1974	SFC, annual awards dinner, Vancouver, British Columbia, January 1975
1975	SFC, annual awards dinner, Montreal, Quebec, January 1976
1976	NIB, annual general assembly, Winnipeg, Manitoba, September 1977
1977	NIB, ceremonial banquet, Fredericton, New Brunswick, August 1978
1978	NIB, ceremonial banquet (no further details provided in the historical records)
1979	NIB, special awards luncheon, Montreal, Quebec, (no month identified) 1980
1980	NIB, special awards luncheon, Penticton, British Columbia, April 1982
1981	AFN, special awards luncheon, Winnipeg, Manitoba, May 1983
1982	AFN, special awards luncheon, Winnipeg, Manitoba, May 1983
1983	Suspended (no funding)
1984	SFC, annual awards banquet, Toronto, Ontario, January 1985
1985	SFC, annual awards banquet, Toronto, Ontario, January 1986
1986	Suspended (lack of nominees)
1987	AFN, annual general assembly, Edmonton, Alberta, (no month identified) 1988
1988	Introduction of the Heroes of Our Times Awards; banquets cancelled; recipients received $2,000 scholarship for education and training

National Indian Brotherhood
Assembly of First Nations
Heroes of Our Time
Tom Longboat Award

Date _Ap B/93_

Instructions to the Applicant

Please provide reproductions of this form for
distribution to persons asked to furnish letters of
appraisal, and insure that the name and address of the
referee is correctly supplied in the space at the bottom

_____

Name of Applicant
typed or printed

Information for the referee from whom the information has been requested:

The person whose name is given above is an applicant for an Assembly of First Nations award. The Selection
Committee will be grateful if you will provide a frank statement regarding this applicant's qualifications.

It is not expected that you will be able to speak from first hand knowledge of the candidate's qualifications under all
these heads. If you are primarily acquainted with the candidate through an academic relationship you are requested
to concentrate particularly on intellectual quality and potential. If, on the other hand, you are better acquainted with
the candidate through non-academic interests, you are requested to concentrate on assessment of character. Your
assessment is welcome to the Selection Committee and will be helpful in reaching a final decision.

Proven intellectual and academic attainment of a high standard is the first quality required of applicants, but they
will also be required to show integrity of character, interest in and respect for fellow human beings, the ability to
lead and the energy to use their talents to the fullest.

Please mail this letter to: _* Letters already Submitted._

Selection Committee   Name of Referee
Heroes of Our Time
The Assembly of First Nations   _____
55 Murray Street 5th Floor   Address
Ottawa, ON
K1N 5M3   _____

                                     _____

                                     Position

                                     _____

__Assembly of First Nations__   __Page 5__

1993 Heroes of Our Time, Tom Longboat Award nomination form. Source: Assembly of First
Nations Archives.

The new format altered the symbolic value of the Tom Longboat
Awards and diminished their visibility. With no formal link to the
mainstream sport system, the AFN amended the Tom Longboat
Awards to fit its members' ideas about self-determination. The
Heroes of Our Times format elevated educational outcomes to match
or exceed athletic achievements so that candidates had to be strong
students as well as demonstrate involvement in sports to be named

Tom Longboat Award recipients. The new format also eliminated the regional category and, instead of a banquet, national recipients received a scholarship of $2,000.

The Tom Longboat Awards had come full circle. Originally used by church and state to assimilate Indigenous youth into broader Canadian society, the awards were now being used by First Nations leaders to facilitate integration on their own terms. In each case, schooling played a critical role in this larger agenda. For the AFN leaders, the awards were no longer a means to encourage assimilation, as they had been for government and church leaders who focused on the residential schools. Instead, the AFN used the awards to cultivate the idea that advanced schooling was central to Indigenous self-determination. Being an athlete was secondary to being a student—these were the real "heroes" according to the AFN. Amid all of the tensions and negative publicity that surrounded Indigenous life in Canada, the awards represented a mechanism by which to counter colonial messages about assimilation by communicating ideas that aligned with an Indigenous vision for what it meant to be First Nations in Canada during this era.

And yet, even with these broader political aspirations in mind, for the next ten years the Tom Longboat Awards would languish under the Heroes of Our Times format, thus diminishing the AFN's political rationale for giving out the award. Perhaps there were too few Indigenous people in post-secondary education also involved in sports for there to be a viable pool of candidates. The cancellation of the Native Sport and Recreation Program in 1981 did not help since it meant far fewer opportunities for Indigenous people to participate in sports. Perhaps information about the award was not circulated far and wide enough through mainstream education and sport systems. Whatever the case, by the late 1990s, the Tom Longboat Award was clearly in need of assistance. This would come from the Aboriginal Sport Circle, whose Indigenous leaders saw the potential for the award to be used once again for broadcasting and reinforcing positive messages about what it meant to be Indigenous in Canada. Sport could help do that.

CHAPTER 4

THE STRUGGLE FOR
MEANINGFUL INCLUSION,
1999–2001

I n 1998, the AFN transferred responsibility for the Tom Longboat
Awards to the ASC, a national multi-sport organization established by Indigenous people in 1995 to advocate for and
coordinate the development of Indigenous sport and recreation
in Canada. The ASC had emerged during politically charged
times that served as a catalyst for broader changes in Indigenous
sport. The crisis at Oka in 1990 was a particularly pivotal event. This
seventy-eight-day standoff between the Mohawks (Kanien'keha:ka)
at Oka, a First Nations community in Quebec, and the Royal
Canadian Mounted Police and Canadian Armed Forces prompted
the Royal Commission on Aboriginal Peoples, a five-year investigation into Indigenous living conditions on- and off-reserve. The
commission based its four-thousand-page final report on data
collected from nearly a hundred meetings with Indigenous people throughout the country, and as such it represented the hopes
and challenges of being Indigenous in Canada.[1] It identified sport
and recreation as essential facets of Indigenous life and important

vehicles for Indigenous community and social development, especially when they were tied to the fostering of healthier lifestyles.[2]

The Royal Commission was the first federal study to show that sport and recreation were not just activities that Indigenous people did for fun in their spare time or strictly for competition, nor were they luxuries to enjoy when other basic needs were met. Rather, they were central to individual and collective well-being, especially for youth, since national concerns revolved around high rates of drug and alcohol abuse, low educational outcomes, and increasing suicide rates. Indigenous people were adamant that sport could help address these problems as well as provide youth with an outlet to feel good about themselves and their culture and find role models to keep them inspired.[3] This vision of sport was radically different from that found in the mainstream system, which treated sports as a source of entertainment or as a vehicle for Canadian nationalism. Significantly, the commission recommended as a first step that an "Aboriginal sport and recreation advisory council" be established and funded to work with federal, provincial, territorial, and Indigenous governments to "meet the sport and recreation needs of Aboriginal people" at all levels, in particular the grassroots.[4]

Although the Royal Commission was important, it was not the only factor paving the way for the creation of the ASC, for the work done by the commission coincided with a renewed state interest in sport, physical activity, and health.[5] The federal government held a series of meetings in the early 1990s to review, discuss, and recommend action in those areas. One of those meetings, the Minister's Task Force on Federal Sport Policy, held the mandate to examine the purpose and place of sport in Canadian society, including how sport contributed to the lives of Canadians and the potential scope for government involvement in amateur sport development.[6] Alwyn Morris, 1984 Olympic medalist and three-time Tom Longboat Award recipient (1974, 1977, and 1984), was at the helm of the push for a new Indigenous sport movement. His experiences as an Indigenous role model after the Olympic Games opened his eyes to the general absence of Indigenous athletes at the Olympic level: "I travelled three days a year, and I went from one end of this country and back and over again for ten years! And as that's happening I'm scratching my head and wondering, something's going wrong here. Something's not right. I shouldn't be the only one."[7] This insight was the impetus for Morris learning about access and equity issues for Indigenous people in Canadian sport. He thus spearheaded talks with political leaders, coordinated discussions among mainstream sport organizations, and took every opportunity he could to make sure Indigenous sport was a government priority.

The task force recommended in its final report, *Sport: The Way Ahead*, published in 1992, that a national Indigenous "secretariat" be established to increase Indigenous participation in national and international sports competitions.[8] As well, the final report of the

Alywn Morris (left), Co-Founder of Aboriginal Sport Circle (est. 1995), with Rick Brant, 2000. Source: Janice Forsyth.

Minister's Steering Committee on Active Living, released in 1993, identified the need to provide Indigenous people with more access and opportunities to ensure physically active lifestyles.[9] These messages further aligned with the 1993 Federal-Provincial-Territorial Conference of Ministers Responsible for Sport and Recreation, which undertook "a widely based examination of sport in Canada" and reaffirmed the need to act on the recommendations laid out in *Sport: The Way Ahead*.[10] From a history of colonialism and violence, realized by the crisis at Oka, came the establishment of the Aboriginal Sport Circle in 1995.[11]

The seeds of the ASC, as a multi-sport organization, were thus firmly rooted in Indigenous politics. Chiefs at the AFN had first supported the idea of the ASC in 1991 with their resolution calling for the establishment of a National Aboriginal Sports Secretariat. This was the "secretariat" referenced by the Minister's Task Force on Federal Sport Policy in its 1992 report and further supported in 1993 by the Confederacy of Nations, a governing body within the AFN.[12] The timeline showed that Indigenous sport leaders, led by Morris, were providing the philosophical and practical leadership for Indigenous sport development in Canada, with the government playing a supporting role—not the other way around. Rick Brant, a member of the Mohawks of the Bay of Quinte, Tyendinaga, in Ontario, and the 1987 national Tom Longboat Award recipient, worked closely with Morris to push the Indigenous sport agenda forward.

Thirteen regional organizations, called Provincial/Territorial Aboriginal Sport Bodies (P/TASBs), were set up in each province and territory of Canada to comprise the ASC. Relevant First Nations, Métis, and Inuit political organizations within their jurisdictions mandated the P/TASBs to represent their interests regionally and nationally. This meant the ASC received its direction from the P/TASBs, making it a grassroots-led organization that used sport to address broader issues of concern to Indigenous people. It was another clear example of Indigenous people working within the mainstream system and adapting the opportunities that it provided to fit their own needs. Making international teams and winning medals, though celebrated, were not the ASC's primary focus. Some of the services it provided in its earliest years included athlete training camps and coaching development clinics as well as tool kits for coaching, such as the *Aboriginal Coaching Manual*, which included a segment on racism in sport. The ASC also advocated for policy change at the federal level.[13] If elite athletes emerged from this otherwise diverse set of programs, then so much the better.

Right from the start, funding for the ASC was an issue. With limited financial resources for sport development in Canada, and especially for Indigenous sport, the ASC had to seek government support and link its policies and programs to those of the mainstream sport system, where a multitude of regional, national, and multi-sport organizations were already competing for recognition and resources, making it easy for the dominant focus on high-performance sport to eclipse Indigenous concerns. For instance, the ASC originally intended its *Aboriginal Coaching Manual* to be integrated fully into the Canadian Coaching Association's National Coaching Certification Program, the main system through which all coaches in Canada had to be certified. This provided an efficient means to ensure that all coaches, in particular non-Indigenous coaches, received some education and awareness on how to make sport more inclusive for Indigenous people.

The *Aboriginal Coaching Manual* focused on the day-to-day realities of coaching on reserves, which was very different from coaching in towns and cities, where the vast majority of human and financial resources for sport development was (and continues to be) directed. For sport to be more inclusive for Indigenous people, coaches had to unlearn what they had been taught in mainstream coaching settings. What was normally considered a "proper" space for sports or the "right" way to organize sports in towns and cities, especially in southern Canada, was not always possible, or even preferred, especially on reserves. The *Aboriginal Coaching Manual* taught coaches that most reserve facilities where sports took place were also where people gathered for community functions, where they hosted meetings and workshops, and where other sport and recreation activities for all ages and levels of ability took place. No specialized spaces existed for specific sports on most reserves, which meant that physical training programs and competitions had to work around community access to those spaces.

The result was that expectations for developing and implementing regular training schedules had to be adjusted for reserve settings. The indoor hockey rink, if there was one, might also be the youth recreation and child-care centre. The school's gymnasium might also be the community meeting place where workshops for quilting or Elders' meetings were held. A school playground might become the community golf course when the children were not around. Communities, or even regions, might not have enough participants in one age group to field a team for a specific event. Participants and teams might show up at the last minute and want to register for an event long after the deadline had passed. They also might not be available for every practice since the daily rhythms of their lives depended on what was going on at the time. Perhaps parents or caregivers had to travel off-reserve for an important meeting or event. Perhaps a community tragedy ground things to a halt for several days or longer to allow for proper mourning, understanding, and healing. Serious environmental issues could also affect sports participation on reserves: the lack of safe drinking water meant that it had to be provided somehow; communities relocated because of flooding or wildfires meant long-term disruptions to training and competition schedules. Additionally, coaches often played critical roles in the lives of Indigenous youth on reserves and therefore needed to consider carefully their positions in the communities in which they worked. They might end up being a surrogate caregiver, a role model, or a confidant. Coaches thus needed to be taught how to adjust their own learned expectations for what sport looked like, how it should be organized, and what their roles might be in a community setting. In a sense, the *Aboriginal Coaching Manual* was more than a coaching program; it was a form of decolonization that educated mainstream coaches about what life was like on reserves.

By integrating this knowledge and awareness into the mainstream coaching system, the ASC hoped that coaches would develop a more flexible and inclusive approach to coaching, especially when working with Indigenous youth. The ASC also hoped that by teaching the coaches how to collaborate with Indigenous community members in the development and delivery of quality sport programs on reserves, there would be a shift away from the deficit approach to Indigenous sport, which viewed reserves as negative spaces where the people had little motivation or hope. ASC leaders thus saw coaching as a broader form of education that could help non-Indigenous people address their fears and prejudices. Not surprisingly, racism in sport—a topic that the Canadian sport system has always been reluctant to address—was an important component of the manual. Although the Canadian Coaching Association provided the seed money to develop the *Aboriginal Coaching Manual*, it did not include it in the National Coaching Certification Program, leaving the ASC to implement the manual in its own programs—essentially teaching Indigenous coaches about coaching on reserves and in Indigenous-specific spaces. As in other facets of Indigenous life, integration into the mainstream system was easier said than done.

The transfer of the awards from the AFN—a political body—to the ASC—a sport organization, even if one with a political heritage—brought about structural and symbolic changes that altered the meanings attached to them. On the one hand, the ASC aimed to build upon the positive association between Indigenous excellence in sport, pride, and self-determination that the NIB and AFN had cultivated. On the other, some of the messages, especially those about self-determination, were diluted because of the broader environment in which they were deployed. In the context of the mainstream sport system, the Tom Longboat Awards became depoliticized, rendering them just another sports award, albeit one intended for Indigenous athletes.

BUILDING THE DOUBLE HELIX

By the mid-1990s, Indigenous people grew to recognize an Indigenous sport system in Canada, one that was distinct from the mainstream system. Soon after the ASC was established, the organization's leaders began to describe the relationship between these two systems as a "double helix," mostly as a way to provide mainstream sport officials with an easily understood model by which to grasp what the ASC was trying to accomplish. Alex Nelson, from the Musgamagwx Dzawada'enuwx First Nation in Kincome Inlet, British Columbia, first proposed the concept. As an Elder with the ASC, he used it in his teachings when leading ASC and Sport Canada officials through national policy discussions on Indigenous sport development in Canada.[14]

The ingenuity of the double helix model rested in its simplicity. Borrowing from molecular science, it refers to parallel strands intertwined around a common axis, forming the building blocks of human DNA. Since most students throughout the country would have learned about the double helix at some point in their high school career, Indigenous sport leaders thought that most people would quickly recognize the image, making the foundation of the relationship, as the ASC saw it, obvious to mainstream sport leaders. Two separate strands—one representing the Indigenous sport system, the other the mainstream sport system—functioned as mutually supportive systems. Although each operated independently from the other, both were joined by links representing the sites where the two systems connected. The image was useful because it drew attention to the existence of an Indigenous sport system and highlighted specific sites where Indigenous sport connected to, and remained distinct from, the mainstream sport model.[15] For nearly twenty-five years, Indigenous sport leaders had been trying to build the Indigenous sport system in Canada and provide opportunities for Indigenous athletes to integrate into mainstream sport if they so desired. Equally important, they had been working toward these goals in ways that contributed to Indigenous self-determination by fostering a greater appreciation of their cultures and identities and, in some cases, their continued connections to the land. The mutually supportive aspect of the double helix model was critical: one strand did not compromise or absorb the other. Rather, the two coexisted in a mutually respectful way. The ASC and the P/TASBs had thus picked up and were building on the structures and opportunities created by the Indigenous leaders involved in the now defunct Native Sport and Recreation Program.

During the 1990s, the North American Indigenous Games (NAIG), a major sporting and cultural festival for Indigenous people in Canada and the United States, was the most visible expression of the double helix model. One of its founders, J. Wilton Littlechild, from the Ermineskin First Nation in Alberta, was a four-time recipient of the Tom Longboat Award, winning it twice at the regional level for Alberta (1965 and 1975) and twice at the national level (1967 and 1974) for his accomplishments in hockey, baseball, golf, tennis, swimming, football, curling, and judo. His achievements outside of sport were equally impressive, if not more so: he had come through the residential school system, graduated from university with a master's degree in physical education, and had gone on to law school, after which he became a leader in the international Indigenous rights movement.[16]

First held in 1990 in Edmonton, the NAIG rapidly evolved into the single largest sporting venue for Indigenous people in Canada. Although the numbers fluctuated over the years, thousands of participants, including athletes, coaches, and mission staff, regularly took part in the games. The most recent events, hosted in 2014 in Regina and in 2017 in Toronto, drew a total of 3,108 and 3,722

The 1990 North American Indigenous Games becomes a reality. Source: *Windspeaker* (Edmonton), April 7, 1989, p. 7.

Canadian participants, respectively. The largest NAIG event for which official data exists was the 2002 games in Winnipeg, in which 4,465 participants from Canada took part.[17]

The NAIG were established to provide a positive space for Indigenous youth to participate in sport and feel proud of their culture. The mainstream sport system, steeped in white middle- and upper-class values and behaviours, was devoid of meaningful Indigenous cultural content and resistant to change, as the example of the *Aboriginal Coaching Manual* showed. Participation in the mainstream system was also too expensive for most Indigenous people. By the 1990s, organized sport was an extravagant habit to maintain, requiring specialized facilities and equipment, coaching, travel, club and team fees, physiotherapy, and all of the ancillary supports that competitive sport demands—provisions that many Indigenous people could not afford and most Indigenous communities did not have the resources to provide. Established by Indigenous people for Indigenous youth, and therefore sensitive to the issues that these youth faced, the NAIG were an alternative to the costly and rule-bound mainstream sporting environment.

Still, as a major international event, the NAIG were expensive to host. Facilities had to be rented. Travel and lodging for thousands of people had to be secured. Staff and volunteers were needed to organize and run everything, as well as to bring teams to the competition and chaperone the youth. The NAIG required significant resources. Securing funding to host the games, as well as to attend them, became a monumental struggle for organizers throughout the country. In the early years of the event, no government policy or legislation existed to ensure consistent funding for the NAIG. During this period, each time Canada hosted the games—1990, 1993, and 1997—organizers at the national and regional levels had to scrounge for money to pay for everything from equipment and facility rentals to clothing and food. This sometimes resulted in chaos, as Indigenous sport leaders tried to accommodate thousands of participants without adequate funding and support. For the 2002 games in Winnipeg, the three levels of government and the host society—the legal entity created for the purposes of hosting the games—entered into a shared-cost agreement that served as the precursor to a funding framework for the NAIG. Indigenous leaders had moved this monumental event forward together, turning it into a resounding success. Their challenge was in trying to secure government interest in working from an Indigenous-led approach to youth and community development through sport.

In 2003, thirteen years after the NAIG were founded, and after years of meetings, negotiations, reports, and lobbying efforts from Indigenous sport leaders, led mostly by the ASC, the Federal-Provincial-Territorial Ministers Responsible for Sport and Recreation agreed to support the costs of hosting the NAIG in Canada. The federal and host provincial/territorial governments agreed to contribute up to 35 percent of the total budget for the games, to a maximum of $3.5 million each. In 2004, this support was enshrined in legislation with the signing of a multi-party funding agreement for hosting the NAIG in Canada.[18] Funding for travel, food, and accommodation remained the responsibility of participants and regional teams until 2017, when money was made available to regions through bilateral government agreements.[19]

In spite of these challenges and frustrations, Indigenous sport leaders continued to build the double helix model through the establishment of the Indigenous sport system, thereby continuing the work that Indigenous sport leaders had begun in the 1970s with the Native Sport and Recreation Program. The NAIG and the ASC exemplified this ongoing commitment.

CONTINUITY AND CHANGE

In November 1998, the ASC approached the AFN with a formal request to take over the Tom Longboat Awards. To the ASC, the transfer was a "national priority" in need of immediate attention.[20] It aimed to "ensure the rich legacy of the Tom Longboat Awards and the memory of the individual from which the award takes its name are preserved within the Aboriginal communities of Canada."[21] The ASC followed a traditional protocol, as suggested by the AFN, to consult with key stakeholders about the appropriateness of the transfer and how the awards should be restructured once the move was complete.[22] Among the individuals from whom the ASC sought advice were Phyllis Winnie, Tom Longboat's daughter, and Jan Eisenhardt, the originator of the awards. The ASC also sought endorsement from the Haudenosaunee (Iroquois) First Nations, including leaders from the Six Nations of the Grand River, Kanawá:ke Mohawk Territory, Akwesasne Mohawk Territory, and Kanesatake Mohawk Territory, since this was Longboat's cultural heritage.[23] These endorsements constituted a culturally appropriate form of consultation, one that took into account the need for discussion and consensus in the decision-making process. This helped to legitimize the transfer of the awards from the AFN to the ASC.

Under ASC control, the Tom Longboat Awards became incorporated into the organization's Athlete Development Program to "serve as a national symbol of excellence in Aboriginal sport."[24] But when the ASC set out to revise the awards, questions surfaced immediately at the board of directors meetings, where the P/TASBs both accepted and challenged the structure and meaning of the awards: Who should be allowed to participate in the program? Which criteria would be the most relevant for assessing the winners? Which venue would be the most appropriate for presenting the awards? Though each organization responsible for the awards had always asked these questions in one form or another, now that Indigenous leaders were giving the awards their full attention in a sporting space, new competing interests came to the fore.

One of the first orders of business for the ASC concerned the criteria for eligibility. For almost fifty years, the awards were limited to athletes with Indian Status as defined by the *Indian Act*. By the 1990s, much had changed politically. Section 35 of the *Constitution Act, 1982* brought First Nations, Inuit, and Métis together under the umbrella term "Aboriginal" and finalized Canada's formal independence from Britain, suggesting the federal government was taking a more comprehensive approach to addressing Indigenous issues in Canada. The Royal Commission on Aboriginal Peoples in the 1990s, which in its final report considered Inuit and Métis populations in addition to First Nations, highlighted this approach. As a national Aboriginal organization, the ASC supported this broader political vision by taking responsibility for building sport and recreation opportunities for all three Indigenous groups. No longer would the awards be exclusive to First Nations with Status; under ASC control, they would include Non-Status, Inuit, and Métis athletes as well.

That is not to say that all Indigenous people uniformly accepted the term "Aboriginal," or even the terms "First Nations," "Inuit," and "Métis." As one might expect, matters of self-identification, especially as they relate to self-determination and sovereignty, are complex and highly politically charged.[25] The construction of Métis identity is a case in point. Sociologist Chris Anderson argues that the Métis have been constituted by race-based understandings of identity, leading to the common characterization of them as a "mixed-blood" people.[26] Since they are defined mostly by biology— unlike First Nations and Inuit, who are defined predominantly by culture and connection to the land—the implication is that the Métis are somehow less Indian and less authentic than First Nations and Inuit. The result is that "Métis" has become the catch-all term for anyone who claims Indigenous heritage but, for one reason or another, has not been categorized as First Nations or Inuit. Anderson further explains how these understandings are generated and reinforced by dominant social institutions, such as the courts and the census, which get to establish the ruling definition of Métis. That definition is then used by political organizations, such as the Métis National Council, to make "public claims to recognition and appeals for resources."[27] In short, the struggle is complex and highly political because it is a relational process in which Indigenous identities are constructed and reconstructed in a web of unequal relations that historically has granted (and still grants) more authority to the state to define Indigeneity and to enforce what it means legally and practically.

By way of comparison, sport is not a generative system in the same way that the courts and the census influence broader understandings of Indigenous self-identification and self-determination. That is to say, sport does not appear to have the same cultural and institutional power to shape the logic surrounding legal identifications of Indigeneity, though it does provide an important public space in which ideas and debates about identity and sovereignty can be shared and tested. As far as the scholarly and grey literature shows, to date there has not been one court case in Canada in which sport was used to arbitrate an Indigenous political issue.

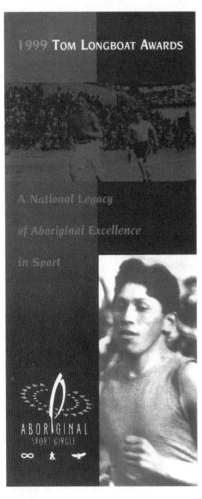

1999 TOM LONGBOAT AWARDS

A National Legacy

of Aboriginal Excellence

in Sport

ABORIGINAL
SPORT CIRCLE

Nomination brochure for 1999 Tom Longboat Awards. Source: Western Archives and Special Collections, Western University, AFC 451, Jan Eisenhardt Fonds / Folder: AFC 451-S5-F18 [Tom Longboat Awards], AFC 451-3/17.

If there was any question about whether or not Tom Longboat, an Onondaga from the Six Nations of the Grand River (who therefore was First Nations and had Indian Status), could or should stand as the symbol of sporting excellence and cultural pride for the Métis and Inuit, the minutes of ASC meetings from 1999 to 2001 are silent on the matter. It seemed that the ASC, through its P/TASBs, which included Métis and Inuit representatives, was comfortable with their blending into a program that was originally meant for Status Indians. Tom Longboat, fifty years after his death, had become an icon for inclusivity in Indigenous sport.

To demonstrate their ancestry, nominees for a Tom Longboat Award now had to produce an official membership card that showed them belonging to one of the three identified groups. If they did not have such a card, then they could supply written confirmation of their heritage from a legitimate Indigenous organization, such as the Métis Nation of Ontario, a Friendship Centre, a traditional council, or a First Nations band council, to name a few. This process would take place at the regional level, where each P/TASB established "a selection committee within its organizational structure to accept nominations, scrutinise the applicants to ensure that all meet the predetermined eligibility criteria, and select the most worthy male and female for the award."[28] Regions without an existing P/TASB needed to "establish a committee comprised of the two ASC board members and representatives from the Aboriginal political bodies of that region" to determine the eligibility and fit of each nominee.[29] Rather than adhering to strict government definitions of who was and who was not First Nations, Inuit, and Métis, the Indigenous sport leaders made these decisions themselves. The awards thus exhibited and validated Indigenous control over matters of self-identification.

And yet media coverage of the regional award recipients, including from Indigenous-owned media organizations such as *Windspeaker*, a national newspaper where we might expect to see more attention paid to Indigenous cultural diversity, did not distinguish between First Nations, Inuit, or Métis recipients; indeed, they tended to list only the winner's name, place of residence, province or territory, and sport. Consider the following summary published in a 2002 issue of *Windspeaker*:

> The regional recipients of the 2001 Tom Longboat Awards include in the female division badminton player Holly Anderson from Makkovik, Labrador; boxer Robin Beaulieu from Fort Smith, N.W.T.; basketball player Denise Wilson from Nanaimo, B.C.; hockey goalie Kayla Narvie from Eel River Bar First Nation, N.B.; hockey player Fallon Head from James Smith Cree Nation in Saskatchewan; and national award winner, wrestler Tara Hedican from Guelph, Ont.[30]

With few details that could allow readers to get a better sense of who these athletes were, the reporting on the Tom Longboat Awards, while bringing recognition to the recipients, nonetheless reinforced the view that Indigenous people were one homogenous group.

National award winners typically received more media coverage. Still, these reports focused primarily on their sporting accomplishments, with only passing mention of their heritage, their history, or their experiences in sport. The political messages that were sometimes evident under NIB and AFN control were nowhere to be found after the awards were transferred to the ASC. Instead, the summaries that the ASC produced for media, and any follow-up reporting carried out by journalists, typically promoted traditional sporting narratives. The following excerpt, pulled from the same 2002 issue of *Windspeaker*, offers an instructive example of this reporting style:

This year's [national] Tom Longboat Award recipients are Tara Hedican and Shawn Bobb. Tara Hedican, a member of the Eabametoong First Nation in Ontario, has been involved in women's freestyle wrestling for nine years. In 2001, she was the World Junior Champion, the National Junior Champion, the CIAU (Canadian Interuniversity Athletic Union) Champion, and Most Valuable Player. In addition to her wrestling accomplishments, Hedican is also a level two certified coach, a mentor, and a referee, and is a second-year history student at Guelph University.

Shawn Bobb is a member of the Spuzzum Nation in the Nlaka'pamux territory in B.C. Bobb, who will graduate from the University of British Columbia with his law degree in May, was co-captain of the University of British Columbia (UBC) men's soccer team this past season when the team took silver at the Canadian Interuniversity Sport (CIS) championships in Halifax. His teammates named him Most Inspirational Player, and he was recognized as a First Team Canada West Conference All Star, and named to the Tournament All Star Team. Bobb is also a member of the Westside Soccer Club, which was a silver medallist at the National Club Soccer Championships held in Saskatoon in October 2000. He also was involved in the UBC's summer soccer camp program, working to teach and motivate camp participants.[31]

The broader political meanings that the NIB and AFN had cultivated for the Tom Longboat Awards had been suppressed. Instead, meanings attached to Indigenous athletes' accomplishments were now being redeployed to serve a narrative of progress that linked performance outcomes to notions of social and cultural advancement.

In addition to opening up the Tom Longboat Awards to all Indigenous athletes, the ASC created a female category at both the regional and the national levels. No longer would the accomplishments of girls and women be eclipsed by those of boys and men.[32] In previous eras, from the 1950s to the 1980s, a number of overlapping factors, including lack of opportunity and gendered expectations for proper sporting behaviour, worked to exclude female athletes from the awards. However, by the time the ASC was established in 1995, girls and women throughout Canada had more options for sport than ever before. They also had more access through the public and private school systems at the high school and post-secondary levels, amateur sports teams, city leagues, as well as semi-professional events.

Founded in 1981, the Canadian Association for the Advancement of Women in Sport and Physical Activity (CAAWS) was at the forefront of this movement, advocating for changes in sport for girls and women at the level of both policy and programs. Similar to the ASC, CAAWS faced an uphill battle in trying to bring about fundamental changes in sport.[33] For instance, in 2002, the secretary of state for amateur sport rejected efforts by the women's association to include gender-equity provisions in the new *Physical Activity and Sport Act* of 2003, offering instead to include accountability mechanisms in the Sport Funding and Accountability Framework of 2004, the evaluation tool used by Sport Canada to identify which organizations would receive financial support and to measure and assess their compliance with the government's stated goals for sport.[34] In theory, including accountability measures in the framework made sense because it tied federal funding for national sports organizations to a clear set of expectations for female participation in sport. However, an earlier funding framework incorporating similar measures had failed to produce the desired results; it remained to be seen whether the 2004 framework would be any more effective in encouraging gender equity in sport.[35] Thus, although organizations were required to identify programs for girls and women in their Sport Canada funding applications as part of their eligibility requirements, between 1999 and 2001 there was no mechanism to ensure the implementation of these programs or monitor their outcomes.

For the ASC, addressing gender equity at the symbolic level by adding a female category to the Tom Longboat Awards was one thing; actually having girls and women engage in the sport system—whether as athletes, coaches, or administrators—was an altogether different matter. As with most sport organizations in Canada, gender equity at the decision-making level proved hard to achieve. Between 1999 and 2001, the total number of women on the ASC's twenty-six-member board of directors never exceeded nine (34.6 percent).[36] How did that number compare with other boards of directors for national multi-sport organizations in Canada? Unfortunately, data for the late 1990s and early 2000s was never collected because gender equity was not a policy priority for sport funding at the time. The closest year for which data exists is 2011. It shows that women occupied about one-third of board of director positions for the fifteen national multi-sport organizations in Canada (such as the ASC and CAAWS) and about one-quarter of board of director positions for national single-sport organizations (such as Hockey Canada).[37] While the numbers for the ASC were low, they were on par with the rest of the system.

In other areas, such as programming, gender equity differences could sometimes be quite stark. In 2001, the ASC agreed to provide financial support to the AFN to deliver international opportunities for male hockey players through Team Indigenous, an initiative that focused on creating an Indigenous-only hockey team. Although the ASC normally distributed its resources evenly between male and female athletes, it did not do so in its support for this hockey program.[38] Soon thereafter, the ASC withdrew its support for Team Indigenous, not because female hockey players had been left out of the venture but because of problems associated with the lack of communication between the two organizations.[39] The structural inequalities that prevented many girls and women from gaining access to sports resulted in less recognition for their achievements, especially in prestige sports like hockey and lacrosse. The fact that women's lacrosse was only added to the NAIG in 2017, twenty-seven years after the games were founded, speaks volumes about the ongoing struggles for gender equity in Indigenous sport.

These gender-based challenges were reflected in the Tom Longboat Awards, which at the regional level always fell shy of an equal slate of male and female recipients. In 1999, 8 male and 7 female athletes were named regional recipients. In 2000, these numbers increased to 10 male and 9 female athletes. And in 2001, the numbers dropped slightly to 9 male and 6 female athletes.[40] Some regions struggled more than others with their nominations; Nova Scotia, for example, had no female nominees between 1999 and 2001, while the Northwest Territories nominated only one. The creation of a female category for the awards thus served a double function: it undoubtedly provided female role models to the public at the same time that it obscured larger issues of gender equity by painting a picture of relative gender parity among the recipients, especially at the national level, where there was always one male and one female winner.

Another important matter for the ASC was the need to balance regional and national priorities for the Tom Longboat Awards. Previously, with the exception of the AFN's Heroes of Our Times program, all Tom Longboat Awards nominations passed through two rounds of assessment. This two-tier structure remained intact after the awards came under the control of the ASC. At the regional level, the P/TASBS selected the regional recipients. A selection committee, consisting of ASC-appointed members, determined the national winners. This structure, outlined in Illustration 4, shows that with the creation of a female category, the total number of recipients at the regional level—including male and female award winners—was potentially twenty-six (thirteen regions with two recipients per region).

ILLUSTRATION 4. Structure of the Tom Longboat Awards, 1999–2001.

With a national award, the ASC faced the challenge of achieving nationwide participation, which was part of its marketing plan to secure corporate sponsorship. It circulated details about its Tom Longboat Awards primarily through the Indigenous and mainstream sport systems, with the P/TASBs, provincial, national, and multi-sport organizations being the principal conduits for such information. Yet, for an organization intent on recognizing Indigenous athletic achievements throughout the country, full national participation in the program proved to be elusive. Of the twenty-six regional awards available annually for male and female athletes, only fifteen were given out in 1999; in 2000, the number increased slightly to nineteen, only to slip back to fifteen in 2001.[41]

With the awards being open to athletes at any level, the question remains: Why was the number of nominees so low? The emphasis on high performance outcomes, broadcast informally by the recipients' sporting credentials, might have been a factor, deterring family members and friends from nominating eligible candidates. It might have also led some P/TASBs to withhold their support for nominees whose accomplishments they thought were not outstanding enough to be considered for an award. Indeed, the national recipients' sporting biographies set high expectations for future winners. Between 1999 and 2001, all six national recipients had competed at either the world-class or the Olympic level. This was stiff competition for a population struggling just to gain access to sport.

In terms of material rewards, the regional recipients received a hand-carved medallion, whereas the national recipients got an all-expenses-paid trip to Toronto to receive their trophy at the annual Canadian Sport Awards, a cash bursary of $500, a custom-made gold ring, and had their names engraved on the Tom Longboat Trophy. As in the past, the P/TASBs or relevant Indigenous organizations paid for the awards ceremonies and banquets for the regional recipients. This pattern, established in 1951, raised the profile of the national recipients but did little for the regional award winners. The P/TASBs, most of which were already struggling financially, had to find their own ways to share and celebrate the achievements of their athletes.

The P/TASBs challenged this imbalance by calling for a more equitable distribution of resources and enhanced media coverage for all levels of the Tom Longboat Awards. At the ASC's 2000 annual general assembly in Victoria, one representative recommended that the sporting achievements of the regional winners be publicized alongside those of the national recipients. Their accomplishments, the delegate argued, were in fact more tangible than those of the national recipients, so they should be highlighted to increase Indigenous participation in sport and to foster healthier lifestyles at the community level, which was fundamentally what the ASC was about.[42] A year later, delegates at the assembly in Whitehorse repeated the need for more monetary support and media attention at the regional level and further recommended the establishment of a youth award to provide more tangible role models for Indigenous youth.[43] The lives of world-class athletes, whose successes undoubtedly generated pride among their communities, were simply too far removed from the day-to-day realities of most Indigenous youth to serve as catalysts for change. In a sense, they were too exceptional.

Yet the debate about regional- and national-level priorities spoke to a deeper issue, one tied to the use of performance measures to assess Longboat nominees. If the P/TASBs were dissatisfied with the use of such measures, at no time did they express their concerns. Instead, they focused their attention on the differential treatment of regional and national award winners, sidestepping important discussions about criteria—namely whether the measures should privilege youth and community development through sport, or

Tom Longboat Trophy, est. 1951. Source: Collections of Canada's Sports Hall of Fame.

whether they should focus on Indigenous athletic excellence. It was impossible for the awards to do both.

Although it is tempting to think of performance measures as an objective, unbiased set of criteria, that would be a misrepresentation. Casting them in such a way reinforces inequities by making the system they support appear meritocratic, as though it was natural and fair for everyone.[44] Even though the notion of meritocracy in sport has been exposed as a myth, the normative principles that underpin such thinking remain intact, making it seem perfectly normal for more resources to be directed to individuals and teams that produce winning results.[45] According to this logic, the most accomplished athletes and teams are the most deserving because they have worked the hardest for their achievements. To rationalize this way of thinking, all one needs to do is point to sports scores for evidence.

While such performance measures provide a reference point for understanding how good an athlete or a team is relative to other athletes and teams, they nonetheless suppress the cultural differences that underpin these achievements. For instance, some athletes and teams have more access to the types of resources that enable them to do better at sports, or they come from backgrounds in which competitive individualism is valued and rewarded and thus encouraged in their everyday lives, making them more amenable to elite sport culture. It follows that performance measures also demonstrate that underperforming athletes and teams need to "train more" and "change their attitude." In effect, self-improvement discourses linked to meritocracy mask the societal and structural constraints by which some individuals are marginalized; in the process they are made to assume responsibility for fitting in and are criticized if they do not.

The scoring system initially developed for the Tom Longboat Awards by the NIB and SFC in 1977 buttressed that logic by awarding the least points to athletes whose highest level of competition was local and the most points to those who had competed internationally in mainstream sports competitions. When the AFN transferred its files on the Tom Longboat Awards to the ASC, it did not include any information on this system. As a result, in 2001 the ASC developed its own guidelines for the national selection process (see Illustration 5).

It created a scoring grid that assigned different numerical weights to various levels of competition, with major mainstream events such as the Olympic Games, World Championships, and Commonwealth Games garnering the most points. All-Indigenous events received less weight. Even the NAIG, the cornerstone of the Indigenous sporting system, was weighted the same as a national championship, while the Arctic Winter Games, which attracted the best athletes in the circumpolar region, were weighted equally with provincial events.[46]

In contrast, each P/TASB had its own method of selecting its regional recipients. In keeping with established protocol at the ASC, which aimed to respect the autonomy of the regional sport bodies, the P/TASBs did not have to disclose their process to the national office. Thus, no official record of their selection processes exists.

These performance-based measurements were offset somewhat by the inclusion of criteria for leadership and role modelling. In the leadership category, nominees who had received special honours or awards in sport—such as being recognized as an MVP, a most improved athlete, or team captain—received points. The role model category awarded points to athletes who demonstrated the principles of fair play and sportsmanship and showed a clear commitment to holistic living, which referred to balancing the demands of work, school, family, culture, and sport.[47] The addition of such criteria made it theoretically possible for an athlete whose highest level of competition was the NAIG and who scored high in the leadership and role model categories to win the national award if the other candidates, even those who had competed at the highest levels of sport, had not demonstrated sufficient leadership or role model qualities. Except this did not actually happen. From 1999 to 2001, community participants and athletes who competed wholly in the all-Indigenous sport system consistently ranked lower than high-performing mainstream athletes, as evidenced by the national recipients, all of whom excelled in the elite mainstream model. Indeed, soon after the ASC took responsibility for the Tom Longboat Awards, a distinct gap emerged between what the P/TASBs were attempting to achieve with their focus on youth, community, and social development, and the ASC's focus on bringing attention to the "best" Indigenous athletes in Canada.

1. Circle one category that describes the athlete's highest level of competition. Give them full marks for the category that you have selected.

/30	Participation in Olympic Games
/27	Participation in World/International Championships
/24	Participation in International Games (Commonwealth, Pan-Am)
/21	National/Provincial Teams or Canada Summer/Winter Games
/18	Participation in National Championships or Aboriginal Games (naig)
/15	Participation in Provincial Championships, Dene or Arctic Games
/12	Community Level (Local Leagues or Tournaments)

2. Give a score in one category that reflects the athlete's highest rankings/results within their sport. Give them full or part marks for this section.

/20	Rankings in Olympic Sport
/17	International Rankings in Non-Olympic Sport
/14	National Rankings or Results
/11	Provincial Rankings or Results
/8	Community Rankings or Tournament Results

3. Give a score according to their other accomplishments. Give them full or part marks for this section.

/10	MVP, Most Improved Player, Most Sportsmanlike, Captain/Co-Captain, or others

4. Give a score in each of the following four (4) categories. Give them full or part marks for this section.

/10	Commitment to Athletic Development
/10	Positive Role Model in Sport and Community
/10	Demonstration of Fair Play and Sportsmanship
/10	Holistic Balance; Physical, Mental, Emotional, Cultural, Spiritual Balance

FINAL SCORE

Add: _____ (1) + _____ (2) + _____ (3) + _____ (4) = _____ /**100**

ILLUSTRATION 5. Scoring system for the 2001 national Tom Longboat Awards.

The tensions that the ASC experienced about fitting into the mainstream sport system were made even more obvious when it sought to include the Tom Longboat Awards in the Canadian Sport Awards, an annual gala that brought together some of the most influential people in mainstream sport to recognize Canada's top amateur athletes. Sponsors, government officials, and national sport leaders all congregated at the awards ceremony; simply attending this black-tie affair afforded a degree of status that those who circulated within this social milieu would have readily understood.

When the ASC assumed control of the Tom Longboat Awards in 1998, it sought to find the most appropriate and highly visible venue for presenting its national awards. It considered keeping the ceremonies within an Indigenous setting, such as the AFN's annual general assembly and the National Aboriginal Achievement Awards, which had emerged in the late 1990s as a prominent venue for recognizing Indigenous achievements in arts, culture, science, and politics. These sites would have provided the ASC with an opportunity to share the Tom Longboat Awards with a specifically Indigenous audience. However, the ASC determined that the presentation of its national awards were more appropriately suited to an integrated setting in which Indigenous athletic achievements could be celebrated alongside those of non-Indigenous athletes, in much the same way Longboat's achievements had been. By way of rationalization, it argued that "the presentation of the national awards warrants a significant…national profile both within the Aboriginal community and mainstream Canadian society" and should thus be hosted at the Canadian Sport Awards.[48] The possibility of gaining mainstream media attention and securing corporate sponsors also played a role in this decision. In sum, the ASC believed hosting its awards alongside the Canadian Sport Awards to be the best way to honour Longboat, transmit messages about the awards, profile the recipients, and capitalize on the media and sponsorships that hopefully would flow its way.[49]

In the end, the merger of the two ceremonies did not go well at all. The seating arrangements alone made clear who had status in the upper echelons of sport. For example, at the 2001 gala event, ushers directed Canadian Sport Awards recipients to the plush seating near the front of the stage, while the remainder of the assembly, mostly special interest groups, were steered to the bleachers behind the reserved area. The ASC staff, their guests, and the national Tom Longboat Award winners found their seats in the stands as well.

Television coverage of the event posed a different problem. The Canadian Sport Awards had contracted the CBC to televise the event. Between 1999 and 2001, sport organizations could buy airtime from the CBC to profile their awards, with each segment costing approximately $5,000. To have the CBC broadcast the male and the female Tom Longboat Awards would have cost roughly $10,000. Since the ASC could not afford to pay such a high price, it found its awards consigned to the untelevised portion of the night, where they served as a sort of warm-up to the main show featuring Canada's "best" athletes. Even if the ASC had managed to pay this fee, the CBC retained the right to select which awards it thought would generate the most public attention. The ASC decided against such a gamble: Why pay a small fortune when the money could be spent providing athletes with more opportunities to engage in sport?

Finally, there was the broader issue of Indigenous representation at the Canadian Sport Awards—or lack thereof. By 2001, the Canadian Sport Awards were already twenty-nine years old, and yet in all that time not one Indigenous person had won a Canadian Sport Award—this in spite of the fact that there were five separate categories of awards at the Canadian Sport Awards: Athletic Performance Awards, Leadership Awards, Corporate Excellence Awards, Spirit of Sport Stories of the Year, and True Sport Communities. The absence of Indigenous athletes from these honours was just one more visible reminder of their marginal status in the mainstream sport system.

Tom Longboat Award recipients, especially the national award winners, have clearly made significant contributions to Canadian sports through their success in the Olympic Games and World Championships and as national team members competing in other major international events. More importantly, they represent the innovative ways in which Indigenous people have moved forward in mainstream sport environments while keeping their identities and cultures intact. Yet even under ASC control, the awards reinforced deeply rooted convictions about how Indigenous athletes should participate in Canadian amateur sports and what counted as a contribution to Canadian society. In this way, the awards highlighted the contradictory space occupied by Indigenous people in

Canada: widespread public recognition was possible for Indigenous athletes only when their accomplishments could be understood and appreciated by the masses. And so nearly fifty years after the death of Tom Longboat, the famed Onondaga whose life was circumscribed by blatant racism, his legacy, specifically in the form of the Tom Longboat Awards, remained beholden to more subtle but equally harmful ideas that hindered the growth and visibility of an Indigenous sporting culture in Canada.

CHAPTER 5

TELLING OUR STORIES: CHALLENGING DOMINANT VIEWS

There are heart-warming stories of athletic striving and achievement in Aboriginal communities in every part of Canada, but unfortunately we hear very little about them. The Tom Longboat Awards affirm the best of those athletes, and bring their stories to a wider audience. Like Tom Longboat almost a century ago, the Awards stimulate athletic excellence and show that Aboriginal athletes rank among the very best. —BRUCE KIDD, TOM LONGBOAT HISTORIAN[1]

So far, I have constructed this history of the Tom Longboat Awards primarily from written documents gathered from official repositories and the personal collection of Jan Eisenhardt, the founder of the awards. These sources privilege the activities of the decision-makers and reinforce a sense that their views are the most legitimate. These perspectives are captured in the hundreds of letters, memos, reports, journal articles, and newspaper clippings dealing with the awards. But however valuable these sources are, there is a danger in writing a history that privileges the dominant voices. Indeed, were I to end this story having presented only those voices, I would have created what historian Paul Thompson described as a "power structure…shaping the past in its own image."[2] Other outlooks, from different sources, were needed to balance my reliance on the written documents.

Enter the Tom Longboat Award recipients. Were they aware of the meanings that the organizers attached to the awards? Did they share the same beliefs about the awards as the organizers? What meanings did *they* attach to them? How did these meanings align with or challenge those of the organizers? These were the general research questions that guided my interviews with the award recipients.

In this chapter, I focus on the interviews that I conducted with seven recipients from Ontario, with segments from all seven interviews included here. Ontario provided an interesting case for several reasons: it offered a balance between male and female perspectives; it included regional- and national-level recipients (including three female national winners); and the winners spanned all three managerial eras of the awards. Also, since most of the recipients are from southwestern Ontario, their perspectives offer a unique window through which to view the varied experiences of people from the same geographic region. The recipients, in order of the year that they won their awards, are

1. Bill Kinoshameg, 1954 regional recipient
2. John Lee Stonefish, 1960 regional recipient
3. Beverly Beaver, 1967 regional recipient and 1980 national recipient
4. Phyllis Bomberry, 1968 national recipient
5. Kenneth Joseph ("Joe") Montour, 1970 national recipient
6. Rick Brant, 1987 national recipient
7. Tara Hedican, 2001 national recipient[3]

The recipients talked about how sport fit into their lives. Indeed, it was so intertwined with their sense of community and place, their family histories and their individual identities, that to talk about sport as only something that happened on the field or the ice was not only trivial but also unimaginable.

Not surprisingly, all of the recipients talked about the struggles that they encountered as Indigenous athletes competing in a system governed by money—even when they had the financial resources to become involved in sports—and in which geography and schooling, along with race and gender, shaped their opportunities and experiences. Their stories bring attention to a number of critical issues, such as how sports are linked to residential school legacies; how racism and sexism in society structure opportunities for involvement in sports; how geography and economics ensure that Indigenous athletes from reserve, rural, and remote settings have to pay more to take part in sports; and how those issues (and more) relate to educational outcomes, social determinants of health, power and resource distribution, community identity, policy, and legislation. Furthermore, their stories accentuate the ideological underpinnings of the Tom Longboat Awards by calling attention to the differences between the dominant discourses constructed by the organizers and the everyday realities of the recipients. If we accept the premise that the awards comprise a cultural text that conveys important meanings about what it means to be Indigenous in Canada, then we need to shine a light on the stories that have been excluded from the dominant discourses and examine the significance of these forms of exclusion.[4]

In other words, the recipients deserve a place to tell their side of the story without having their experiences buried or distorted by the messages that the award organizers wished to convey. Rarely, if ever, have they been provided with such an opportunity, notwithstanding suggestions to the contrary, such as the "heart-warming" quotation from historian Bruce Kidd that I used to open this chapter. Those words were featured on the Tom Longboat Awards nomination brochure that the ASC produced in the early 2000s and used for nearly a decade. To say that the awards "bring [Indigenous] stories to a wider audience" is quite a stretch. Certainly, they pointed to people's athletic achievements: how fast recipients ran, how many goals they scored, which teams they made, and how many medals they won. And certainly they brought attention to the organizers' perspectives and aspirations. Beyond that narrow scaffolding, however, the awards provide no indication of what the recipients experienced, thought, or felt. Instead, the focus on performance, framed by the official narratives, carved the award recipients' biographies into neat and palatable sound bites about progress and advancement more easily understood in the context of sport.

Why are these individual stories important? Above all, they allow us to explore and understand how the recipients rationalized and made sense of the complex spaces in which they found themselves— spaces in which economics, geography, family, history, culture, schooling, race and racism, gender, and other factors intersected on a daily basis. They also highlight the unequal power relations that made it difficult for the recipients to address the challenges they faced. Theirs are not the heartwarming stories that we crave in order to fortify sport's image as a meritocracy based on determination and talent, where everyone is welcomed and accepted. These accounts are raw and real and better viewed through lenses that focus on and tease out how Indigenous people have tried to make better lives for themselves and their families by adapting to the changes that have occurred around them. Finally, the recipients' stories demonstrate how they have participated in the construction of the Tom Longboat Awards by weaving their own meanings into them.[5] Their stories, then, tell us a great deal about Indigenous lives in Canada.

This does not mean that the recipients' perspectives are missing completely from existing sources. The article on Doug Skead, the 1971 national award winner, in the *Indian News* is a case in point. It recorded Skead advising youth to get more schooling, to hold on to their culture, and to speak their "native" language. Media, therefore, occasionally printed stories that captured some of the recipients' views about sport and life—but this was rare. Usually their stories were represented through the letters included in their nomination package. As well, the recipients, or people close to them, sometimes wrote to the administrative organizations asking when they would be receiving their medals or trophies, which suggests that some people thought enough of the awards to make an official written inquiry. And, as far as the documents show, no one ever refused a Tom Longboat Award. Clearly, the recipients valued the recognition at some level.

The fact that I situate these stories in the last chapter of this book does not mean that these perspectives are somehow less important than the official stories constructed by the organizers. Quite the opposite: the decision to position recipients' voices at the end is a strategic one insofar as it allows me to layer these stories on top of the perspectives analyzed in previous chapters, thereby affording them pride of place and narrative power. I use "transitions" as the overarching theme to organize what follows. This structure made the most sense when I looked at the interviews as a whole, since that was how the recipients talked about their experiences, situating their narratives in specific social and geographic settings (e.g., going to school, moving into the mainstream) and describing how different factors—such as economics, race, and gender—intersected in those spaces to affect the totality of their lives.

TRANSITIONS
Defeating the Residential School System

I begin with Bill Kinoshameg[6] from the Wikwemikong Unceded Indian reserve, occupying the northeastern portion of Manitoulin island, in Lake Huron. Of the seven interviewees, Bill was the only recipient to go to a residential school. He was sent to the St. Peter Claver School for Boys for his elementary education when he was seven years old and then continued on at Garnier, an all-boys high school situated on the same plot of land as St. Peter Claver. Both schools, though funded by the federal government, were established and run by the Jesuits. Administratively, St. Peter Claver and Garnier, along with an all-girls institution called St. Joseph's School, were known as Spanish Indian Residential School, named after the nearby town of Spanish, Ontario. Bill was at Garnier for twelve years, from 1942 to 1954.

Bill graduated from Garnier in 1954 at the top of his class, the same year that he was named the regional recipient of the Tom Longboat Award for Ontario. By that time, he was nineteen years old and had developed into a fine athlete, playing basketball, lacrosse, rugby, softball, football, and volleyball at school. He had also honed his leadership skills by coordinating various sport and social events for his classmates. Sports played an important role in his residential school experience. But when I commented that Garnier seemed to have provided him with many opportunities for sports, Bill was quick to point out my error: "Garnier didn't offer me any opportunities," he said. If he or the other students wanted to make something of themselves, they had to do so using their own ingenuity and determination. To him, all that Garnier seemed to care about was harnessing unpaid student labour to keep the school running.

Part of that labour was expended on sport. In Bill's estimation, the boys were responsible for all sports activities at the school: they were the ones who constructed the facilities, fundraised for travel and equipment, and sewed their own uniforms. Bill learned that, if you wanted something, you had to do it yourself. He used the covered ice rink that the boys built as an example:

> We had a rink that the boys had built from the year before. This was a covered rink, one of the only ones owned by a residential school in the province. They built the whole thing on the labour of the boys. When I said the boys' school was built by the boys, it was. And, for want of a better word, they ended up with a lot of skills about learning how to build things. So we built all this stuff, and it affected me in a lot of different ways.

As at most residential schools, the students at Garnier struggled with poverty and deprivation. The disparities were obvious when they played other teams, especially ones from cities. Defeating better-equipped and better-dressed teams became for them a matter of pride:

Our hockey team was one of the top hockey teams up there. We beat everybody. We always had about thirteen players. We beat schools in towns that had four or five teams. Not only did we beat them, not only did we compete against other high schools, but we competed against teams with older people, higher leagues, stuff like that. Same in baseball. We didn't play against those teenage teams. We played against senior baseball teams. So we were always out of our league in terms of who we played against. Our uniforms? We were about as rag-tagged as you could be. When people looked at us, they wondered how high a score they could run against us. And, when we actually played, they found out they were in the wrong place.

When I mailed the transcript of this interview to Bill asking for clarification on a few points, he responded in a separate letter, explaining what sports meant to him at the residential school:

In beating better-equipped teams the only thing we had was a *win* because whether we won or lost, the reward was the same. We did not get a medal, a handshake, or a better meal. What we got was exactly what we had before the game. The pride we had was to defeat the other teams and the residential school system.[7]

Sport provided a complex social and psychological space in which struggles over economics, social class, race, and gender took place on a regular basis. Sport was much more than just sport—it was part and parcel of a broader outlook on life that did not conform to the messages broadcast by Indian Affairs and the AAUC through the Tom Longboat Awards. Bill's was not a story of assimilation. Within the context of the residential school system, the emphasis on competition and winning in sports took on additional significance for him: "It was us students against the rest of the world." Sport was the one place where he could "defeat," at least symbolically, the residential school system.

Not only did the students at Garnier have to contend with better-equipped and more-experienced teams, there were also fewer athletes at Garnier to field the school team. To Bill, fewer athletes meant more time on the ice and more opportunities to play, which taught him how to be versatile and adaptable:

> We could play whatever way you wanted. We could play
> a very fair game or play the dirtiest game you ever saw.
> And every guy that played on our team could play every
> position. And this came from the fact that we played on
> the teams that came from the residential school. You
> know, maybe you had only seven players, so you had to
> play every position. You played every position around.

These were lessons that Bill translated into other areas of his life. After finishing high school at Garnier, he pursued his goal of becoming a certified electrician and enrolled in courses at York University, the University of Toronto, and Ryerson Institute of Technology (now Ryerson University). Bill spent most of his working life in maintenance and construction, spending more than twenty years with General Electric as a "troubleshooter" and then as an energy management technician and later as supervisor of operations. He retired from Trent in 2000 and passed away in July 2018.

Integrating into the Public School System

Some recipients grew up on a reserve and attended an Indian day school in their community. The day schools usually provided elementary education, though some on the larger reserves, such as Six Nations, also offered schooling at the intermediate level. After that, students had to travel to the nearest city or town for high school. It was an arrangement that restricted their involvement in extracurricular activities, such as organized sports, usually offered outside normal school hours.

For example, John Lee Stonefish,[8] who won the regional Tom Longboat Award in 1960, grew up in Moraviantown, a small reserve located in southwestern Ontario. He was the eldest of six siblings, all members of the Delaware Nation. As did most children from Moraviantown, John attended school on-reserve and then transferred to an integrated public school about sixteen kilometres away in Ridgetown, where he continued his intermediate and high school education. At his new school, John enjoyed volleyball, basketball, soccer, and track and field in the physical education class, but he was unable to join after-school sports programs because of where he lived and the limited transportation to and from home.

Even so, John recalled how his participation in sports at the school "opened up more doors" than was possible on the reserve since most people from Moraviantown lacked the human and financial resources to organize and fund community-based teams and leagues, except in a few sports. Still, John knew that he was luckier than most young people from Moraviantown. Coming from a family whose father was employed full-time, John was provided with opportunities to play hockey on his reserve as well as baseball, a sport that he learned from his father, who played semi-pro baseball in southwestern Ontario.

John was a talented athlete and welcomed his move into the public school system as an opportunity to test his knowledge and physical skills:

> Coming from a small reserve, we only had a core of four or five people that were about the same age. And, when you grow up like that, you have a limited scope on things. Then, when you go into a school that has thirty kids in the class, or whatever it might have been, it's much nicer to have all these different ideas and people around you. And then, when you get into athletics, the competition was there, and I had to learn to train, learn to compete. I didn't just have to beat three, four, or five people—I had to beat thirty people.

John also learned to adjust to the limitations on travel. He focused on track and field at school because it was not a team sport, which meant he could train on his own at home. As for equipment, he was resourceful, using some natural materials to construct equipment in his backyard. He was particularly proud of the pole vault that he made: "I had my own pole that I cut from a tree limb. I had boards for the uprights and a bamboo pole that I bought for the bar."

John was fifteen years old and still in high school when he was named the Tom Longboat Award recipient for Ontario in 1960. He won the award for his accomplishments in hockey and baseball at the community level but mostly because of his outstanding performances in track and field at school. That same year, in addition to winning several medals at local school events, John placed in the top three in four events at the Western Ontario Secondary Schools Athletic Association Championships, in which more than three thousand athletes participated; as a result of these performances, he was named the overall junior champion of the meet.[9] John's accomplishments earned him an invitation to a sports camp at Lake Couchiching during the summer, one of the premier sports camps in Ontario at the time.

Joe Montour[10] also grew up on a reserve but had a different experience than John. Born in 1935, he was raised on Six Nations. His father was a member of the Delaware Nation, while his mother was a member of the Cayuga Nation. Joe spoke eloquently about Delaware history and its connection to Six Nations. It was clear from the start that his sense of place and identity was rooted in that history.

Joe completed his elementary and intermediate schooling on the reserve and was then sent to the town of Hagersville, about nineteen kilometres away, for high school. He left school when he was seventeen to become an ironworker, a traditional occupation among the men in his family and on Six Nations. He joined the ironworkers' union in 1952 and worked fifty years in the high-steel business, retiring in 2002.

Yet in some ways, Joe's experience was similar to John's. As a schoolboy, Joe did not take part in extracurricular activities because he had to catch the bus home as soon as classes ended. For Joe, missing the bus after school meant a long jog home at the end of the day. If for any reason he stayed after school, he usually hitchhiked home. Such were the arrangements for most Indigenous students who lived on-reserve at that time. It meant that they were not even given the choice to try out for teams. They were excluded right from the start because they could not commit for logistical reasons. As Joe pointed out, "If you had a school team, the Indians didn't play on them, because how were you going to get home?"

Joe remembered feeling lonely and isolated in the public school system. Moving into a foreign and predominantly white environment was a daunting task:

> It was such a change when you were in a [reserve] school with thirty-seven kids or something. And when I graduated there were only two of us. And the other guy, he figured he was a professor by the time he finished grade 8. He didn't have to go on, and I had to go on. I didn't know anyone. So I go to school, and there are about three hundred kids there that I never saw before in my life, and they're not Indians. I didn't have anyone to talk to.

Joe left high school after his second year to join his father as an iron-worker. It was then that he committed himself to sports, specifically lacrosse. Being an ironworker and a lacrosse player was a rough-and-tumble lifestyle but one that Joe remembered fondly. The Elders and a few ironworkers taught him how to play, and at one time he played for the Brantford Warriors, helping his team to win the Canadian senior lacrosse title in 1968. Joe acquired these skills not because he made a conscious decision to play the game but because he was too young to drive a car and had to travel everywhere with the men. As he explained, "Whatever they did, I had to do."

When Joe won the national Tom Longboat Award in 1970, he was thirty-five years old and had already served six terms as president of the Six Nations Minor Lacrosse Association and two terms as president of the Six Nations Minor Hockey Association.[11] In 1967, he also helped to spearhead the construction of an indoor arena on the reserve. The facility opened in 1972 and was named the Six Nations Sports and Cultural Memorial Centre, later renamed the Gaylord

Powless Arena, after the famed lacrosse player from Six Nations (Powless was the national Tom Longboat Award recipient for 1964 and was inducted posthumously into the Canadian Sports Hall of Fame in 2017). Joe had also recently retired from competitive sports and had begun channelling his energies into coaching lacrosse, hockey, and baseball. One of the telltale signs of the prominent position that he acquired among the young men in the community was that they spent countless hours playing lacrosse and other games in his backyard, turning the field into a "dustbowl" each summer.

From the Reserve to the City

Although there were more sports opportunities in the mainstream system, gaining access to and staying involved in mainstream sports were not simple for the Tom Longboat Award recipients. The effort required determination and discipline, especially when it came to issues like having to relocate to play sports and dealing with racism in an athletic milieu. Phyllis Bomberry's story is a good example.[12] Phyllis was the second-oldest in a family of seven children (four boys and three girls) who grew up on the Six Nations reserve. Phyllis learned how to play sports at an early age, catching ball for her father and brother, both of whom were accomplished pitchers. She began competing in softball at age eight and in her teens was selected to play for the Ohsweken Mohawk Ladies team on Six Nations.

In 1963, Phyllis was recruited to play for a Toronto-based commercial team called Carpetland. She accepted the offer, found full-time employment working on the assembly line of a major communications factory, and moved to the city. Playing for Carpetland opened up new sporting possibilities previously closed to her. The Ohsweken Mohawk Ladies were talented and successful, but the team did not compete beyond the regional level at that time. For the most part, opportunities for Indigenous women to compete in all-Indigenous sports at the national level did not exist until the late 1970s. In order for Phyllis to pursue her softball career, she had no choice but to leave Six Nations and integrate into the mainstream sport system.

Phyllis was an outstanding catcher and batter, helping Carpet-land to achieve many victories. With her help, in 1967 and 1968 the team won the gold medal at the Ontario Senior A Women's and the Canadian Senior A Women's Championships. For her efforts, Phyllis was named the top batter and all-star catcher at the national championships in 1967 and the all-star catcher in 1968. She was also named the national Tom Longboat Award recipient in 1968 for these achievements. She was the first female athlete to win this honour, seventeen years after the awards were initiated.[13]

Playing for Carpetland was sometimes hard and complicated. Racism permeated the sport that Phyllis loved. As the team's catcher, she was always within earshot of these remarks. There was little that she could do since she was competing in an environment that implicitly supported racial discrimination by not taking action when it surfaced. Indeed, no one tried to rectify these situations—not her teammates, the coaches, or the umpires. This meant that Phyllis had to deal with the racism on her own if she wanted to continue playing on an integrated team. It was a part of the game that Phyllis had to tolerate, and she reacted by "tuning out" and concentrating on the ball. What else could she have done? With few options at hand, she focused on being the best player that she could be and learned to ignore the racism she faced.

Softball was more than just a leisure activity to Phyllis; it was how she created a sense of community for herself and other Indigenous women who had moved to Toronto in search of better lives and more opportunities since the government was not serious about invest-ing in reserves in ways that mattered to Indigenous people. Many of the women she met were interested in playing ball but struggled financially, so Phyllis secured equipment through donations and helped to organize games against other women's teams in the city. She remembers the games as non-competitive, social events. Runs and innings were counted, but the players did not dwell on the out-come of the game. It was a busy time in Phyllis's life. In the day, she worked on the assembly line; after work, she coached the women for a few hours and then scrambled to the other end of the city to make practice for the Carpetland team. These were hectic days, filled from morning to night, but they stood out in her memory as being among the most memorable. Phyllis passed away in January 2019.

Beverly Beaver[14] also played for the Ohsweken Mohawk Ladies softball team on Six Nations, where she was born and raised. And like Phyllis, Beverly was recruited to play for a Toronto-based team, though she chose to stay home to raise her children and to "help the team win championships." Beverly is proud that the Ohsweken Mohawk Ladies never recruited "outside" players when she was on the team, viewing the team's ability to compete at an elite level without having to recruit outsiders as a sign of their autonomy and self-reliance. In her estimation, they did not need anyone from outside Six Nations to help them be successful. From her first days on the field in 1961 to her last event in 2000, Beverly was part of a winning tradition that included five Canadian Native Ladies Fastball titles (1979, 1982, 1983, 1984, 1985), two National Indian Activities Association Championships (1980, 1991), and one North American Native Ladies Tournament (1979). She also received numerous awards as an individual athlete in the MVP, best-pitcher, top-batter, and all-star categories.[15]

Hockey was another sport that Beverly loved to play. She recalled learning to play on a pond that her brother groomed behind their house on Six Nations. She enjoyed spending much of her time there:

> My brother built a dam to stop the water so we had a place to skate. He played hockey too, just on the pond. I remember playing at night. It was dark, and we'd use a tin can instead of a puck so you could hear wherever the can went. You couldn't see it unless there was moonlight, but you could hear it. I'd be out there as soon as I got up in the morning till it got dark at night. I'd be out there a lot by myself.

Beverly mentioned that a group of boys would gather at local ponds to play pick-up games. She wanted to join them to hone her skills, but in order for them to accept her as a legitimate player she had to disguise the fact that she was a girl. She would put her hair up under her hat and call herself "Billy" so that they would let her play with them. Sometimes she even taped her breasts to hide her feminine physique. Whether or not they knew who she was, she believed that she would have been treated differently if she presented herself as a girl, and thus tried to fit in by hiding her identity and manipulating her looks.

When Beverly was growing up, opportunities for girls and women to play organized hockey on Six Nations were limited to exhibition matches; they were not allowed to play in the regular league or championship games.[16] The local minor hockey coach spotted her talent and frequently asked her to play in the exhibition games. To do so, she had to change at home before the games because there were no change rooms for girls at the hockey arena. Her uncle, who also coached youth hockey in Six Nations, did the same, enlisting her skills in special matches against male students from the Mohawk Institute, the Indian residential school in the nearby town of Brantford. She soon wanted more opportunities to play and more respect as a player. With no options on the reserve, Beverly ended up integrating into the mainstream hockey system, playing for teams in Burlington and Brantford. Some of her career highlights include gold medal victories at the Canadian Senior A Women's Hockey Championships (1983), the Dominion Ladies Hockey Tournament Senior A Championships (1967), and the Provincial Senior A Ladies Hockey Championships (1967, 1968, 1969, 1972, 1983), as well as being named top scorer, MVP, and all-star centre in various events.[17]

Beverly is one of only a handful of recipients to be named a Tom Longboat Award winner more than once and she remains the only female recipient with this distinction. From 1967, when she won the regional award for Ontario, to 1980, when she was given the national award, Beverly competed successfully in softball, hockey, and bowling at the local, regional, national, and international level.[18] Tom Longboat Jr.—Tom Longboat's son—nominated her in 1967, while George Beaver, her husband, nominated her in 1980.

Not unlike the other recipients, Beverly also experienced racial discrimination, though it was the opposite of Phyllis's experience. Beverly talked about how her light skin colour helped her integrate into mainstream hockey in Brantford and Burlington while being a challenge for her growing up and going to school on Six Nations:

> I didn't have any problems that way [integrating into mainstream hockey] because I'm fair. Maybe at the time they didn't know I was Native, but they probably knew George [my husband] was because he looks Native. But with me people accepted me more because I don't look Native....I had more problems with discrimination at school on the reserve, where they called me "white girl"! They called me that because I was fair and had blonde hair, so I had to look after myself. Good thing I was big for my age [she said with a playful smile].

Beverly was not alone in talking about how her appearance and skin colour shaped the way people viewed and treated her. This was one of the key themes to emerge from the interviews with all seven recipients. Each was well aware of the racial politics of skin colour and how it created opportunities and tensions in their lives, privileging them in some situations while marginalizing and stigmatizing them in others.

Growing Up in the City

The demands placed on athletes in competitive sports have changed dramatically since the Tom Longboat Awards were first established in 1951. This was especially true for amateur athletes from the 1980s onwards. Increased performance expectations, accompanied by the rapid professionalization of sports, meant that they had to be more talented, receive more training and support, and have more resources than ever before in order to reach the podium.

The recipients of the awards who had competed at the elite level were well aware that athletes from middle- and upper-class backgrounds living in urban areas had distinct advantages over athletes from lower-income levels and those who lived on reserves or came from rural and remote locations. Although the recipients did not deny that hard work was needed to succeed in sports, they understood that it took more than grit and determination to do well at the elite level. Rick Brant, the national recipient in 1987 who went on to become a co-founder and executive director for the ASC, expressed it best: "There are those extraordinary athletes who have emerged from that [reserve] environment. But, with today's sport systems, there are so many barriers for a First Nations athlete to overcome. Unless you have access to a knowledgeable and committed coach, training facilities, the sport sciences, and a significant amount of money to cover the cost of training and competing at an elite level, the odds are stacked against you."[19]

Rick, a member of the Mohawks of the Bay of Quinte, Tyendinaga Mohawk Territory, located near Belleville, Ontario, had many of those opportunities. In the 1980s, he was one of the best middle-distance runners in Canada, but becoming a runner was not what Rick had originally imagined for himself. As a young athlete, he had dreams of playing in the National Hockey League and he competed in minor hockey until high school, at which point he stepped away from the sport, believing that he had reached the peak of his potential. Looking for another activity to occupy his time, Rick channelled his energies into running and found success early in his career, winning a bronze medal in the 800 metres in his first appearance at the Ontario Federation of School Athletic Associations (OFSAA), the premier track and field event for high school athletes in Ontario.[20] At the OFSAA Championships in 1986, Rick tied for first place in the 800 metres and set a Canadian interscholastic record. Later that summer, at the national junior championships, he won the 800-metre race and was part of the gold medal relay team in the 400 metres, qualifying for the 1986 World Junior Track and Field Championships in Greece, where he placed fourteenth overall in the 800-metre event. In the fall of 1986, he enrolled in the Native Studies program at the University of Saskatchewan, where he trained at the national training centre in Saskatoon. Rick went on to win other national and provincial 800-metre championships and competed for the national team, winning competitions in the United Kingdom.

Rick retired from track and field in 1988, when he was twenty-one years old, because of a chronic back injury brought on by the stress and strain of training. After that, he committed himself to rebuilding the Indigenous sport system in Canada by contributing to the organization and realization of the North American Indigenous Games and by supporting the creation of the ASC under the leadership of fellow Tom Longboat Award recipient Alywn Morris. Rick served as the organization's first executive director. It was Rick who spearheaded the transfer of the Tom Longboat Awards from the AFN to the ASC in the late 1990s.

The recipients who had competed at the elite level were aware of and troubled by the widening gap between the realities of modern sports and the social and economic realities of being Indigenous in Canada. They knew that they had more access to sports than most Indigenous people, and this awareness provided them with insightful and incisive views on the matter. Rick, who grew up in Ottawa, was well aware of the disparities between the opportunities available to athletes in major urban areas compared to those on reserves:

> There are significant cost factors, but it was through school that so many doors opened up to me....I think the difference from my perspective, if I was living on-reserve, especially in an isolated community, are the limited opportunities. Would I have had the same opportunity to compete and train at a top facility, under the guidance of expert coaches, and among nationally ranked athletes? I was blessed to have a strong support system that included my family, schoolteachers, and coaches. I don't believe I would have been afforded the same opportunities had I not been living in a large urban centre.

Tara Hedican, a former world-class wrestler and the 2001 Tom Longboat national recipient, was also aware of these disparities and how they privileged her: "I can't compare myself—a girl in the city with a university degree—to a kid who won a local track meet.

I had a huge advantage where I grew up, where other Aboriginal kids from reserve communities are so secluded."[21] Tara, a member of the Eabametoong First Nation, located northeast of Thunder Bay, in northern Ontario, was one of the most accomplished wrestlers in Canada. Born and raised in Guelph, Ontario, she was introduced to wrestling in grade 7 during her physical education class and liked the sport so much that she immediately joined the junior high school team. Although women's wrestling was still a relatively new sport when Tara took an interest in it, she trained hard, spending every available moment practising in the gym. In grade 10, she began training with the varsity athletes at the University of Guelph, where she met older, more experienced, and heavier female wrestlers who not only challenged her physically but also helped her to adapt to a male-dominated sport. By the end of her high school career, Tara had won numerous tournaments, including four OFSAA titles and one national junior championship, at which she was also awarded MVP status.

After high school, Tara chose to stay close to home, enrolling as a student at the University of Guelph and completing her undergraduate degree in history. During her first year, while still adjusting to the demands of university life, she successfully defended her title as junior national champion with MVP status, and, in only her second appearance at the competition, she won the world junior championship. Proud of her daughter's accomplishments, Tara's mother nominated her for the Tom Longboat Award.

Tara went on to become the 2003 Pan American champion and was named the alternative female wrestler for the Canadian team at the 2004 Olympic Games in Athens. Equity issues became even more pronounced for her after reaching the highest level of sport:

> Some people probably think it's unfair for me to be nominated for the [Tom Longboat] Award. People from the city have more opportunities that are not available on reserves. Cities have better facilities and better coaches. I've seen a lot of talented Indigenous athletes, but most don't have the guidance to take sports to a

higher level. The perception is that you need to be rich to play on a national team or make it to the NHL. We have a few Indigenous athletes who have made it really far who win most of the awards like Jordan [Tootoo, drafted by the National Hockey League in 2001]. He was nominated for the [Tom Longboat] Award [and was named a national winner in 2002]....And who's going to win it besides those people? I mean, if you've gone to the Olympics or World Championships, where do you draw the line? I'm really excited that Indigenous peoples are starting to be recognized and I hope to see more inclusion in Canada's athletic program in the near future. The Tom Longboat Award symbolizes our struggles in mainstream sports and should be earned by our best athletes.

This point is well taken. Most of the recipients who have won the national Tom Longboat Award are products of the mainstream high-performance system.

Racism was another complicating factor for elite-level recipients of the Tom Longboat Award. Rick, who described his appearance as "nondescript," explained his experience with racism this way: "There were individuals who would share with me, not necessarily knowing whether I was First Nations or not, their views of Indigenous Peoples, which were outright racist, but when we lined up on the track that didn't affect the outcome. I wasn't banned or excluded from events because I was First Nations. I was either fast enough to race in that event or I wasn't." More subtle forms of racism—rather than banning Indigenous athletes outright—have made it harder to detect and address such discrimination in sport, as Rick suggested.

Tara did not openly acknowledge her Indigenous heritage until she reached university because it was too complicated and too tiring to constantly explain her mixed background to people. Not talking about it was her response to racist thinking that placed people in specific categories like Indigenous, white, black, and so on—categories that did not fit her idea of who she was. As Tara explained,

"I always felt uncomfortable when people ask you what you are because I'm such a mixture of different things anyway." Her father can trace his roots back to various European heritages, a point that most people choose to ignore: "When I start going into all that, people tend not to believe me. They just want to hear that I'm Spanish or Native or whatever. They don't care. They just want to know why I'm so dark." Tara preferred not to be drawn into such conversations; similar to Phyllis Bomberry, who ignored the racist taunts on the ball field, for Tara, silence was a means to resist racist thinking.

Like Rick, Tara was thoughtful and observant about matters of racism toward Indigenous people in sport and broader society. Using her own experience as an example, she talked about how Indigenous athletes were viewed as being different from other athletes and how their difference resulted in their objectification: "I think it's the reason I've been on TV so many times or in magazines. I don't think I would have had the publicity I had unless I was Native….People want to hear about what it's like being Native. People want me to go everywhere [to do public speaking]." This was similar to what Beverly from Six Nations, a two-time Tom Longboat Award recipient, experienced. Beverly also referred to the way that her Indigeneity could be used for commercial profit. She recalled the Ohsweken Mohawk Ladies being invited to play against non-Indigenous baseball teams so as to profit from their otherness: "We were invited to a lot of tournaments because we were a Native team. I guess we were like a drawing card for them. People would come out because they knew a Native team was going to be there." Beverly's husband George, who frequently travelled with her to competitions, also recalled how non-Indigenous people attended the games "looking for anything unusual" to watch.

Life Went on as Usual

What ultimately emerges from these interviews is a wide range of attitudes about the Tom Longboat Awards and what they mean to the recipients. No matter how the organizers promoted the awards, the recipients attached their own meanings to them—meanings shaped by the contexts in which the individual athletes lived and competed. The result is a range of options for understanding the role of sport, and the Tom Longboat Awards, in Indigenous lives.

At one end of the spectrum is Bill Kinoshameg, the 1954 recipient who won his award while at Garnier Indian Residential School. Sport was important to his survival at residential school—it helped him to "defeat" the system, as he put it—and shaped his attitude toward life in general. In a similar way, Bill looked for the instrumental value in the awards and saw none. He was living in Sudbury, Ontario, when he was invited to return to Garnier to attend a ceremony that he did not know was being held in his honour. When I interviewed him, he had a vague memory of that day, and what he remembered was the "comical" aspect of it all:

> I had no idea what I was going back for. I borrowed my mother's car, and I drove down there in the morning and found out that there was some big dinner for an award. At the end of the day, I had all this stuff, everybody was shaking my hand, and then I went home. I still had no idea what was going on. All I knew was I had a medal.

Bill's memory of that day was shaped by the fact that he did not know who Tom Longboat was and he was only vaguely aware of the awards prior to 1954. What possible significance could he have found in being named a recipient? Indeed, as he put it, "In essence, the Tom Longboat Award didn't really do me any good because I had to take a day off of work to go down there, and they had to take a day off of school." Instead, the awards benefitted the school authorities by bringing attention to their educational mission, with the school responsible for organizing the ceremony, sponsoring the dinner, and cancelling the school day (but not the daily chores) to prepare for the event.

Joe Montour, the 1970 national recipient who left school to become an ironworker, was proud of his contributions to sport but ambivalent about what the awards meant. He found out that he had won the award when a reporter from the *Brantford Expositor* called for an interview. Joe was surprised to hear the news because he thought it was an award for athletes; although he had played lacrosse, he was honoured primarily for his involvement as a coach and organizer. When I asked him if the award held any special meaning for him, he had this to say:

> The thing was, it wasn't given to me for being a great athlete, so it didn't really faze me thinking I was this big superstar lacrosse player or whatever. The way I had won it, I thought, well, I guess I must be deserving of it, but it didn't seem to be a big deal at the time....And the thing is it didn't seem to make a difference to anyone else. So what's the use of me blowing a whistle around saying that I won it?

Joe passed away in January 2012. For him, as for Bill, sport—but not the Tom Longboat Awards, at least initially—occupied an important role in his life.

The issue of the ceremony, raised by Bill and Joe, came up time and again during my interviews with all seven recipients. For instance, Tara Hedican, the 2001 national recipient, was presented with her national award at the Canadian Sport Awards in Toronto, where the best amateur athletes were recognized annually for their achievements. At the ceremony, she observed how Indigenous athletes, among other targeted populations, were marginalized both spatially and symbolically, as the major media attention afforded to the other award winners was withheld from Indigenous athletes. Not only were they assigned to the bleachers behind the plush chairs reserved for the other recipients, presenters, and the corporate sponsors of the high-profile mainstream awards, but they were also rendered invisible to a wider audience when, in Tara's words, "they didn't televise the Tom Longboat Awards."

Other recipients developed a strong attachment to the awards. John Lee Stonefish, the 1960 recipient who constructed his own track and field equipment at home, was informed by his school coach that he had been nominated for the award. At the time, this did not strike John as "anything out of the ordinary" because, in his words,

"I didn't know the significance of it, or why they were putting in my name, or if I had a chance of winning, or anything else like that." But when he was named the regional recipient, he received letters of congratulations from his local MP and MPP, and a special awards dinner was held for him in Moraviantown. It was then that he began learning about Tom Longboat and the awards by talking to other people on Six Nations. As he later told me, "When you think about how many people have won this award, there's not that many. To be part of that group is nice." John, who went on to become chief of the Delaware Nation from 2005 to 2007, credits his training in sport with the fact that he became a political leader. Sport prepared him for life. During his time as chief, he was inducted into the Ridgetown District High School Hall of Excellence for his accomplishments in sport as well as for his community leadership. He was in northern Ontario when the induction ceremony took place, so his brother went on his behalf.

Rick Brant, the 1987 recipient, learned about the awards through his father, who instilled in him a great respect for Tom Longboat and the awards:

> I was aware of the award because it was brought to my attention by my father years before I had achieved national-level performances in middle-distance running. It was one of those things where my dad would say, "This is something you could win someday." And I was thinking, "Yeah, whatever!" I understood how prestigious the award was and to be honest, I didn't think it was something I could ever attain. And so, when I did win, I was able to reflect on how far I had come....I was on the flight to Edmonton to receive the award when I thought, "Wow, this is huge," because it's the acknowledgement and recognition of your achievements by Indigenous leaders from across Canada. I held it in such high esteem when I was younger and never thought I would have the chance to win an award like that. It had a profound impact on me. I figure I must be doing

something right if communities are acknowledging me for it. And then to be presented the award in front of all the [AFN] Chiefs, wow! I was still fairly young at the time, being nineteen years old. I was very nervous and excited. It was one of those experiences I will never forget. I said to myself, "I am a Tom Longboat recipient."

When Rick became the executive director of the ASC, one of his first priorities was to work with the AFN to transfer the Tom Longboat Awards to the ASC. When that was achieved, the program was restructured and the Tom Longboat Trophy refurbished after years of travel-related wear and tear. Today, the Tom Longboat Awards remain a core ASC program.

Phyllis Bomberry remembered the day when she found out that she won the national award. It was in 1969, and she was playing for the Toronto Carpetland Senior A team. After a game at the Cayuga Longhouse on Six Nations, Renson Jamieson, the 1966 national recipient of the Tom Longboat Award and the coach of the Ohsweken Mohawk Ladies team, approached Phyllis while she was sitting with her teammates on the bench getting ready to go home. Jamieson told her that she had won the Tom Longboat Award for being the "best Indian athlete in Canada," handed her a certificate, and showed her the big trophy. She was surprised but not excited—indeed, this was the first that she had ever heard about the award, even with Jamieson being a former winner. She was promised a small replica of the large trophy, but it never materialized, and she never saw the big trophy again. She did, however, receive the traditional medallion, given to each regional recipient since the awards were established. When I met Phyllis, she had her medallion stored in a box with other memorabilia from her sports days and could not put into words what the Tom Longboat Awards meant to her. The fact that she kept the medallion all those years was indication enough that it meant a great deal.

While the recipients have woven their own meanings into the awards—meanings rooted in their own social, cultural, and material interests—the meanings that the organizers attached to the awards were hardly well known or even accepted by the recipients. In fact, no one really cared what the organizers thought. When I told John what the awards were originally intended to do, he honed in on their essence, emphasizing how their meaningfulness can vary from person to person and group to group, and claimed the ability to define their significance for himself and for Indigenous people: "It doesn't matter who started it. It doesn't matter what it's supposed to be. It's what it is in our eyes that is important."

The question remains: Have the Tom Longboat Awards shifted how Canadians see and understand Indigenous people or Indigenous athletes in sport? Not likely. Part of the problem is the silence surrounding the recipients' stories. This silence is arguably one of the most striking features of the awards. Although the same could be said of most other sports awards in Canada, what makes the quietness surrounding the Tom Longboat Awards so poignant is the fact that the substance of the awards relies in large part on the continued excision of their stories. Although the organizers have always altered the meanings attached to the awards, they nevertheless retained control of what information is published. In doing so, they have effectively achieved what sociologist Richard Gruneau calls "the ruling definition of the social" by regulating what messages can be attached to the awards, at least publicly.[22] Under other conditions, more complex (to say nothing of truthful) versions of the recipients' stories would mean that Canadians would have to take Indigenous stories, and therefore stories about Canada, more seriously.

TRUTH, RECONCILIATION, AND SPORT

The act of giving out sport awards is a popular cultural practice, not just in Canada but globally as well. In every country that has an organized competitive sport system, there are certain to be awards that recognize the outstanding achievements of athletes, teams, coaches, officials, volunteers, and builders. What is more, these broad categories are often broken down into discrete forms of recognition, whether by particular sports (e.g., track and field or hockey), specific segments of society (e.g., amateur/professional, junior/senior, male/female, able/disabled athletes, Indigenous), geopolitical areas (e.g., province, region, or state), or any other way of distinguishing one group from another. This widespread practice covers a lot of territory since most countries in the world are involved in some type of organized sport.

All sport awards, including the Tom Longboat Awards, serve a deeper social function, one that goes well beyond their stated purpose of recognizing participants for their achievements—they teach participants and the public subtle lessons about who should be admired and why we should admire them. Whether intentional or not, sport awards thus communicate and reinforce the values, beliefs, and practices of broader society—of the people who created

them, the people who receive them, and the community of follow-
ers who valorize them. It is precisely that invisible curriculum—the
aspirations and ideologies, reinforced through specific practices
(such as who controls which part of the nomination process and
how recipients are assessed)—that needs to be explored in order for
us to understand who and what is being celebrated. As cultural theorist Stuart Hall explains, it is "our use of things, and what we say,
think, and feel about them—how we represent them" that makes
something meaningful and therefore culturally significant.[1] In the
case of the Tom Longboat Awards, it is our "use" of the awards
that makes it a unique site for critical analysis and reflection on
Indigenous involvement in sport and what that involvement tells us
about Indigenous-settler relations in Canada.

Organized sports have always played a valuable role in nation
building. Canada is no exception. By the late 1800s, the Department
of Indian Affairs, along with the churches, used organized sports
to transform Indigenous people's sense of themselves as distinct
groups with their own languages, histories, cultures, and unique
ways of interacting with the environment. Any change to one aspect
of Indigenous life affected the others. Indian agents and missionaries understood this and aimed to undermine the deep fabric that
held Indigenous lives together using sports to advance this agenda.
They encouraged Indigenous people to adopt new physical practices
and, in some cases, forced changes upon them. Their use of sports
to help replace religious customs that had been banned through the
Potlatch Laws is a clear reminder of how sport is entangled with
Canada's colonial history. The Potlatch Laws were in place from 1885
to 1951, at which point the federal government revised the *Indian Act*
while still working toward Indigenous assimilation.

The late 1800s to the mid-1900s were thus formative years for
sport and colonization in Canada. That era set the stage for five of
the most damaging beliefs about the role of sports in Indigenous
life: first, that sports were suitable alternatives to Indigenous physical practices that were slowly being made to disappear; second,
that sports could help Indigenous people to cultivate the values
and behaviours that they needed to succeed in broader society;

third, that Indigenous people would naturally prefer the new activities over their own cultural practices because they were thought to be more legitimate and worthwhile; fourth, that Indigenous physical practices, such as snowshoeing, lacrosse, and canoeing, were acceptable sports only when they had been taken up and transformed by settler society; and fifth, that Indigenous involvement in sports required constant supervision to ensure that the remedial effects were being properly administered. Individually and together, these assumptions fuelled the colonial imagination, providing settlers with the moral authority to use sports to fundamentally alter Indigenous ways of life. The growing institutionalization of sports—with its constructed facilities divorced from a deeper connection to the land, its rapidly expanding set of tightly bound rules that defined who could play and how, and its middle-class governing bodies policing and enforcing those rules—thus served as an important form of civic advancement to eradicate Indigenous cultural practices while fostering new, more socially acceptable ones.

The Tom Longboat Awards were part of this broader process of cultural transformation. They emerged in 1951 out of a complicated history involving Indian Affairs and the churches—a powerful superstructure that consumed award founder Jan Eisenhardt's sincere love for physical culture and crippled his attempt to bring more resources and support for sports and recreation to Indigenous people. As a state-led tool for assimilation, the awards sought to encourage Indigenous youth, especially students in the residential school system, to appreciate new bodily practices that would presumably replace their traditional ways of life and instil in them a new sense of self, one rooted in and expressed through physical movement and a functional and civil relationship to the land. In other words, the Tom Longboat Awards were much more than a sport award: they were a mechanism for breaking down Indigenous cultural values and behaviours as well as an annual public celebration of that process. Yet, their meaningfulness was not set in stone; it would change over time as administrative responsibility gradually shifted from government to Indigenous control.

From 1951 to 1972, Indian Affairs and the Amateur Athletic Union of Canada co-managed the Tom Longboat Awards. Although the awards were open to Status Indians of all ages in Canada, information about the awards was circulated primarily through the residential schools, ensuring that the focus remained squarely on the young. Educators and administrators worked to identify potential recipients and took great pride in having award winners chosen from their institutions. Successful Indigenous athletes were a gold mine of symbology for school, government, and church leaders, who could put to effective use the positive assumptions about organized sport to counter the negative aspects of residential schooling. The changes made in 1951 to the *Indian Act* repealing the Potlatch Laws also signalled official recognition of the failure of the residential school system. Thus began the slow process of dismantling this system and channelling Indigenous students into public schools that were neither ready nor willing to accommodate them. The Tom Longboat Awards helped to obfuscate and deflect criticism of the residential schools by pointing to Indigenous "success" stories. Sometimes success came from the public schools too. As important as the award recipients were symbolically—perhaps even because of this fact—they were rarely granted an opportunity to say something about being an award winner; this created an opening that decision-makers filled with redemptive descriptions of the relationship between sport, schooling, and assimilation.

At the request of Indian Affairs, the AAUC became formally involved in the Tom Longboat Awards. In promoting a strict adherence to its amateur code, the organization implicitly endorsed a white, male, middle-class approach to sport that restricted the involvement of Indigenous athletes, most of whom could not afford to play without some form of compensation. The focus on the youth in the residential schools sidestepped this issue since the students were generally too young to play professionally anyway (if they were allowed to play at all). Residential schools provided tightly regulated spaces where the AAUC could cast its brand of sport to a vulnerable population with little to no resistance from the students, or from school, government, or church officials. Although the Tom

Longboat Awards signalled the growing acceptance of Indigenous athletes in Canadian amateur sports, they had their limitations. Formal exclusion of certain types of Indigenous athletes was not necessary because the very definition of sport, and the criteria used to determine who could win an award, typically ensured that the winners would be male, mainstream, and amateur. Certainly, only a handful of female athletes won the award between 1951 and 1972. Furthermore, not one athlete who competed exclusively in all-Indigenous environments or in traditional Indigenous sports was ever named a recipient, in any era of the award.

Changes in the broader political landscape, including the emergence of vocal Indigenous groups seeking to redress systemic inequalities and to reconfigure state involvement in organized sports, led to the transfer of the Tom Longboat Awards. In 1970, worn out from its attempt to administer amateur sports in Canada, the AAUC disbanded. Yet it remained committed to the awards until its successor, the Sports Federation of Canada, assumed responsibility for the national program. Without Indigenous input or approval, the AAUC unilaterally empowered the SFC to make substantive decisions about the awards, ensuring continuity in the values and practices that the awards promoted. Indian Affairs did not object to this transfer since it also sought to minimize its involvement in the awards. With the closing of the residential schools well under way (the last federally funded school closed in 1996), sports and games were not as useful for the government as they had once been. For a short while, sport had been woven into the community-development program at Indian Affairs, but the department's interest in sport as a tool for community development had quickly waned. Instead, it deferred to the new SFC as *the* knowledge holder and capacity builder for sport. This left Indigenous people who wanted to participate in the mainstream sport system to their own devices. They had to find their own resources to support their interests, and this included everything from facility construction, to coaching development, to travel for competition: Indian Affairs withdrew what little support it had provided for Indigenous involvement in this area of life. Under the guise of restructuring the awards, Indian Affairs sought to have the newly established National Indian Brotherhood take them over, but in fact it only wanted to transfer the responsibility for selecting regional recipients. Once it secured NIB involvement, it washed its hands of the program after federal officials concluded that the awards had outlived their usefulness as a state-sponsored initiative.

For fourteen years, from 1973 to 1987, the NIB and SFC co-managed the Tom Longboat Awards, with the NIB directing activities regionally and the SFC managing activities nationally. With NIB involvement, new political messages calling attention to Indigenous self-determination were layered into the awards. To be sure, Indigenous people had always used sport as a vehicle to maintain and enhance their position in Canadian society, but now they were doing so openly and even more strategically. Sport was one of the few areas in which they could gain widespread public attention for their accomplishments and still broadcast messages about who they were as people to mainstream audiences. The NIB helped to transmit a limited set of political messages to a broad audience by capitalizing on the symbolic power the awards provided. To the NIB, the awards focused on and celebrated Indigenous cultural resurgence and pride, not assimilation. At the same time, however, the awards, by honouring Indigenous male excellence in the mainstream amateur sport system, continued to regulate who and what would be celebrated.

By the 1980s, the federal government had fully shifted its priorities to high-performance sport while the Assembly of First Nations had replaced the NIB as the national political body for First Nations in Canada. As a result, in 1987, the SFC completely withdrew its involvement in the awards, leaving the AFN to assume full responsibility for the program. Indigenous leaders reshaped the awards, adding an educational component to the eligibility criteria to align and integrate them into the newly established Heroes of Our Times program, which tied all of its awards to educational outcomes. This deliberate move subverted previous links between sport and education designed by Indian Affairs and the AAUC for the purpose of assimilation. Set within the the Heroes of Our Times program, however, the Tom Longboat Awards became just one of several Indigenous awards, advertised alongside a suite of other honours. When the Aboriginal Sport Circle was established in 1995, one of its first objectives was to seek responsibility for the Tom Longboat Awards and heighten their visibility within the Canadian sport system. They intended to bring awareness to the thousands of Indigenous athletes playing and competing in a system in which their contributions, accomplishments, and issues were habitually overlooked or ignored altogether.

By the dawn of the twenty-first century, decades of Indigenous political organizing had resulted in the widespread recognition of three distinct Indigenous groups in Canada: First Nations, Métis, and Inuit. The Royal Commission on Aboriginal Peoples, with its five-volume report published in 1996, devoted specific segments on sports and recreation and recommended the creation of a national organization led by Indigenous people to oversee the development of Indigenous sport in Canada; this organization would become the ASC. Unlike traditional sport organizations, which tended to eschew any links to formal politics (at least on the surface), one of the most striking aspects of the ASC lay in its connections to a broader political project—specifically Indigenous political activism; the ASC received its mandate from the three national Indigenous political bodies: the AFN, the Métis National Council, and the Inuit Tapiriit Kanatami. In other words, the ASC derived its power and authority from outside of mainstream sporting institutions.

Between 1999 and 2001, the ASC set about transforming several long-standing traditions connected to the Tom Longboat Awards. Taking a cue from the broader political environment, it adopted a wider definition of Indigeneity that included First Nations, Métis, and Inuit people and created an organizational structure that allowed for meaningful input from all three groups. This meant that the awards were no longer confined only to Status Indians as defined by the *Indian Act*. Contemporary politics surrounding gender inequality in sport also shaped the structure of the awards, resulting in the creation of a category for female athletes. Although girls and women had won regional and national awards in the past, such examples were few and far between. Creating a separate category for females helped break down this disadvantage in sport, at least symbolically.

Under ASC control, the Tom Longboat Awards became firmly rooted in the competitive sports model, such that the criteria guiding the selection process focused on performance outcomes as the principal markers of success. This shift was expressed most clearly by the scoring grid, which placed the highest value on podium finishes as well as on participation in major mainstream international games. Finally, in seeking to elevate the profile of the awards and the accomplishments of Indigenous athletes in the mainstream sport system, the ASC decided to seek inclusion in the Canadian Sport Awards, even though the Tom Longboat Awards were repeatedly positioned as adjunct to and lesser than the mainstream awards. The ASC's efforts in this regard speak to its determination to carve out a meaningful niche for Indigenous athletes in Canadian amateur sport in the face of challenges from the mainstream system.

What about the recipients of the Tom Longboat Awards? No matter what messages the organizers promoted, they attached their own meanings to the awards, in effect turning them into personal symbols of their lives. Each of their stories varied greatly. Where they grew up, their school experiences, their relationship to their Indigenous heritage, their age, economic background, and family dynamics, whether they were male or female, and even what they "looked like"—each played a critical role in shaping their views of the awards and of sports in general. One recipient, Bill Kinoshameg, offered a powerful critique of the awards as trivial and inconsequential; indeed, he dismissed them as irrelevant. Yet the fact that Bill still recalled important details of the day in 1954 when he received his award at Garnier Indian Residential School speaks to the value that he attached to this experience in the first place. He believed that he could parlay his success in sport into success in business, only to realize that, as an Indigenous man, he faced different social codes than other athletes. Being good at sports and being an award winner did little to help him find a stable job that paid the bills. Instead, for Bill, as for other recipients, the awards became a flashpoint for talking about the social inequalities that he and other Indigenous people faced, whether in sports or other areas of life. Any attempt to create an overarching narrative that consolidates their diverse experiences into a neat package undermines the potential value that comes from understanding each story in its own context.

The Tom Longboat Awards thus offer an array of unique entry points for examining what it means to be Indigenous in Canada—experiences that for the recipients go well beyond talking about memorable moments in sports, describing what it felt like to win a particular championship, or accounting for the records that they amassed. Narrowing these stories down to popular sports clichés deflects our attention away from more important matters, such as how sport aligns with other institutions, like education, economics, and the law, to reinforce unequal power relations that ascribe lesser status to Indigenous people, not just to their sports accomplishments. It also diverts attention away from how Indigenous people exert their own agency through sport, using the platform that organized sports provide to emphasize what matters to them as Indigenous people. Doug Skead's advice to youth, telling them to "hold on to their culture and speak their native language," is just as relevant today (and perhaps more so) than it was when he shared that comment with media in 1972. Therefore, the emphasis that the organizers wanted to promote through the awards only tells part of the story. The agency of the award winners also mattered in determining what the awards meant.

TELLING THE NATIONAL STORY

In 2015, the Truth and Reconciliation Commission of Canada concluded its investigation into the history of the Indian residential school system and released a suite of reports that documented its findings. Totalling more than four thousand pages, the reports dissected and explained how the state, in collaboration with other institutions—such as churches, courts, schools, and the media—tried to eradicate Indigenous ways of life through residential schools and pointed to the lasting effects that this had on the survivors, their families, and their communities. It was the most comprehensive examination of the system ever undertaken and it formed the capstone to more than twenty-five years of investigation into the kind of thinking and support structures behind what has been called Canada's "national crime."[2]

The fact that the TRC was triggered at all is a critical but often neglected point in public discussions about the investigation. As Naomi Angel and Pauline Wakeham explain, when the federal government first launched the TRC in 2008, "Canada became the first G8 nation and long-standing liberal democracy to initiate such a forum—an act that, in summoning the idioms and mechanisms of transitional justice typically employed in the aftermath of oppressive regimes, articulated a self-proclaimed liberal democratic nation to the scene of apartheid in South Africa, civil war in El Salvador, and military dictatorship in Chile."[3] By agreeing to engage in the commission's process, Canada thus acknowledged its attempt at genocide, placing itself alongside nations that it had condemned for atrocities committed elsewhere. The Canadian case involved not only cultural genocide—the loss of languages, traditions, and customs, which has led to profound problems on its own—but also the wilful extermination of people through such means as starvation, inadequate health care, and environmental destruction. Canada admitted its guilt. But the question remained: What was the state going to do to repair its relationship with Indigenous people?

Never before had Canadians been confronted in such a public way and all at once with the darkest aspects of their history, sparking a bewildering clamour over the nation's past, present, and future. The disharmony ranged from staunch rejections of the findings, to questions about why this history had not been taught in schools, to thoughtful reflections on how to move forward from a shameful past, to the type of anger that comes from someone who has been held down so long and lost so much that what comes out is a big ball of fury. This last reaction was especially true for Indigenous people acutely aware of what their ancestors and Elders had given up so that they could endure and perhaps one day even thrive.

One of the reports that the TRC produced was a list of "94 Calls to Action," ninety-four discrete items to serve as a roadmap to reconciliation. They were more than recommendations offered up for debate and consideration. Rather they detailed clear tasks designed to lead to systemic change in key areas such as child welfare, education, language and culture, and health—essentially any aspect of Indigenous life that the state had negatively affected.

Of the 94 Calls to Action, numbers 87 to 91 focused specifically on sport. Broadly speaking, they identified the need to support the development of the Indigenous sport system and traditional physical practices, to develop a better understanding of Indigenous sports experiences, to ensure that Indigenous needs and concerns regarding health and physical activity are enshrined in policy and legislation, and to involve Indigenous people in the hosting of major games so that Indigenous people can benefit from these billion-dollar spectacles taking place on their lands. The Calls to Action thus spoke to Indigenous people's ongoing commitment to use sport to advance their social, political, cultural, and economic interests, which are not necessarily aligned with the state. Although Indigenous lives have undoubtedly changed since Confederation, how Indigenous people express themselves through sport and other physical practices remains a key part of their identities as distinct groups and nations.

Canada's sport system responded to the Calls to Action haphazardly. Government agencies and organizations throughout the country jumped on efforts at reconciliation without giving careful thought to what needed to be addressed or how to implement ideas for change. Instead, they marshalled their already considerable resources and their high-level connections in government and business, sidestepping the need to develop meaningful relationships with Indigenous organizations so as to secure more opportunities for themselves and their corporate partners. Now that increased funding for Indigenous sport is finally being made available through TRC-inspired initiatives, mainstream third-party organizations as well as different divisions of government want access to this money to promote their agendas and fuel their administrative needs, thus developing their own capacity at the expense of Indigenous communities. This means fewer resources going directly to Indigenous systems. The long-term forecast for this type of funding is well known: once it dries up, the mainstream establishments move on to the next pot of money, wherever that might be, leaving Indigenous people without the core funding or capacity they need to lead the projects on their own.

Canada's major media institutions, and specifically the CBC, have not helped. In March 2018, it produced "Beyond 94: Where Is Canada at with Reconciliation?," a searchable online "report card" measuring the progress made on each Call to Action.[4] There was no detailed information on how the CBC actually assessed this progress, though it did claim to have "reached out to relevant governments, faith groups, professional and community organizations for comment" and "fact-checked each response with invested stakeholders." Nor did the CBC state how long it would continue to provide updates, even though it promised to "monitor the progress of that journey." To this end, it gave each item one of four labels: "not started," "in progress—projects proposed," "in progress—projects under way," and "complete." It condensed all the Calls to Action, not just those for sport, into short excerpts, with the full TRC descriptions following below them. When I last checked the website in December 2019, the CBC considered ten of the 94 Calls to Action to be complete. Three of those relate to sport: number 87: "Tell the national story of Aboriginal athletes in history"; number 88: "Continued support for the North American Indigenous Games"; and number 90: "Ensure that national sports policies, programs and initiatives are inclusive of Aboriginal Peoples."[5]

With few accompanying details, "Beyond 94" did more harm than good in terms of educating the public about how well Canadians are faring on their journey toward reconciliation. For many readers, especially those uninformed about the people, organizations, and issues that defined each sector, the report card could have easily been viewed as an authoritative document accurately assessing the state of each Call to Action. Yet for people trying to untangle the ideas and structures that have held Indigenous people back, the report card's limitations were yet another reminder of how the potential for change can be compromised by a lack of meaningful, collaborative effort. In other words, "Beyond 94" reduced the moral imperative to change a complex colonial system to a simple checklist.

Call to Action 87 is of particular interest to me because of my research area and for this reason it has special relevance to this book. The way that the CBC framed it is not quite how the TRC put it when it talked of the need for "all levels of government, in collaboration with Aboriginal Peoples, sports halls of fame and other relevant organizations, to provide public education that tells the national story of Aboriginal athletes in history."[6] In its "summary" of this item, the CBC declared it complete because Canada's Sports Hall of Fame had included a segment on "prominent Indigenous athletes through Canada's history" in its online exhibit. Yet this website is a veritable maze without a clear indication of anything specific to Indigenous athletes except for a few pages under the tab for "Cultural and Racial Diversity," wherein readers could select "Aboriginal Athletes" from a drop-down menu. Segments on "Black Athletes" and "Newcomers to Canada" were the other two options.[7]

The site includes sections devoted to Tom Longboat and Sharon and Shirley Firth, whose Tom Longboat Award nomination as part of the Northwest Territories Cross-Country Ski Team was rejected in 1974 on the grounds that the awards were for individuals only and that the Firth sisters were not First Nations. The Sports Hall of Fame's entries for the Firths include about three hundred words and several photos of the athletes. Included in the entry for Longboat are photos and captions for four other Indigenous athletes, presumably in this section because they, like Longboat, had persisted in sport despite the circumstances they faced. They are all male athletes: Harry Manson, a member of the Snuneymuxw First Nation who competed in soccer in the early 1900s; Bill Isaacs, from Six Nations of the Grand River, who competed in lacrosse in the 1930s and '40s; Alwyn Morris, the Olympic paddler from Kahnawake who helped to establish the Aboriginal Sport Circle in the 1990s; and Steve Collins, a member of the Fort William First Nation (identified on the site as "Ojibwa First Nation") who competed as a world-class ski jumper in the 1970s and '80s and was named the 1979 national Tom Longboat Award recipient. The final section of this three-part segment on Indigenous athletes returns to the exploits of Tom Longboat.

Though not included in its summary, CBC mentions four more activities, all occurring in 2017, that demonstrate why it considers Call to Action 87 complete: Sport Canada "educated Canadians about Aboriginal athletes through their financial support of the 2017 North American Indigenous Games," which is a curious statement given that Sport Canada had been directed by the Federal-Provincial-Territorial Ministers Responsible for Sport and Recreation in 2003 to financially support the NAIG, long before the TRC was even initiated; Canada's Sports Hall of Fame inducted Gaylord Powless, one of Canada's standout lacrosse players and the 1964 national Tom Longboat Award recipient; the Saskatchewan Sports Hall of Fame launched a six-month special exhibit called *The Stories of Indigenous Athletes: Rights and Wrongs*; and the Hockey Hall of Fame in Toronto honoured a hockey team made up of mostly residential school survivors from Sagkeeng First Nation in Manitoba by putting their memorabilia on display.[8]

This, according to the CBC, constitutes "telling the national story" of Indigenous athletes throughout Canadian history. This is not nearly good enough. It ignores the complex ways in which Indigenous people have continued to pick up sport and weave it into their lives. It renders insignificant the cultural importance that Indigenous people attach to sport and physical culture and obscures the real challenges that they face in trying to use sport and physical activities to reaffirm who they are as people. It discounts the wide range of mainstream sporting activities in which Indigenous athletes—male, female, and persons with disabilities—have been successful. What is true is that Canada's Sports Hall of Fame, along with the other four initiatives, are merely five responses to Call to Action 87. Yet the CBC's coverage positioned them as an appropriate collective response for reconciliation.

Just as sport and the Tom Longboat Awards have been used in the past to break down Indigenous societies, so, too, can they be used in the future to build them back up. The extent to which that is possible depends to a large degree on the stories that are told about Indigenous involvement in sport. To aid this movement, the recipients need to be provided with opportunities to tell their stories from their own perspectives, identifying the ways in which their experiences are connected to Indigenous values and interests, thereby providing a more authentic response to Call to Action 87. The Tom Longboat Awards, and the hundreds of people who have been named a recipient, provide the occasion to begin this important conversation.

Listening carefully to their complex stories is equally important. Their experiences are a foundational part of the history of Indigenous sport in Canada, as well as Indigenous history more broadly, touching on matters that are sport specific but are also tied to issues that extend well beyond the playing fields and ice rinks. Understood in this larger context, their stories—not filtered through mundane sporting narratives—will help us all to reflect on our own lives, as well as the state of Indigenous-settler relations in Canada.

Last, but not least, it is time for stewards of sport awards, including the Tom Longboat Awards, to reflect on what they are representing to Canadians, as well as to Indigenous people, when they give out an award. Now that we know the Tom Longboat Awards have always been a platform for broadcasting important social and political messages, what might the future themes be? By the end of 2019, British Columbia and the Northwest Territories will be the first two regions in Canada that write into law the United Nations Declaration on the Rights of Indigenous Peoples. It states that Indigenous people have the right to self-determination and to benefit from state services in ways that advance their collective interests, including their interests in sport. Perhaps this message, grounded in rights derived from the UN Declaration could structure and guide the pathway moving forward. These rights, reaching well beyond sport, might also be just the kind of aspirations that Tom Longboat would have supported.

NOTES ON ARCHIVAL SOURCES

Much of the information on the years 1949 to 1951 I drew from the personal files of Jan Eisenhardt, the director of physical education and recreation at Indian Affairs during this period. Eisenhardt, of course, was the originator of the Tom Longboat Awards, and he went to great lengths to cultivate support for them. His collection includes official departmental letters, reports, personal journals, photos, and memorabilia, much of which cannot be found in Library and Archives Canada. This is largely because, when he resigned from Indian Affairs in 1951, he took all of his files with him "to remember his work among the Indians."¹ Eisenhardt was a historian's dream, for he recorded in great detail much of what he did and thought about in life and kept these items with him through the years. When I met him in the summer of 2003, he was ninety-seven years old and living independently in his home in Dorval, Quebec. His massive collection was stored throughout his home and he knew where every bit of information was located. He was also training to run a marathon on his one hundredth birthday. He passed away in December 2004. In 2015, his daughter, Lisa Spillane, donated her father's collection to Weldon Archives and Special Collections at Western University in London, Ontario. The collection is open to the public.

Records on the years 1951 to 1972 I collected primarily from Library and Archives Canada in Ottawa, Weldon Library at Western

University, and the Woodland Cultural Centre in Brantford, Ontario. The RG10 file at LAC is the most significant here since it contains official departmental correspondence regarding management of the awards, completed nomination forms, and letters of support from local instructors, school administrators, Indian agents, and super-intendents of schools. The archives at Weldon Library contain the minutes of the meetings of the Amateur Athletic Union of Canada in which the regional and national award winners are identified. I had to build the list of recipients, especially at the regional level, from scratch. I cross-checked the information from Weldon Library with the information collected from RG10 files to ensure accuracy. Regrettably, the AAUC did not record minutes of its executive or committee meetings, making it impossible to gain official insight into how the union selected the national award winners.

The *Indian School Bulletin* (1946–57), which can be found at the Departmental Library of Indigenous and Northern Affairs Canada in Gatineau, Quebec, was another indispensable source of informa-tion. It can also be found at LAC, but its copy is not as complete as the departmental one. The *Bulletin* was a publication of Indian Affairs and it was used for in-service training of residential school teachers. The Departmental Library does not let the *Bulletin* cir-culate; interested readers must travel to the facility in Gatineau to access it. Matters pertaining to sport, recreation, and physical edu-cation in Canadian residential schools were featured regularly in this news source.

I sought records for the years 1973 to 1998 directly from two of the principal organizations involved in the Tom Longboat Awards during this era. First, the Departmental Library in Gatineau con-tains much information on the transfer of the awards from Indian Affairs to the National Indian Brotherhood (later the Assembly of First Nations), as well as on the role of the Sports Federation of Canada in managing the awards. It includes official letters, detailed nomination forms, newspaper clippings, photos of award winners, and reports of public celebrations. Upon my request, these doc-uments were sent to the regional office in Toronto, where I could easily access them. Second, the NIB/AFN archive, located in Ottawa, includes official letters and memos, completed nomination forms, and committee selection notes, though information on the awards from 1985 to 1998 is scarce. I also used the *Indian News* (1968–82), a publication sponsored by what was then the Department of Indian Affairs and Northern Development, for this study. This news journal periodically reported on the award winners. The complete collection (1954–82) is now available online through the University of Winnipeg's WinnSpace Repository. Selected primary source documents related to the Native Sport and Recreation Program are from the Provincial Archives of New Brunswick.

I gathered information on the years 1999 to 2001 from the office of the Aboriginal Sport Circle, then located in Akwesasne Mohawk Territory, Ontario, as well as from my own collection from my time working at the ASC. Included are the minutes of meetings from its annual general assembly and its annual general meeting from 1998 to 2001, board of directors' manuals from 1999 to 2001, as well as official letters and reports on the Tom Longboat Awards. These documents are historically significant, not only for their detailed information on the awards but also for the way they reflect the primary issues and concerns among Indigenous sports leaders throughout the country.

NOTES

INTRODUCTION

1   Bruce Kidd, "In Defense of Tom Longboat," *Canadian Journal of History of Sport* 14, no. 1 (1983): 41. Later in the article, Kidd speculates that someone, perhaps Lou Marsh—one of two attendants accompanying Longboat in the race by bicycle—administered a stimulant to him during the race, causing his collapse. Kidd offers this theory based upon the medical report filed by J.H. Crocker, the Canadian team manager who oversaw Longboat's care at the games, who mentioned the possibility that the runner was administered "an overdose of some stimulant." Kidd also acknowledges, however, that if a stimulant was indeed given to Longboat the report is unclear about whether it was administered before or after his collapse (51). No evidence to support this speculation has ever been found.

2   Fergus Cronin, "The Rise and Fall of Tom Longboat," *Maclean's*, February 4, 1956, 21.

3   Bruce Kidd, *Tom Longboat* (Don Mills, ON: Fitzhenry and Whiteside, 1980).

4   Kidd, "In Defense of Tom Longboat," 47.

5   William Brown, "Remembering Tom Longboat: A Story of Competing Narratives" (MA thesis, Concordia University, 2009), 54–61.

6   Ibid., 72–3.

7   Examples include Jack Batten, *The Man Who Ran Faster than Everyone: The Story of Tom Longboat* (Toronto: Tundra Books, 2002); Peter Unwin, "Who Do You Think I Am? A Story of Tom Longboat," *The Beaver*, April–May 2001, 20–6; and Brenda Zeeman, *To Run with Longboat: Twelve Stories on Indian Athletes in Canada* (Edmonton: GMS2Ventures, 1988), 13.

8   *Tom Longboat: Canadian Indian World Champion*, film strip (Department of Citizenship and Immigration, Indian Affairs Branch, 1952).

9   *Wildfire: The Tom Longboat Story*, made-for-television movie, produced by David Tucker (Canadian Broadcasting Corporation, 1993).

10   *Longboat*, video, produced by David Story (Dereck Van Lint and Associates, 1993).

11 Jack Granatstein, "Tom Longboat," *Maclean's*, July 1, 1998, 49–50.

12 Legislative Assembly of Ontario, Bill 120, *Tom Longboat Day Act*, 2008, https://www.ola.org/en/legislative-business/bills/parliament-39/session-1/bill-120.

13 Bruce Kidd, *The Struggle for Canadian Sport* (Toronto: University of Toronto Press, 1996), 48.

14 M. Ann Hall, *The Girl and the Game: A History of Women's Sport in Canada*, 2nd ed. (Toronto: University of Toronto Press, 2016), 72.

15 Ibid., 159n33.

16 Bruce Kidd, "Springstead, Velma Agnes," in *Dictionary of Canadian Biography*, vol. 15 (Toronto: University of Toronto; Laval: Université Laval, 2005), http://www.biographi.ca/en/bio/springstead_velma_agnes_15E.html.

17 Don Morrow and Kevin B. Wamsley, *Sport in Canada: A History*, 4th ed. (Don Mills, ON: Oxford University Press, 2017), 140–7.

18 For a thorough assessment of media representations of Longboat, see Brown, "Remembering Tom Longboat."

19 Kidd, "In Defense of Tom Longboat," 48.

20 Don Morrow, "Lou Marsh: The Pick and Shovel of Canadian Sports Journalism," *Canadian Journal of History of Sport* 14, no. 1 (1983): 25.

21 Malcolm Kelly, "Tom Longboat: A Man Called Everything," CBC *Sports*, April 17, 2017, https://www.cbc.ca/sports/canada-150/canada-150-tom-longboat-1.4067560.

22 *The Un-Canadians*, documentary, directed by Len Scher, produced by Joanne Muroff Smale and Michael Allder (National Film Board of Canada, 1996), available at https://www.nfb.ca/film/un-canadians/.

23 Throughout this book, I use the term "Indigenous" to refer collectively to the First Nations, Métis, and Inuit people in Canada. Distinctions between the three groups are made where needed. At times, I also use the terms "Native," "Indian," and "Aboriginal" when referring to proper nouns, such the National Indian Brotherhood, the Native Sport and Recreation Program, and the Aboriginal Sport Circle, as well as for specific eras when those terms were more common. Lastly, I use specific nation-based names where appropriate.

CHAPTER I

1 Morrow and Wamsley refer specifically to physical education, but the perspective applies just as well to sport or any other physical cultural practice. See Morrow and Wamsley, *Sport in Canada*, 187.

2 In this book, I use the term "discourse" in a general Foucauldian sense to refer to the ideas attached to the active (and inactive) body. These ideas are constructed, reinforced, and communicated to the public in a number of different ways, such as through images and words (e.g., speeches, brochures, posters, textbooks, policies, etc.), which come to be inherently meaningful to people. It is important to note that, even though such meaningfulness is constructed, it feels real because real consequences flow from believing in that construction. The description of discourse as an "organized system of knowledge" is apt here since it links to the allocation and distribution of material resources, which, as Mary Louise Adams explains, allow "certain discourses to become more powerful than others." Mary Louise Adams, *The Trouble with Normal: Postwar Youth and the Making of Heterosexuality* (Toronto: University of Toronto Press, 2003), 6.

3 Taiaiake Alfred, *Peace, Power, Righteousness: An Indigenous Manifesto* (Don Mills, ON: Oxford University Press, 1999), 48.

4 The Numbered Treaties are dealt with extensively in Sheldon Krasowski, *No Surrender: The Land Remains Indigenous* (Regina: University of Regina Press, 2019).

5 Canada, *Looking Forward, Looking Back*, vol. 1 of the *Report of the Royal Commission on Aboriginal Peoples* (Ottawa: Minister of Supply and Services, 1996), 255–332.

6 General histories include Terry Wotherspoon and Vic Satzewich, *First Nations: Race, Class, and Gender Relations* (Regina: Canadian Plains Research Center, 2000), and J.R. Miller, *Skyscrapers Hide the Heavens: A History of Indian-White Relations in Canada*, 3rd ed. (Toronto: University of Toronto Press, 2000).

7 Maria Campbell, *Half-Breed* (Toronto: McClelland and Stewart, 1973), 10.

8 Ovide Mercredi and Mary Ellen Turpel, *In the Rapids: Navigating the Future of First Nations* (Toronto: Viking, 1993), 81.

9 Sally Weaver, *Making Canadian Indian Policy: The Hidden Agenda, 1968–1970* (Toronto: University of Toronto Press, 1981).

10 Canada, *Looking Forward, Looking Back*, 257.

11 Thomas King, *The Truth about Stories: A Native Narrative* (Toronto: Anansi, 2003), 142–3.

12 Ibid., 143.

13 For a detailed discussion of the genocidal aspects of legislative assimilation, see Dean Neu and Richard Therrien, *Accounting for Genocide: Canada's Bureaucratic Assault on Aboriginal Peoples* (London: Zed, 2003). For analyses that include the Canadian and American contexts, see Alexander Laban Hinton, Andrew Woolford, and Jeff Benvenuto, eds., *Colonial Genocide in Indigenous North America* (Durham, NC: Duke University Press, 2014).

14 Although it was not the focus of her book, Pettipas's research helps us to understand the connection between Euro-Canadian sports and games and cultural repression on the Prairies. Katherine Pettipas, *Severing the Ties that Bind: Government Repression of Indigenous Religious Ceremonies on the Prairies* (Winnipeg: University of Manitoba Press, 1994).

15 Quoted in "Historical Notes, the Indian Act, 1876," *Indian News* 14, no. 6 (1971): 3.

16 Vicky Paraschak, " 'Reasonable Amusements': Connecting the Strands of Physical Culture in Native Lives," *Sport History Review* 28, no. 1 (1998): 124.

17 Jacqueline Gresko, "Creating Little Dominions within the Dominion: Early Catholic Indian Schools in Saskatchewan and British Columbia," in *Indian Education in Canada, Volume 1: The Legacy*, eds. Jean Barman, Yvonne Hébert, and Don McCaskill (Vancouver: UBC Press, 1986), 100.

18 Examples of how sports days helped to maintain and renew Indigenous family, social, and political networks along the West Coast, especially among the Coast Salish, can be found in Allan Downey, *The Creator's Game: Lacrosse, Identity, and Indigenous Nationhood* (Vancouver: UBC Press, 2018), 127–38, and Allan Downey and Susan Neylan, "Raven Plays Ball: Situating 'Indian Sports Days' within Indigenous and Colonial Spaces in Twentieth Century Coastal British Columbia," *Canadian Journal of History* 50, no. 3 (2015): 442–68.

19 Pettipas, *Severing the Ties that Bind*, 160.

20 Ibid.

21 J.R. Miller, *Shingwauk's Vision: A History of Native Residential Schools* (Toronto: University of Toronto Press, 1996), 15. A poignant example of the difference

between schooling and education can be found at the end of the book, in the moving letter from an unidentified mother to an unidentified teacher (441–2).

22   Quoted in Michael Heine, *Dene Games: A Culture and Resource Manual, Traditional Aboriginal Sport Coaching Resources, Volume 1* (Yellowknife: Sport North Federation and MACA [GNWT], 2006), 1–15.

23   The mouth pull involves two competitors who stand beside each other. The arm touching the other person is wrapped around the opponent's head, and the middle finger is placed in the opponent's mouth. The objective is to move the opponent's head out of position by pulling his or her mouth. For the ear lift, two participants stand facing each other with a leather strap looped around their ears. The contestant who pulls the leather loop from the opponent's ear wins. Michael Heine, *Arctic Sports: A Training and Resource Manual, Traditional Aboriginal Sport Coaching Resources, Volume 2* (Yellowknife: Arctic Sports Association and MACA [GNWT], 2002), 1-28–1-31.

24   Downey, *The Creator's Game*, 3–12.

25   James Daschuk, *Clearing the Plains: Disease, Politics of Starvation, and the Loss of Aboriginal Life* (Regina: University of Regina Press, 2013).

26   See, for example, Augustine Shingwauk, *Little Pine's Journal: The Appeal of a Christian Chippeway Chief on Behalf of His People* (Toronto: Copp, Clark, 1872).

27   Miller, *Shingwauk's Vision*; John Milloy, *A National Crime: The Canadian Government and the Residential School System, 1879–1986* (Winnipeg: University of Manitoba Press, 1999).

28   David Kirk, *Schooling Bodies: School Practice and Public Discourse, 1880–1950* (London: Leicester University Press, 1998).

29   Canada, *Looking Forward, Looking Back*, 340–1.

30   Educational leaders, government officials, medical specialists, and religious authorities have always been interested in student health, whether in the Indian residential school system, the public school system, or the private boarding school system in Canada or abroad. However, their interests and approaches to student health vary depending on the group of students in question. As a result, different types of health and physical education curricula have been developed and implemented for different groups of students. For a thorough analysis of the ideologies that underpinned educational leaders' approaches to student health in the post-secondary school system in Canada, see Catherine Gidney, *Tending the Student Body: Youth, Health, and the Modern University* (Toronto: University of Toronto Press, 2015). A similar argument can be made about the state and the general population more broadly. For an international comparative analysis, see Charlotte Macdonald, *Strong, Beautiful and Modern: National Fitness in Britain, New Zealand, Australia and Canada, 1935–1960* (Vancouver: UBC Press, 2011).

31   John Bloom, *To Show What an Indian Can Do: Sports at Native American Boarding Schools* (Minneapolis: University of Minnesota Press, 2000).

32   Denominational rivalry for students was one of the key factors driving the development of residential schools throughout the country. See Miller, *Shingwauk's Vision*, for a more detailed examination of this rivalry.

33   Mary-Ellen Kelm, *Colonizing Bodies: Aboriginal Health and Healing in British Columbia, 1900–1950* (Vancouver: UBC Press, 2001), 57–80.

34   Ibid., 77.

35   Ibid., 64.

36   Department of Indian Affairs, *Calisthenics and Games, Prescribed for Use in All Indian Schools* (Ottawa: Government Printing Bureau, 1910).

37   Don Morrow, "The Strathcona Trust in Ontario, 1911–1939," *Canadian Journal of History of Sport and Physical Education* 8, no. 1 (1977): 71–90.

38   Evan J. Habkirk, "From Indian Boys to Canadian Men? The Use of Cadet Drill in the Canadian Indian Residential School System," *British Journal of Canadian Studies* 30, no. 2 (2018): 227–48.

39   Department of Indian Affairs, *Calisthenics and Games*, 6.

40   Michael Heine, "Gwich'in Tsii'in: A History of Gwich'in Athapaskan Games" (PhD diss., University of Alberta, 1995), 155–8.

41   Instructors sometimes withheld recreational privileges to instill respect for authority among the students. For some examples, see Gresko, "Creating Little Dominions within the Dominion," 96, and Diane Persson, "The Changing Experience of Indian Residential Schooling: Blue Quills, 1931–1970," in *Indian Education in Canada, Volume 1: The Legacy*, eds. Jean Barman, Yvonne Hébert, and Don McCaskill (Vancouver: UBC Press, 1986), 153.

42   Andrew Woolford, *This Benevolent Experiment: Indigenous Boarding Schools, Genocide, and Redress in Canada and the United States* (Winnipeg: University of Manitoba Press, 2015), 141.

43   Ibid.

44   Moss E. Norman, Michael Hart, and LeAnne Petherick, "Indigenous Gender Reformations: Physical Culture, Settler Colonialism, and the Politics of Containment," *Sociology of Sport Journal* 36, no. 2 (2019): 118.

45   Many former residential school students have mixed feelings about their sports experiences there. This ambivalence is rendered in a beautiful but heartbreaking way in Richard Wagamese, *Indian Horse: A Novel* (Madeira Park, BC: Douglas and McIntyre, 2013).

46   Basil Johnston, *Indian School Days* (Toronto: Key Porter Books, 1988), 24–5.

47   Martha H. Verbrugge, *Active Bodies: A History of Women's Physical Education in Twentieth-Century America* (New York: Oxford University Press, 2012).

48   Martha Hill attended the Mohawk Institute from 1912 to 1918. Hill is quoted in Elizabeth Graham, *The Mush Hole: Life at Two Indian Residential Schools* (Waterloo, ON: Heffle Publishing, 1997), 356.

49   Quoted in Jo-Anne Fiske, " 'And Then We Prayed Again': Carrier Women, Colonization, and Mission Schools" (MA thesis, University of British Columbia, 1981), 36.

50   Miller, *Shingwauk's Vision*, 273–4.

51   Johnston, *Indian School Days*, 197–209.

52   Persson, "The Changing Experience of Indian Residential Schooling," 163.

53   Ward Churchill, Norbert S. Hill, Jr., and Mary Jo Barlow, "An Historical Overview of Twentieth-Century Native American Athletics," *Indian Historian* 12, no. 4 (1979): 31–2.

54   John Bloom, " 'There Is Madness in the Air': The 1926 Haskell Homecoming and Popular Representations of Sports in Federal Indian Boarding Schools," in *Dressing in Feathers: The Construction of the Indian in American Popular Culture*, ed. Elizabeth Bird (Boulder, CO: Westview Press, 1996), 98.

55   Johnston, *Indian School Days*, 206.

56 John Dewar, "The Introduction of Western Sports to the Indian People of Canada's Prairie West," in *Sport, Culture, Society: International Historical and Sociological Perspectives*, Proceedings of the Eighth Commonwealth and International Conference on Sport, Physical Education, Dance, Recreation, and Health, eds. James Mangan and Roy Small (London: E. and F.N. Spon, 1986), 30.

57 Tsianina Lomawaima, *They Called It Prairie Light: The Story of Chilocco Indian School* (Lincoln: University of Nebraska Press, 1995), 125.

58 Quoted in Celia Haig-Brown, *Resistance and Renewal: Surviving the Indian Residential School* (Vancouver: Tillacum Library, 1988), 72.

59 Don Morrow, "The Knights of the Snowshoe: A Study of the Evolution of Sport in Nineteenth-Century Montreal," *Journal of Sport History* 15, no. 1 (1988): 23.

60 Ibid., 21.

61 Frank Cosentino, "A History of the Concept of Professionalism in Canadian Sport," *Canadian Journal of History of Sport and Physical Education* 6, no. 2 (1975), 78–9, and Frank Cosentino, *Afros, Aboriginals, and Amateur Sport in Pre–World War One Canada* (Ottawa: Canadian Historical Society, 1998), 19.

62 Morrow, "The Knights of the Snowshoe," 23n68.

63 Donald Fisher, *Lacrosse: A History of the Game* (Baltimore: Johns Hopkins University Press, 2002), 38.

64 Morrow, "The Knights of the Snowshoe," 23.

65 Michael Heine and Kevin Wamsley, " 'Kickfest at Dawson City': Native Peoples and the Sports of the Klondike Gold Rush," *Sport History Review* 27, no. 1 (1996): 80.

66 Paraschak, "Reasonable Amusements," 122.

67 Fisher, *Lacrosse*, 27–8.

68 John Bale and Joe Sang provide a detailed exploration of this historical process in an African context in *Kenyan Running: Movement Culture, Geography, and Global Change* (London: Frank Cass, 1996).

69 Malcolm MacLean, "Ambiguity within the Boundary: Rereading C.L.R. James' *Beyond a Boundary*," in *Beyond C.L.R. James: Shifting Boundaries of Race and Ethnicity in Sport*, eds. John Nauright, Alan G. Cobley, and David K. Wiggins (Fayetteville: University of Arkansas Press, 2014), 18.

70 Selected recent publications, in addition to the materials cited throughout this book, include Murray Phillips, Russell Field, Christine O'Bonsawin, and Janice Forsyth, eds., *Indigenous Resurgence, Regeneration, and Decolonization through Sport History*, special issue of *Journal of Sport History* 46, no. 2 (2019); Tricia D. McGuire-Adams and Audrey R. Giles, "Anishinaabekweg Dibaajimowinan (Stories) of Decolonization through Running," *Sociology of Sport Journal* 35, no. 3 (2018): 207–15; Tricia McGuire-Adams, "Anishinaabeg Women's Stories of Wellbeing: Physical Activity, Restoring Wellbeing, and Dismantling the Settler Colonial Deficit Analysis," *Journal of Indigenous Wellbeing* 2, no. 3 (2018): 90–104; and Chris Hallinan and Barry Judd, eds., *Native Games: Indigenous Peoples and Sport in the Post-Colonial World* (Bingley, UK: Emerald, 2013).

71 MacLean, "Ambiguity within the Boundary," 27.

72 Ibid.

73 J.A. Mangan, *The Games Ethic and Imperialism: Aspects of the Diffusion of an Ideal* (London: Frank Cass, 1986).

CHAPTER 2

1 Victor Satzewich, "Indian Agents and the 'Indian Problem' in Canada in 1946: Reconsidering the Theory of Coercive Tutelage," *Canadian Journal of Native Studies* 17, no. 2 (1997): 227–57.

2 Ibid., 229.

3 Ibid., 245.

4 Ibid., 246.

5 Don Morrow and Kevin B. Wamsley, *Sport in Canada: A History*, 3rd ed. (Don Mills, ON: Oxford University Press, 2013), 68–73, 76–7; Kidd, *The Struggle for Canadian Sport*, 35–7.

6 Bernard Neary, Superintendent of Education, to General Secretary, Central YMCA, Montreal, July 6, 1949, Library and Archives Canada (hereafter LAC), RG 32, Public Service Commission, Series C-2, Volume 1408.

7 Ibid.

8 Bernard Neary, Superintendent of Education, memorandum to Major Mackay, Director of Indian Affairs, November 30, 1948, LAC, RG 32, Public Service Commission, Series C-2, Volume 1408.

9 Civil Service Commission, notice to Jan Eisenhardt, February 10, 1950, LAC, RG 32, Public Service Commission, Series C-2, Volume 1408.

10 Neary to General Secretary, July 6, 1949, LAC, RG 32, Public Service Commission, Series C-2, Volume 1408.

11 Jan Eisenhardt, Supervisor of Physical Education and Recreation, letter of resignation to Major Mackay, Director of Indian Affairs, November 3, 1951, LAC, RG 32, Public Service Commission, Series C-2, Volume 1408.

12 For a detailed study of his involvement with Pro-Rec, see Barbara Schrodt, "A History of Pro-Rec: The British Columbia Recreation Programme, 1934–1953" (PhD diss., University of Alberta, 1979). Also see Barbara Schrodt, "Federal Programs of Physical Recreation and Fitness: The Contributions of Jan Eisenhardt," *Canadian Journal of History of Sport and Physical Education* 15, no. 2 (1984): 45–61. A synopsis of Pro-Rec and Eisenhardt's role in this movement is also found in Kidd, *The Struggle for Canadian Sport*, 247–54.

13 Schrodt, "A History of Pro-Rec," 197.

14 Ibid., 200.

15 Jan Eisenhardt, "Report on Inspection of Schools and Reserves in Saskatchewan and British Columbia," prepared for Indian Affairs, 1950, 3, personal collection of Jan Eisenhardt.

16 George Beete, Kamloops resident, to Father O'Grady, Preceptor, Kamloops Indian Residential School, June 25, 1950, personal collection of Jan Eisenhardt.

17 This was also the case for Australian schoolchildren. See Kirk, *Schooling Bodies*, 68–70.

18 Job advertisement from the Civil Service of Canada for the position of Supervisor of Physical Education and Recreation, Indian Affairs Branch, Department of Mines and Resources, March 23, 1949, LAC, RG 32, Public Service Commission, Series C-2, Volume 1408.

19 Personal interview with Jan Eisenhardt, Dorval, QC, March 10, 2004.

20 Jan Eisenhardt quoted in "New Deal in Education for Brant Indians," *Brantford Expositor*, March 16, 1950, 1, 2.

21 V.A. Bower, "Inaugurate New Deal for Canadian Indians," *Evening Citizen* (Ottawa), March 29, 1950, 21.

22 Bernard Neary, Superintendent of Education, Indian Affairs Branch, memorandum to Jan Eisenhardt, Supervisor of Physical Education and Recreation, April 1, 1950, personal collection of Jan Eisenhardt.

23 Ibid.

24 Jan Eisenhardt, "Tentative Plans in Regard to the Program of Physical Education, Sports, Games, and Recreation for the Indian Population," report prepared for Philip Phelan, Superintendent of Education, Indian Affairs Branch, March 1950, section B, item 1 (a)(ii), "Residential Schools, Indoor Facilities," personal collection of Jan Eisenhardt.

25 Major Mackay, Director of Indian Affairs, memorandum to Deputy Minister, April 2, 1949, LAC, RG 32, Public Service Commission, Series C-2, Volume 1408.

26 Ibid.

27 Eisenhardt, "Tentative Plans," section B, item 1 (c)(ii), "Residential Schools."

28 "The Indians Show Us How," *Sudbury Star*, circa 1950, personal collection of Jan Eisenhardt.

29 Eisenhardt, "Report on Inspection," 13.

30 Father Irvine Leclerc, Tzouhalem Catholic Rectory, Duncan, BC, to Jan Eisenhardt, Supervisor of Physical Education and Recreation, Indian Affairs Branch, September 27, 1950, personal collection of Jan Eisenhardt.

31 Eisenhardt, "Report on Inspection," 6.

32 Financial support from Indian Affairs was meant to supplement sport and recreation programs on reserves, not to be the sole provider. This approach was noted in a 1979 review of departmental funding for the Native Sport and Recreation Program. See David Elkins, "Evaluation Report: Recreation Program Review," Department of Indian Affairs and Northern Development, March 1979, 16–18.

33 "Wikwemikong," *Manitoulin Expositor* (Little Current, ON), May 25, 1950, 4.

34 Canada, Department of Citizenship and Immigration, *Report of Indian Affairs Branch for the Fiscal Year Ended March 31, 1953*, 52, LAC, Indian Affairs Annual Reports, 1864–1990.

35 Eisenhardt, "Report on Inspection," 7.

36 Eisenhardt, "Tentative Plans," section A, item 2(e).

37 Jan Eisenhardt, "General Report on Visits to Residential and Day Schools as Well as Indian Reserves in the Provinces of Alberta and Saskatchewan," prepared for Indian Affairs, 1950, 4, personal collection of Jan Eisenhardt.

38 Brian Titley, *The Indian Commissioners: Agents of the State and Indian Policy in Canada's Prairie West, 1873–1932* (Edmonton: University of Alberta Press, 2009), 207.

39 Personal interview with Jan Eisenhardt, Dorval, QC, March 10, 2004.

40 Ibid.

41 "A Commentary for the Filmstrip on Tom Longboat," *Indian School Bulletin* 6, no. 4 (1952): 10.

42 Ibid., 9.

43 Jan Eisenhardt, "The Canadian Red Man of Today," *Journal of the American Association for Health, Physical Education, and Recreation* 22, no. 6 (1951): 9–10.

44 Ibid., 10.

45   Ibid., 9.

46   Ibid., 10.

47   Bernard Neary, Superintendent of Education, memorandum to Director of Indian Affairs, September 29, 1950, personal collection of Jan Eisenhardt.

48   Jan Eisenhardt, President, Dominion Life Assurance Company, to Kahn-Tineta Horn, May 1, 1964, personal collection of Jan Eisenhardt.

49   Canada, Department of Citizenship and Immigration, *Report of Indian Affairs Branch for the Fiscal Year Ended March 31, 1954*, 60, LAC, Indian Affairs Annual Reports, 1864–1990.

50   Canada, Department of Citizenship and Immigration, *Report of Indian Affairs Branch for the Fiscal Year Ended March 31, 1953*, 60, LAC, Indian Affairs Annual Reports, 1864–1990.

51   Braden Paora Te Hiwi, "Physical Culture as Citizenship Education at Pelican Lake Indian Residential School, 1926–1970" (PhD diss., Western University, 2015); Fatima Ba'abbad, "History of Sioux Lookout Black Hawks Hockey Team, 1949–1951" (MA thesis, Western University, 2017).

52   "Twelve Indian Puck-Toters Here for Bantam Series," *Evening Citizen* (Ottawa), April 12, 1951, 20.

53   Ibid.

54   "Bush-to-Bank-Streak Leaves Boys Bug-Eyed," *Ottawa Journal*, April 12, 1951, 18.

55   E.S. Cole, Principal of Old Sun Residential School, to Jan Eisenhardt, Supervisor of Physical Education and Recreation, Indian Affairs Branch, April 1, 1951, and E.S. Cole, Principal of Old Sun Residential School, to Jan Eisenhardt, Supervisor of Physical Education and Recreation, Indian Affairs Branch, May 5, 1951, personal collection of Jan Eisenhardt.

56   Reverend O.N. Rushman, Holy Cross Mission, Manitoulin Island, ON, to Jan Eisenhardt, Supervisor of Physical Education and Recreation, Indian Affairs Branch, October 15, 1951, personal collection of Jan Eisenhardt.

57   "Playing Field: Recreation Program for District Indians," *Daily Times Journal* (Thunder Bay, ON), June 22, 1951, 1.

58   Ibid.

59   "How Can I Start a Physical Education Programme?" *Indian School Bulletin* 4, no. 6 (1950): 16.

60   "Sault Agrees to Assist Garden River Sports Plan," *Sault Daily Star*, July 4, 1951, 14.

61   Ibid.

62   Personal interview with Jan Eisenhardt, Dorval, QC, March 10, 2004.

63   Schrodt, "A History of Pro-Rec," 182.

64   Amateur Athletic Union of Canada, Minutes of the Fifty-Eighth Annual Meeting, Vancouver, November 15–17, 1951, 91, Weldon Library.

65   Amateur Athletic Union of Canada, Minutes of the Fifty-Seventh Annual Meeting, Montreal, November 30–December 2, 1950, 71, Weldon Library.

66   George Machum, AAUC, to Jan Eisenhardt, Supervisor of Physical Education and Recreation, Indian Affairs Branch, April 23, 1951, LAC, RG 10, Volume 8581, File 1/1-2-15-2, Part 1.

67   Personal interview with Jan Eisenhardt, Dorval, QC, March 10, 2004.

68   Keith Lansley, "The Amateur Athletic Union of Canada and Changing Concepts of Amateurism" (PhD diss., University of Alberta, 1971), 239.

69   Ibid., 252–3.

70   Ibid., 254.

71   Jan Eisenhardt, Supervisor of Physical Education and Recreation, Indian Affairs Branch, to George Machum, AAUC, January 23, 1951, LAC, RG 10, Volume 8581, File 1/1-2-15-2, Part 1.

72   Jan Eisenhardt, Supervisor of Physical Education and Recreation, Indian Affairs Branch, memorandum to Bernard Neary, Superintendent of Education, Indian Affairs Branch, January 23, 1951, LAC, RG 10, Volume 8581, File 1/1-2-15-2, Part 1.

73   George Machum, AAUC, to Jan Eisenhardt, Supervisor of Physical Education and Recreation, Indian Affairs Branch, February 5, 1951, LAC, RG 10, Volume 8581, File 1/1-2-15-2, Part 1.

74   George Machum, AAUC, to Jan Eisenhardt, Supervisor of Physical Education and Recreation, Indian Affairs Branch, February 12, 1951, LAC, RG 10, Volume 8581, File 1/1-2-15-2, Part 1.

75   George Machum, AAUC, to Major Mackay, Director of Indian Affairs, April 5, 1952, LAC, RG 10, Volume 8581, File 1/1-2-15-2, Part 1.

76   AAUC, Minutes of the Fifty-Eighth Annual Meeting, 1951, 91.

77   Philip Phelan, Superintendent of Education, to Regional Supervisors, September 7, 1951, LAC, RG 10, Volume 8581, File 1/1-2-15-2, Part 1.

78   The 1951 selection committee for British Columbia was typical of most committees from 1951 to 1972, as can be discerned in the available documents. It included the Indian commissioner and the regional inspector of Indigenous schools for the province, the superintendent of the Vancouver Indian Agency, and a regional member of the AAUC. See W.S. Arneil, Indian Commissioner of British Columbia, to Jan Eisenhardt, Supervisor of Physical Education and Recreation, Indian Affairs Branch, November 2, 1951, LAC, RG 10, Volume 8581, File 1/1-2-15-2, Part 1.

79   Eisenhardt, letter of resignation, to Mackay, November 3, 1951.

80   A "gross" is equivalent to 144, suggesting an order of 1,728 lacrosse sticks. Jan Eisenhardt to Grand Chief Phil Fontaine, Assembly of First Nations, March 4, 1998, personal collection of Jan Eisenhardt.

81   Eisenhardt, "Tentative Plans," section C, "Budget."

82   Machum to Eisenhardt, February 12, 1951.

83   Eisenhardt to Machum, January 23, 1951.

84   Philip Phelan, Superintendent of Education, to George Machum, AAUC, May 3, 1951, LAC, RG 10, Volume 8581, File 1/1-2-15-2, Part 1.

85   Jan Eisenhardt, Supervisor of Physical Education and Recreation, to Frederick Baker, Squamish, BC, November 26, 1951, LAC, RG 10, Volume 8581, File 1/1-2-15-2, Part 1.

86   Indian Affairs Branch, circular to Indian Commissioner of British Columbia, Regional Supervisors, Superintendents of Indian Agencies, Regional School Superintendents, District School Superintendents, Supervising Principals, and Counsellors, June 17, 1965, LAC, RG 10, Volume 8582, File 1/1-2-15-2, Part 4.

87   Andrew Paull, President, Grand Council of the North American Indian Brotherhood, to Colonel H.M. Jones, Director of Indian Affairs, January 25, 1957, LAC, RG 10, Volume 8581, File 1/1-2-15-2, Part 2.

88   "Sherlock Paull and Prize," The Province (Vancouver), February 5, 1957, 14.

89   Reverend D. Hannin, Holy Cross Mission, Wikwemikong, Manitoulin Island, ON, nomination of Henry Wibokamigad and Maxi Simon, to C.R. Johnston, Superintendent, Manitoulin Island Indian Agency, November 3, 1951, LAC, RG 10, Volume 8581, File 1/1-2-15-2, Part 1.

90   Reverend Harry B. Miller, Old Sun Anglican Indian Residential School, Gleichen, AB, letter of support for Randy A. Youngman, June 1958, LAC, RG 10, Volume 8582, File 1/1-2-15-2, Part 3.

91   Peter Kelly, Coordinator, Grand Council Treaty No. 3, ON, nomination of Doug Skead, December 17, 1971, Department of Indian Affairs (hereafter DIA), 1/1-2-15-1, Volume 10.

92   "Tom Longboat Winner," *Indian News* 14, no. 10 (1972): 8.

93   "Strong Contenders Take Area Medals: Longboat Medallists, Good Sportsmen," *Indian News* 1, no. 1 (1954): 5.

94   R.J. Stallwood, Superintendent of Six Nations Agency, to Indian Affairs Branch, May 26, 1954, LAC, RG 10, Volume 8581, File 1/1-2-15-2, Part 2.

95   "Thomas Davey Awarded Tom Longboat Medal," *Brantford Expositor*, May 25, 1954, LAC, RG 10, Volume 8581, File 1/1-2-15-2, Part 2.

96   R.F. Davey, Superintendent of Education, to R.J. Stallwood, Superintendent of Six Nations Agency, June 7, 1954, LAC, RG 10, Volume 8581, File 1/1-2-15-2, Part 2.

97   R.J. Stallwood, Superintendent of Six Nations Agency, to Indian Affairs Branch, July 27, 1954, LAC, RG 10, Volume 8581, File 1/1-2-15-2, Part 2.

98   By the 1950s, lacrosse was not played at most day and residential schools in Canada. If it was played, the sport had been stripped of its link to any traditional aspects connected to land, language, or ceremony.

99   "Cecilia Jeffrey Indian Residential School Held Sports Day on Wednesday," newspaper clipping, circa 1950, personal collection of Jan Eisenhardt.

100   J. O'Neil, Superintendent, Sault Ste. Marie Agency, to Regional Supervisor at North Bay, October 8, 1959, LAC, RG 10, Volume 8581, File 1/1-2-15-2, Part 3.

101   Vicky Paraschak, "An Examination of Sport for Aboriginal Females on the Six Nations Reserve, Ontario, from 1968 to 1980," in *Women of the First Nations: Power, Wisdom, and Strength*, eds. Christine Miller and Patricia Chuchryk (Winnipeg: University of Manitoba Press, 1996), 85–86, and Vicky Paraschak, "Organized Sport for Native Females on the Six Nations Reserve, Ontario, from 1968 to 1980: A Comparison of Dominant and Emergent Sport Systems," *Canadian Journal of History of Sport* 21 (1990): 76.

102   Tom Longboat Award nomination form, 1951, LAC, RG 10, Volume 8581, File 1/1-2-15-2, Part 1.

103   J.E. Morris, Regional Supervisor, Southern Ontario, circular to Superintendents, Southern Ontario Region, July 9, 1956, LAC, RG 10, Volume 8581, File 1/1-2-15-2, Part 2.

104   See R.F. Matters, Regional Supervisor of Indian Agencies, to Indian Affairs Branch, September 27, 1955, and R.F. Davey, Superintendent of Education, to E.K. Yost, AAUC, October 12, 1955, LAC, RG 10, Volume 8581, File 1/1-2-15-2, Part 2.

105   R.F. Davey, Superintendent of Education, to E.K. Yost, AAUC, November 29, 1955, LAC, RG 10, Volume 8581, File 1/1-2-15-2, Part 2.

106   E.K. Yost, AAUC, to R.F. Davey, Superintendent of Education, December 28, 1955, LAC, RG 10, Volume 8581, File 1/1-2-15-2, Part 2.

107　R.F. Matters, Regional Supervisor of Indian Agencies, to Indian Affairs Branch, March 9, 1956, LAC, RG 10, Volume 8581, File 1/1-2-15-2, Part 2.

108　Bomberry won the national award in 1968. See Paraschak, "An Examination of Sport," 85–6.

109　Ibid., 86. Paraschak has repeated this claim elsewhere; see Vicky Paraschak, "Invisible but Not Absent: Aboriginal Women in Sport and Recreation," *Canadian Women's Studies* 15, no. 4 (1995): 71–2; Paraschak, "Native American Games and Sports," in *International Encyclopedia of Women and Sport*, eds. Karen Christensen, Allen Guttmann, and Gertrude Pfister (New York: Macmillan Reference USA, 2001), 788–91; and Paraschak, "Organized Sport," 76.

CHAPTER 3

1　Little has been written about the historical development of the NIB and AFN. A general overview can be found in Miller, *Skyscrapers Hide the Heavens*, 311–35. George Manuel's role in establishing the NIB is described in Peter McFarlane, *Brotherhood to Nationhood: George Manuel and the Making of the Modern Indian Movement* (Toronto: Between the Lines, 1993).

2　The history of sport organizing in Canada in the latter half of the 1900s involves a complex web of advocacy, policy, and administrative bodies. The organizations that have occupied the advocacy role include the Canadian Sport Advisory Council (1951–63), the Canadian Amateur Sports Federation (1963–72), and the Sports Federation of Canada (1972/73–93). At present, Sport Matters fulfills this role for Canadian sport organizations.

3　Arthur Laing to Gordon Robertson, October 19, 1963, quoted in Weaver, *Making Canadian Indian Policy*, 48.

4　Truth and Reconciliation Commission of Canada, *Honouring the Truth, Reconciling for the Future: Summary of the Final Report of the Truth and Reconciliation Commission of Canada* (Winnipeg: Truth and Reconciliation Commission of Canada, 2015), 68.

5　National Indian Brotherhood, *Tradition and Education: Towards a Vision of Our Future, Volume 1* (Ottawa: NIB/AFN, 1988), 57.

6　Truth and Reconciliation Commission of Canada, *Honouring the Truth*, 68.

7　H.B. Hawthorn, *A Survey of the Contemporary Indians of Canada: A Report on the Economic, Political, Educational Needs and Policies: Part 2* (Ottawa: Indian Affairs Branch, 1967), 35.

8　Holy A. McKenzie, Colleen Varcoe, Annette J. Browne, and Linda Day, "Disrupting the Continuities among Residential Schools, the Sixties Scoop, and Child Welfare: An Analysis of Colonial and Neocolonial Discourses," *International Indigenous Policy Journal* 7, no. 2 (2016): 2.

9　Cindy Blackstock, Nico Trocmé, and Marlyn Bennett, "Children Maltreatment Investigations among Aboriginal and Non-Aboriginal Families in Canada," *Violence Against Women* 10, no. 8 (2004): 905.

10　Jorge Barrera, "Indigenous Child Welfare Rates Creating 'Humanitarian Crises' in Canada, says Federal Minister," CBC *News*, November 2, 2017, https://www.cbc.ca/news/indigenous/crisis-philpott-child-welfare-1.4385136.

11　Hawthorn, *Contemporary Indians of Canada*, 88.

12   In 1971, the Standing Committee on Indian Affairs reported that the dropout rate for Indigenous students in Canada was four times the national average, with approximately 96 percent of Indigenous youth never completing high school. Verna Kirkness and Sheena Selkirk Bowman, *First Nations and Schools: Triumphs and Struggles* (Toronto: Canadian Education Association, 1992), 14–15.

13   NIB, *Tradition and Education*, 57–8.

14   For a detailed critique of the school strike in northeastern Alberta, see Harold Cardinal, *The Rebirth of Canada's Indians* (Edmonton: Hurtig, 1977). Also see Arthur Manuel and Grand Chief Ronald M. Derrickson, *Unsettling Canada: A National Wake-Up Call* (Toronto: Between the Lines, 2015).

15   Kirkness and Bowman, *First Nations and Schools*, 15.

16   National Indian Brotherhood, *Indian Control of Indian Education* (Ottawa: NIB/AFN, 1972), 3.

17   Ibid., 20, 24.

18   Ibid., 26.

19   Arthur Laing, notes for an address, February 12, 1967, quoted in McFarlane, *Brotherhood to Nationhood*, 91.

20   Weaver, *Making Canadian Indian Policy*, 28.

21   McFarlane, *Brotherhood to Nationhood*, 46.

22   Neu and Therrien, *Accounting for Genocide*, 125.

23   The annual reports can be found at http://www.bac-lac.gc.ca/eng/discover/aboriginal-heritage/first-nations/indian-affairs-annual-reports/Pages/search.aspx. As well as reading the relevant sections in each report from 1947 to 1975, I conducted a keyword search for the terms "sport," "recreation," "physical education," and "physical culture." The reports last mention physical education in 1966. After that year, the terms "sport" and "recreation" are used in the context of sport fishing and hunting as means to encourage tourism on reserves.

24   Canada, Department of Citizenship and Immigration, *Report of Indian Affairs Branch for the Fiscal Year Ended March 31, 1960*, 58, LAC, Indian Affairs Annual Reports, 1864–1990.

25   L.J. Hyslop, "The Tom Longboat Awards: An Examination of the Administrative Procedures for These Awards and the Selection Process and Qualifications for Nominees," report prepared for the Indian Affairs Branch, August 13, 1968, 3, Department of Indian Affairs and Northern Development (hereafter DIAND), 1/1-2/15/2, Volume 8.

26   Amateur Athletic Union of Canada, Minutes of the Seventy-Fifth Annual Meeting, Saskatoon, November 1968, 15, Weldon Library.

27   Hyslop, "The Tom Longboat Awards," 1.

28   Ibid.

29   Donald MacIntosh, Tom Bedecki, and C.E.S. Franks, *Sport and Politics in Canada: Federal Government Involvement Since 1961* (Montreal and Kingston: McGill-Queen's University Press, 1988), 63.

30   Margaret Lord, Chair, Honours and Awards Committee, AAUC, to L.J. Hyslop, Social Development Officer, Indian Affairs Branch, November 17, 1968, DIAND, 1/1-2/15/2, Volume 8.

31   Hyslop, "The Tom Longboat Awards," 2.

32   AAUC, Minutes of the Seventy-Fifth Annual Meeting, 1968, 32.

33   Lord to Hyslop, November 17, 1968.

34   In addition to the Norton H. Crowe Trophy and Viscount Alexander Trophy, the AAUC managed the J.W. Trophy for the most outstanding Canadian athlete who competed in track and field, the marathon, or harrier (cross-country) races, the Frederick N.A. Rowell Trophy for the most outstanding field athlete, and the Tees Trophy for the best intercollegiate athlete in Canada.

35   Lansley, "Changing Concepts of Amateurism," 260.

36   V.M. Gran, Chief, Band Management Division, Indian Affairs Branch, circular to All Regional Directors, November 10, 1971, DIAND, 1/1-2/15/2, Volume 10.

37   Vicky Paraschak, "The Native Sport and Recreation Program, 1972–1981: Patterns of Resistance, Patterns of Reproduction," *Canadian Journal of History of Sport* 26, no. 2 (1995): 1.

38   Fred Sappier, Acting Chairman, National Indian Sport Council, to the Honourable Jean Chrétien, Minister of Justice, House of Commons, March 6, 1981, Provincial Archives of New Brunswick, Fitness and Amateur Sport Indian Support Program—Submission, MC 1795, Box 26, Content ID 3683.

39   Ibid., 12–13.

40   George Manuel, President, NIB, to Jean Chrétien, Minister, Indian Affairs Branch, July 31, 1972, 1, DIAND, 1/1-2/15/2, Volume 11.

41   Ibid., 2.

42   NIB, *Tradition and Education*, 53.

43   National Indian Brotherhood, Minutes of the Recreation Meeting, Ottawa, October 1973, 12, LAC, RG 29, Volume 3242, File 7320/I38.

44   V.M. Gran, Chief, Band Management Division, Indian Affairs Branch, to All Presidents, Regional Indian Associations, November 6, 1973, 1, DIAND, 1/1-2/15/2, Volume 11.

45   Ibid.

46   Keene Johnston, Social Development Section, Band Management Division, Indian Affairs Branch, to Clive Linklater, Vice-President, NIB, September 11, 1974, 1, LAC, RG 10, Series B-3-e-xiv, Volume 12712, File 1/1-2-15-2, Part 12.

47   R.M. Connelly, Director, Community Affairs, Indian Affairs Branch, to Peter Lesaux, Assistant Deputy Minister, Indian and Eskimo Affairs, March 20, 1974, LAC, RG 10, Series B-3-e-xiv, Volume 12712, File 1/1-2-15-2, Part 12.

48   Johnston to Linklater, September 11, 1974, 2.

49   Ibid., 1.

50   NIB, Minutes of the Recreation Meeting, Ottawa, October 1973, 12.

51   J.K. Johnston, Social Development Section, Band Management Division, Indian and Northern Affairs, to File, January 9, 1975, LAC, RG 10, Series B-3-e-xiv, Volume 12712, File 1/1-2-15-2, Part 12.

52   J.R. Tully, Acting Director, Local Government, Operations, Indian Affairs Branch, to Director General, Ontario Region, May 4, 1976, LAC, RG 10, Series B-3-e-xiv, Volume 12712, File 1/1-2-15-2, Part 12.

53   Tom Longboat Awards Committee, NIB, memorandum to Provincial/Territorial Organizations and Chiefs, March 23, 1982, 1, AFN Archives.

54   See, for example, Tom Longboat Awards Committee, AFN, memorandum to First Nations Organizations and Tribal Councils and Chiefs, October 9, 1985, AFN Archives.

55 Minutes of the Meeting of the Selection Committee for the Tom Longboat Award, June 24, 1977, LAC, RG 29, Volume 3242, File 7320/I38.

56 George Erasmus, National Chief, AFN, to Tom Erasmus, September 5, 1986, AFN Archives.

57 Personal interview with Jan Eisenhardt, Dorval, QC, March 10, 2004.

58 "The Tom Longboat Awards: A Short History," 2, attachment to memorandum from Clive Linklater, Vice-President, to Executive Directors, Provincial and Territorial Member Organizations, October 10, 1975, LAC, RG 10, Series B-3-e-xiv, Volume 12712, File 1/1-2-15-2, Part 12.

59 "Criteria for Selection of the Tom Longboat Trophy, Revised Deed of Gift," September 1974, attachment to memorandum from Clive Linklater, Vice-President, to Executive Directors, Provincial and Territorial Member Organizations, October 10, 1975, LAC, RG 10, Series B-3-e-xiv, Volume 12712, File 1/1-2-15-2, Part 12.

60 Indian Brotherhood of the Northwest Territories, telex to Tim Steward, Social Development Division, Indian Affairs Branch, November 29, 1976, LAC, RG 10, Series B-3-e-xiv, Volume 12712, File 1/1-2-15-2, Part 12.

61 J.R. Wright, Local Government—Operations, Social Development, message to Indian Brotherhood of the Northwest Territories, December 12, 1976, LAC, RG 10, Series B-3-e-xiv, Volume 12712, File 1/1-2-15-2, Part 12.

62 Sharon and Shirley Firth competed in the 1972, 1976, 1980, and 1984 Olympic Winter Games. In 1987, the twin sisters were awarded the Order of Canada for their contributions to Canadian sport. As M. Ann Hall explains, their Gwich'in mother lost her Indian Status when she married a Loucheauz Métis man of Scottish heritage. See Hall, *The Girl and the Game*, 245. For a detailed history of the Northwest Territories Cross-Country Ski Team, see Christine O'Bonsawin, "Failed TEST: Aboriginal Sport Policy and the Olympian Firth Sisters" (MA thesis, University of Western Ontario, 2002).

63 From 1974 to 1998, complete records were located for only six years (1974, 1975, 1976, 1981, 1982, 1987) and partial records for twelve years, limited primarily to the names of the national recipients (1977, 1978, 1979, 1980, 1984, 1985, 1988, 1989, 1994, 1995, 1997, 1998). Records for five years (1990, 1991, 1992, 1993, 1996) are missing completely. The awards were suspended for two years (1983 and 1986).

64 The six national recipients, and the regions for which they won the award, include Beverly Stranger, Quebec, 1976; Carole Polchies, Maritimes, 1979; Beverly Beaver, Ontario, 1980; Mona Jones, region unknown, 1988; Alanaise O. Ferguson, British Columbia, 1994; and Francis Debassiaee, region unknown, 1995.

65 The Ontario Games are referred to as the "Ontario Summer Games" in *Native Perspective* but were properly known as the Ontario Games for the Physically Disabled. "Tom Longboat Trophy Winners," *Native Perspective* 2, no. 6 (1977): 48.

66 "Portage Indian Student Wins T. Longboat Medal," *Daily Graphic* (Portage, SK), December 1, 1952, LAC, RG 10, Volume 8581, File 1/1-2-15-2, Part 1.

67 Minutes of the Meeting of the Selection Committee for the Tom Longboat Award, June 24, 1977.

68 Points System for the Tom Longboat Awards, 1977, AFN Archives.

69 Minutes of the Meeting of the Selection Committee for the Tom Longboat Award, June 24, 1977.

70 Ibid. The historical record does not indicate if nominations were actually pulled for 1977 or any other year, and how this affected the regional awards, since only partial information was available for the years 1977, 1978, 1979, 1980, 1984, 1985, 1988, 1989, 1994, 1995, 1997, and 1998.

71 Points System for the Tom Longboat Awards, 1977.

72 Mrs. Olga Stusick, Cote Field Nurse, to Regional Director, Saskatchewan, Indian Affairs Branch, February 28, 1974, 2, LAC, RG 10, Series B-3-e-xiv, Volume 12712, File 1/1-2-15-2, Part 12.

73 Ibid.

74 "Cote Wins Longboat Award," *Saskatchewan Indian* 4, nos. 6–7 (1974): 40.

75 Neeghani-Binehse, Grand Chief of Manitoba, nomination for John C. Courchene, to Clive Linklater, Vice-President, NIB, December 8, 1975, 1, LAC, RG 10, Series B-3-e-xiv, Volume 12712, File 1/1-2-15-2, Part 12.

76 Ibid.

77 Backgrounder on John C. Courchene, circa 1976, 1, LAC, RG 10, Series B-3-e-xiv, Volume 12712, File 1/1-2-15-2, Part 12.

78 Ibid., 2.

79 Because the organization was incorporated under the National Indian Brotherhood name, it had to keep the moniker for financial reasons.

80 Patricia Simon, Recreation Coordinator, Sarcee Seven Chiefs Sportsplex, nomination for Gordon Lee Crowchild, to Dawn Thompson, Special Projects Coordinator, AFN, February 28, 1983, AFN Archives.

81 David Ahenakew, National Chief, AFN, to Gordon Lee Crowchild, May 6, 1983, AFN Archives.

82 David Ahenakew, National Chief, AFN, to Tyler Sunday, May 6, 1983, AFN Archives.

83 Assembly of First Nations, Budget for Tom Longboat Awards Submitted for the 1985–86 Fiscal Year, 1984, AFN Archives.

84 Ibid.

85 AFN, Budget for Tom Longboat Awards, 1984.

86 Email communication with Alwyn Morris, November 30, 2004.

87 Tom Longboat Awards Committee, AFN, memorandum to First Nations Organizations, Tribal Councils, and Chiefs, October 9, 1985, AFN Archives.

88 Sam Bull, Chief, Whitefish Lake Band, nomination for Tom Erasmus, January 6, 1986, AFN Archives.

89 AFN, Budget for Tom Longboat Awards, 1984, part C1, point 5.

90 Briefing Note, AFN Scholarships and Awards, 1988, 1, AFN Archives.

91 Personal interview with Rick Brant, Kanata, ON, September 24, 2004.

92 In the latter case, for instance, the archives included nomination packages for the Tom Longboat Awards that had little to do with sports. Likewise, nomination packages submitted for the awards other than the Tom Longboat Awards highlighted extensive sports experiences.

CHAPTER 4

1 Canada, *Report of the Royal Commission on Aboriginal Peoples: Looking Forward, Looking Back, Volume 1* (Ottawa: Royal Commission on Aboriginal Peoples, 1996), xvi.

2   Sport is mentioned five times in the recommendations of the final report. See recommendations 4.4.3, 4.4.4, 4.4.5, 4.4.8, and 4.7.11. The overall objectives are expressed therein. Canada, *Report of the Royal Commission on Aboriginal Peoples, Renewal: A Twenty-Year Commitment, Volume 5* (Ottawa: Royal Commission on Aboriginal Peoples, 1996), 239, 240, 249.

3   Briefing note on the Aboriginal Sport Circle, February 23, 1998, AFN Archives.

4   Canada, *Report of the Royal Commission on Aboriginal Peoples: Perspectives and Realities, Volume 4* (Ottawa: Royal Commission on Aboriginal Peoples, 1996), 177.

5   A general overview of these interests is documented in Chris Szabo, "Historical Overview of Government Involvement in Aboriginal Sport and Recreation," Leisure Information Network, 2011.

6   Minister's Task Force on Federal Sport Policy, *Sport: The Way Ahead: Minister's Task Force on Federal Sport Policy* (Ottawa: Minister of Supply and Services Canada, 1992), mandate.

7   Personal interview with Alwyn Morris, Kahnawake, Quebec, October 27, 2009.

8   Ibid., 156.

9   Canada, *Minister's Steering Committee on Active Living: Final Report* (Ottawa: Minister of State, Fitness and Amateur Sport, 1993), 37.

10 Canada, Communiqué of the Federal-Provincial-Territorial Conference of Ministers Responsible for Sport and Recreation, Regina, March 9, 1993, document 830-473/016.

11 A general history and analysis of factors that contributed to the establishment of the ASC and Indigenous sport development (from a policy perspective) in Canada can be found in Janice Forsyth and Vicky Paraschak, "The Double Helix: Aboriginal People and Sport Policy," in *Sport Policy in Canada*, eds. Lucie Thibault and Jean Harvey (Ottawa: University of Ottawa Press, 2013), 267–93; Vicky Paraschak, "Aboriginal Peoples and the Construction of Canadian Sport Policy," in *Aboriginal Peoples and Sport in Canada: Historical Foundations and Contemporary Issues*, eds. Janice Forsyth and Audrey R. Giles (Vancouver: UBC Press, 2013), 95–123; and Vicky Paraschak, " 'Get into the Mainstream': Aboriginal Sport in Canada, 1967–2002," in *2002 North American Indigenous Games Research Symposium Proceedings*, eds. Vicky Paraschak and Janice Forsyth (Winnipeg: University of Manitoba, 2003), 23–30.

12 Ron Ahenakew, Aboriginal Sport Circle, briefing package to A.J. Felix, Vice-Chief, Assembly of First Nations, May 24, 1995, 6, AFN Archives.

13 Janice Forsyth, "Aboriginal Sport Circle," in *Native Americans in Sports, Volume 1*, ed. Richard King (Armonk, NY: Sharpe Reference, 2004), 2–3.

14 Forsyth and Paraschak, "The Double Helix," 269.

15 Ibid.

16 The only other athlete named a recipient four times was Charles Ross Smallface, also from Alberta, who competed in boxing, track and field, and rifle shooting. He won the regional award in 1951, 1952, and 1953, and the national award in 1954. Littlechild and Smallface remain the only athletes to date who have won the award four times.

17 Tim Berrett, *2016 Aboriginal Sport, Physical Activity, and Recreation Survey: Data Analysis, Final Report*, prepared for Caminata Consulting and submitted to Sport Canada, 2017, 29.

18   Forsyth and Paraschak, "The Double Helix," 281.

19   In February 2019, the ministers committed to a new funding framework, with the NAIG being hosted in Canada every four years beginning in 2024; they also finally agreed to provide regular financial support for athletes and team preparation.

20   Alwyn Morris, Chair, Aboriginal Sport Circle, to Phil Fontaine, National Chief, Assembly of First Nations, November 12, 1998, 1, AFN Archives.

21   Aboriginal Sport Circle, Proposed Transfer and Restructuring of the Tom Longboat Awards, 1998, 2, AFN Archives.

22   Ahenakew to Felix (briefing package).

23   Morris to Fontaine, 1.

24   Aboriginal Sport Circle, Resolution Regarding the Tom Longboat Awards, Board of Directors Meeting, Halifax, October 21, 1998, AFN Archives.

25   Glen Sean Coulthard, *Red Skin, White Masks: Rejecting the Colonial Politics of Recognition* (Minneapolis: University of Minnesota Press, 2014).

26   Chris Anderson, *"Métis": Race, Recognition, and the Struggle for Indigenous Peoplehood* (Vancouver: UBC Press, 2014).

27   Ibid., 9.

28   Aboriginal Sport Circle, the Tom Longboat Award, National Awards for Excellence in Aboriginal Sport, nomination form, 1999, ASC Files.

29   Ibid.

30   "Regional Athletic Award Recipients Shine," *Windspeaker* 19, no. 12 (2002): 25.

31   "Awards Recipients Serve as Role Models," *Windspeaker* 19, no. 12 (2002): 24.

32   Aboriginal Sport Circle, Proposed Transfer and Restructuring of the Tom Longboat Awards, 1998, 3, AFN Archives.

33   This argument has been developed elsewhere. See, for example, Pam Ponic, "A Herstory, a Legacy: The Canadian Amateur Sport Branch's Women's Program," *Avante* 6, no. 2 (2000): 51–63; Donald MacIntosh and David Whitson, *The Game Planners: Transforming Canada's Sport System* (Montreal and Kingston: McGill-Queen's University Press, 1990), 81–91; and Ann Hall and Dorothy Richardson, *Fair Ball: Towards Sex Equality in Canadian Sport* (Ottawa: Canadian Advisory Council on the Status of Women, Minister of Supply and Services, 1983), 89.

34   "Women Urge Sports Minister to Revise Legislation," *Canada NewsWire*, May 27, 2002, 1; "Minister Opposes Enshrining Women Despite Pressure [Bill C-54]," *Globe and Mail* (Toronto), May 30, 2002, S4; "Women Withdraw Gender Equity Demand," *Ottawa Citizen*, June 6, 2002, C8.

35   Sport Canada, *Sport Gender Snap Shot, 1997–1998: Survey Results Report* (Ottawa: Canadian Heritage, 1999).

36   The P/TASBs comprised the ASC Board of Directors. Each of the thirteen P/TASBs were represented by two members, thus making the ASC a twenty-six-member board. Aboriginal Sport Circle, Board of Directors Contact List, 1999–2001, ASC Files.

37   Lori Johnstone and Sydney Millar, *Actively Engaging Women and Girls: Addressing the Psycho-Social Factors, a Supplement to Canadian Sport Life* (Ottawa: CAAWS, 2012), 10.

38   Report Prepared for the Aboriginal Sport Circle, Annual General Assembly, September 6–8, 2001, ASC Files.

39   Ibid.

40   Report on the 2001 Tom Longboat Awards Prepared for the Aboriginal Sport Circle, Annual General Assembly, Ottawa, September 11–14, 2002, 2, ASC Files.

41   Ibid.

42   Aboriginal Sport Circle, Minutes of the Annual General Assembly, Victoria, September 22–24, 2000, 9, ASC Files.

43   Aboriginal Sport Circle, Minutes of the Annual General Assembly, Whitehorse, September 6–8, 2001, 10, ASC Files.

44   Douglas Booth, "The Consecration of Sport: Idealism in Social Science Theory," *International Journal of the History of Sport* 10, no. 1 (1993): 12.

45   Richard Gruneau, *Class, Sports, and Social Development* (Champaign, IL: Human Kinetics, 1999), 106.

46   Report on the 2001 Tom Longboat Awards, 1.

47   Report on the ASC Criteria for Ranking Tom Longboat Nominations Prepared for the Aboriginal Sport Circle, Annual General Assembly, Ottawa, September 11–14, 2002, 5, 6, ASC Files.

48   Aboriginal Sport Circle, Proposed Transfer and Restructuring of the Tom Longboat Awards, 1998, 5, AFN Archives.

49   Ibid.

CHAPTER 5

1   Quoted in Aboriginal Sport Circle, press release, March 23, 2004, ASC Files.

2   Paul Thompson, "The Voice of the Past: Oral History," in *The Oral History Reader*, eds. Robert Perks and Alistair Thomson (London: Routledge, 1998), 22.

3   Three of the recipients have passed away since these interviews were conducted: Kenneth Joseph "Joe" Montour on January 13, 2012; Bill Kinoshameg on July 22, 2018; and Phyllis Bomberry on January 3, 2019.

4   Gruneau, *Class, Sports, and Social Development*, 106.

5   Popular Memory Group, "Popular Memory: Theory, Politics, Method," in *The Oral History Reader*, eds. Robert Perks and Alistair Thomson (London: Routledge, 1998), 76.

6   Unless otherwise noted, the following information on and quotations from Bill Kinoshameg are from a personal interview with him, North Bay, ON, January 16, 2005.

7   Bill Kinoshameg to Janice Forsyth, May 30, 2005.

8   Unless otherwise noted, the following information on and quotations from John Lee Stonefish are from a personal interview with him, London, ON, November 17, 2004.

9   Nomination for John Lee Stonefish from Bruce Foster, Principal, Ridgetown District High School, October 6, 1960, LAC, RG 10, Volume 8582, File 1/1-2-15-2, Part 4.

10   Unless otherwise noted, the following information on and quotations from Joe Montour are from a personal interview with him, Six Nations, ON, December 20, 2004.

11   Department of Indian Affairs and Northern Development, press release, Tom Longboat Award, 1970, 2–3, DIAND, 1/1-2/15/2, Volume 9.

12   Unless otherwise noted, the following information on and quotations from Phyllis Bomberry are from a personal interview with her, Brantford, ON, November 10, 2004.

13   Lucy Koserski, "Indians Triumph," *The Spectator* (Hamilton, ON), June 6, 1969, 45. I would like to thank Phyllis Bomberry for sharing this article with me.

14   Unless otherwise noted, the following information on and quotations from Beverly Beaver are from a personal interview with Beverly and George Beaver, Wilsonville, ON, November 29, 2004.

15   Between 1961 and 2000, Beverly was named MVP eleven times, best pitcher nine times, top batter two times, and all-star player two times.

16   Ann Hall, "Beverly (Bev) Beaver," unpublished biography. I am grateful to Ann Hall for sharing this information with me.

17   Between 1963 and 1991, Beverly was the top scorer in nine tournaments, received six MVP awards, and was twice named an all-star centre.

18   For brief biographies of Beverly, see M. Ann Hall, *The Girl and the Game: A History of Women's Sport in Canada* (Peterborough, ON: Broadview Press, 2002), 154; Paraschak, "An Examination of Sport for Aboriginal Females," 92; and Paraschak, "Organized Sport for Native Females," 71, 79.

19   Unless otherwise noted, the following information on and quotations from Rick Brant are from a personal interview with him, Kanata, ON, September 24, 2004.

20   Rick Brant, "Rick Brant," in *Heroes in Our Midst: Top Canadian Athletes Share Personal Stories from Their Lives in Sport*, eds. Robin Mednick and Wendy Thomas (Toronto: McClelland and Stewart, 2001), 194–5.

21   Unless otherwise noted, the following information on and quotations from Tara Hedican are from a telephone interview with her, Montreal, QC, December 18, 2004.

22   Gruneau, *Class, Sports, and Social Development*, 106.

CONCLUSION

1   Stuart Hall, "Introduction," in *Representation: Cultural Representations and Signifying Practices*, ed. Stuart Hall (London, UK: SAGE and Open University, 2007), 3.

2   See Milloy, *A National Crime*.

3   Naomi Angel and Pauline Wakeham, "Witnessing in Camera: Photographic Reflections on Truth and Reconciliation," in *Arts of Engagement: Taking Aesthetic Action in and beyond the Truth and Reconciliation Commission of Canada*, eds. Dylan Robinson and Keavy Martin (Waterloo, ON: Wilfrid Laurier University Press, 2016), 94.

4   Donna Carreiro, "Beyond 94: Where Is Canada at with Reconciliation?," CBC *News*, https://www.cbc.ca/news/indigenous/beyond-94-truth-and-reconciliation-1.4574765.

5   Of the two remaining sports-related Calls to Action, one is listed as "not started" (number 89: "Amend the *Physical Activity and Sport Act* to ensure policies are inclusive to Aboriginal Peoples"), and the other as "in progress—projects proposed" (number 91: "Ensure that Indigenous Peoples' territorial protocols are respected by officials and host countries of international sporting events").

6   Truth and Reconciliation Commission of Canada, *Truth and Reconciliation Commission of Canada: Calls to Action*, 2015, http://trc.ca/assets/pdf/Calls_to_Action_English2.pdf, 10.

7   Canada's Sports Hall of Fame, "Aboriginal Athletes Introduction," 2017, http://www.canadasports150.ca/en/aboriginal-athletes/aboriginal-athletes-introduction/118.

8   Ibid.

NOTES ON ARCHIVAL SOURCES

1   Personal interview with Jan Eisenhardt, Dorval, QC, March 10, 2004.

BIBLIOGRAPHY

PRIMARY SOURCES

Archival Collections
Aboriginal Sport Circle, Ottawa, ON
Assembly of First Nations, Ottawa, ON
Indigenous and Northern Affairs Canada, Gatineau, QC
    DIAND, 1/1-2/15/2, Volume 8
    DIAND, 1/1-2/15/2, Volume 9
    DIAND, 1/1-2/15/2, Volume 10
    DIAND, 1/1-2/15/2, Volume 11
Library and Archives Canada, Ottawa, ON
Indian Affairs Annual Reports, 1864–1990
    RG 10, Series B-3-e-xiv, Volume 12712, File 1/1-2-15-2, Part 12
    RG 10, Volume 8581, File 1/1-2-15-2, Part 1
    RG 10, Volume 8581, File 1/1-2-15-2, Part 2
    RG 10, Volume 8582, File 1/1-2-15-2, Part 3
    RG 10, Volume 8582, File 1/1-2-15-2, Part 4
    RG 29, Volume 3242, File 7320/I38
    RG 32, Public Service Commission, Series C-2, Volume 1408
Provincial Archives of New Brunswick, Fredericton, NB

Weldon Archives and Special Collections, Western University, London, ON
   AFC 451, Jan Eisenhardt Fonds
Weldon Library, Western University, London, ON
Woodland Cultural Centre, Brantford, ON

INTERVIEWS AND PERSONAL COMMUNICATIONS

Beaver, Beverly, and George Beaver, personal interview, Wilsonville,
   ON, November 29, 2004
Bomberry, Phyllis, personal interview, Brantford, ON, November 10,
   2004
Brant, Rick, personal interview, Kanata, ON, September 24, 2004
Eisenhardt, Jan, personal interview, Dorval, QC, March 10, 2004
Hedican, Tara, telephone interview, Montreal, QC, December 18, 2004
Kinoshameg, Bill, personal interview, North Bay, ON, January 16, 2005
Montour, Joe, personal interview, Six Nations, ON, December 20, 2004
Morris, Alwyn, personal interview, Kahnawake, QC, October 27, 2009
Morris, Alwyn, email to the author, November 30, 2004
Stonefish, John Lee, personal interview, London, ON, November 17, 2004

SECONDARY SOURCES

Articles, Chapters, Books

Adams, Mary Louise. *The Trouble with Normal: Postwar Youth and
   the Making of Heterosexuality*. Toronto: University of Toronto
   Press, 2003.
Alfred, Taiaiake. *Peace, Power, Righteousness: An Indigenous Manifesto*.
   Don Mills, ON: Oxford University Press, 1999.
Anderson, Chris. *"Métis": Race, Recognition, and the Struggle for
   Indigenous Peoplehood*. Vancouver: UBC Press, 2014.
Angel, Naomi, and Pauline Wakeham. "Witnessing in Camera:
   Photographic Reflections on Truth and Reconciliation." In
   *Arts of Engagement: Taking Aesthetic Action in and beyond
   the Truth and Reconciliation Commission of Canada*, edited

by Dylan Robinson and Keavy Martin, 93–134. Waterloo, ON: Wilfrid Laurier University Press, 2016.

Bale, John, and Mike Cronin, eds. *Sport and Postcolonialism*. New York: Berg, 2003.

Bale, John, and Joe Sang. *Kenyan Running: Movement Culture, Geography, and Global Change*. London: Frank Cass, 1996.

Batten, Jack. *The Man Who Ran Faster than Everyone: The Story of Tom Longboat*. Toronto: Tundra Books, 2002.

Berbrugge, Martha H. *Active Bodies: A History of Women's Physical Education in Twentieth-Century America*. New York: Oxford University Press, 2012.

Berrett, Tim. *2016 Aboriginal Sport, Physical Activity, and Recreation Survey: Data Analysis, Final Report*. Prepared for Caminata Consulting and submitted to Sport Canada, 2017.

Blackstock, Cindy, Nico Trocmé, and Marlyn Bennett. "Children Maltreatment Investigations among Aboriginal and Non-Aboriginal Families in Canada." *Violence Against Women* 10, no. 8 (2004): 1–16.

Bloom, John. "'There Is Madness in the Air': The 1926 Haskell Homecoming and Popular Representations of Sports in Federal Indian Boarding Schools." In *Dressing in Feathers: The Construction of the Indian in American Popular Culture*, edited by Elizabeth Bird, 97–110. Boulder, CO: Westview Press, 1996.

———. *To Show What an Indian Can Do: Sports at Native American Boarding Schools*. Minneapolis: University of Minnesota Press, 2000.

Booth, Douglas. "The Consecration of Sport: Idealism in Social Science Theory." *International Journal of the History of Sport* 10, no. 1 (1993): 1–19.

Brant, Rick. "Rick Brant." In *Heroes in Our Midst: Top Canadian Athletes Share Personal Stories from Their Lives in Sport*, edited by Robin Mednick and Wendy Thomas, 193–97. Toronto: McClelland and Stewart, 2001.

Brayboy, Tim, and Bruce Barton. *Playing before an Overflow Crowd: The Story of Indian Basketball in Rebeson, North Carolina, and Adjoining Counties*. Chapel Hill, NC: Chapel Hill Press, 2003.

Brown, David. "Canadian Imperialism and Sporting Exchanges: The Nineteenth-Century Cultural Experience of Cricket and Lacrosse." *Canadian Journal of History of Sport* 18, no. 1 (1987): 55–66.

Bumsted, Jack. *Louis Riel v. Canada: The Making of a Rebel.* Winnipeg: Great Plains Publications, 2001.

Campbell, Maria. *Half-Breed.* Toronto: McClelland and Stewart, 1973.

Canada. Department of Indian Affairs. *Calisthenics and Games, Prescribed for Use in All Indian Schools.* Ottawa: Government Printing Bureau, 1910.

——. Minister's Steering Committee on Active Living. *Minister's Steering Committee on Active Living: Final Report.* Ottawa: Minister of State, Fitness and Amateur Sport, 1993.

——. Royal Commission on Aboriginal Peoples. *Report of the Royal Commission on Aboriginal Peoples: Looking Forward, Looking Back, Volume 1.* Ottawa: Minister of Supply and Services Canada, 1996.

——. Royal Commission on Aboriginal Peoples. *Report of the Royal Commission on Aboriginal Peoples: Perspectives and Realities, Volume 4.* Ottawa: Minister of Supply and Services Canada, 1996.

——. Royal Commission on Aboriginal Peoples. *Report of the Royal Commission on Aboriginal Peoples: Renewal: A Twenty-Year Commitment, Volume 5.* Ottawa: Royal Commission on Aboriginal Peoples, 1996.

——. Sport Canada. *Sport Gender Snap Shot, 1997–1998: Survey Results Report.* Ottawa: Canadian Heritage, 1999.

Cardinal, Harold. *The Rebirth of Canada's Indians.* Edmonton: Hurtig, 1977.

——. *The Unjust Society.* Vancouver: Douglas and McIntyre, 1969.

Chalmers, John. *Education behind the Buckskin Curtain: A History of Native Education in Canada.* Edmonton: self-published, circa 1972.

Churchill, Ward, Norbert S. Hill, Jr., and Mary Jo Barlow. "An Historical Overview of Twentieth-Century Native American Athletics." *Indian Historian* 12, no. 4 (1979): 22–32.

Ciaccia, John. *The Oka Crisis: A Mirror of the Soul.* Dorval, QC: Maren Publications, 2000.

Clark, Warren. "Kid's Sports." Statistics Canada Catalogue No. 82-003-XPE, 2008. http://www.statcan.gc.ca/pub/11-008-x/2008001/article/10573-eng.htm.

Cosentino, Frank. *Afros, Aboriginals, and Amateur Sport in Pre–World War One Canada*. Ottawa: Canadian Historical Society, 1998.

———. "A History of the Concept of Professionalism in Canadian Sport." *Canadian Journal of History of Sport and Physical Education* 6, no. 2 (1975): 75–81.

Coulthard, Glen Sean. *Red Skin, White Masks: Rejecting the Colonial Politics of Recognition*. Minneapolis: University of Minnesota Press, 2014.

Cronin, Fergus. "The Rise and Fall of Tom Longboat." *Maclean's*, February 4, 1956, 21.

Daschuk, James. *Clearing the Plains: Disease, Politics of Starvation, and the Loss of Aboriginal Life*. Regina: University of Regina Press, 2013.

Dewar, John. "The Introduction of Western Sports to the Indian People of Canada's Prairie West." In *Sport, Culture, Society: International Historical and Sociological Perspectives*, Proceedings of the Eighth Commonwealth and International Conference on Sport, Physical Education, Dance, Recreation, and Health, edited by James Mangan and Roy Small, 27–32. London: E. and F.N. Spon, 1986.

Donnelly, Peter. "Sport Participation." In *Sport Policy in Canada*, edited by Lucie Thibault and Jean Harvey, 177–213. Ottawa: University of Ottawa Press, 2013.

Downey, Allan. *The Creator's Game: Lacrosse, Identity, and Indigenous Nationhood*. Vancouver: UBC Press, 2018.

Downey, Allan, and Susan Neylan. "Raven Plays Ball: Situating 'Indian Sports Days' within Indigenous and Colonial Spaces in Twentieth Century Coastal British Columbia." *Canadian Journal of History* 50, no. 3 (2015): 442–68.

Edwards, Peter. *One Dead Indian: The Premier, the Police, and the Ipperwash Crisis*. Toronto: Stoddart, 2001.

Elkins, David. "Evaluation Report: Recreation Program Review." Department of Indian Affairs and Northern Development, 1979.

Fisher, Donald. *Lacrosse: A History of the Game.* Baltimore: Johns Hopkins University Press, 2002.

Forsyth, Janice. "Aboriginal Sport Circle." In *Native Americans in Sports, Volume 1,* edited by Richard King, 2–3. Armonk, NY: Sharpe Reference, 2004.

———. "Bodies of Meaning: Sports and Games at Canadian Residential Schools." In *Aboriginal Peoples and Sport in Canada: Historical Foundations and Contemporary Issues,* edited by J. Forsyth and A. Giles, 15–34. Vancouver: UBC Press, 2013.

———. "The Indian Act and the (Re)Shaping of Canadian Aboriginal Sport Practices." *International Journal of Canadian Studies* 35 (2007): 95–111.

———. "Make the Indian Understand His Place: Politics and the Establishment of the Tom Longboat Awards at Indian Affairs and the Amateur Athletic Union of Canada." *Sport in History* 35, no. 2 (2015): 241–70.

Forsyth, Janice, and Vicky Paraschak. "The Double Helix: Aboriginal People and Sport Policy." In *Sport Policy in Canada,* edited by Lucie Thibault and Jean Harvey, 267–93. Ottawa: University of Ottawa Press, 2013.

Fournier, Suzanne. *Stolen from Our Embrace: The Abduction of First Nations Children and the Restoration of Aboriginal Communities.* Vancouver: Douglas and McIntyre, 1997.

Furniss, Elizabeth. *Victims of Benevolence: Discipline and Death at the Williams Lake Indian Residential School, 1891–1920.* Williams Lake, BC: Cariboo Tribal Council, 1992.

Gidney, Catherine. *Tending the Student Body: Youth, Health, and the Modern University.* Toronto: University of Toronto Press, 2015.

Goodleaf, Donna. *Entering the War Zone: A Mohawk Perspective on Resisting Invasions.* Penticton, BC: Theytus Books, 1995.

Graham, Elizabeth. *The Mush Hole: Life at Two Indian Residential Schools.* Waterloo, ON: Heffle Publishing, 1997.

Granatstein, Jack. "Tom Longboat." *Maclean's,* July 1, 1998, 49–50.

Grant, Agnes. *No End in Grief: Indian Residential Schools in Canada.* Winnipeg: Pemmican Publications, 1996.

Gresko, Jacqueline. "Creating Little Dominions within the Dominion: Early Catholic Indian Schools in Saskatchewan and British Columbia." In *Indian Education in Canada, Volume 1: The Legacy,* edited by Jean Barman, Yvonne Hébert, and Don McCaskill, 93–109. Vancouver: UBC Press, 1986.

Gruneau, Richard. *Class, Sports, and Social Development.* Champaign, IL: Human Kinetics, 1999.

Habkirk, Evan J. "From Indian Boys to Canadian Men? The Use of Cadet Drill in the Canadian Indian Residential School System." *British Journal of Canadian Studies* 30, no. 2 (2018): 227–48.

Haig-Brown, Celia. *Resistance and Renewal: Surviving the Indian Residential School.* Vancouver: Tillacum Library, 1988.

Hall, M. Ann. "Beverly (Bev) Beaver." Unpublished biography.

———. *The Girl and the Game: A History of Women's Sport in Canada.* Peterborough, ON: Broadview Press, 2002.

———. *The Girl and the Game: A History of Women's Sport in Canada.* 2nd ed. Toronto: University of Toronto Press, 2016.

Hall, M. Ann, and Dorothy Richardson. *Fair Ball: Towards Sex Equality in Canadian Sport.* Ottawa: Canadian Advisory Council on the Status of Women, Minister of Supply and Services, 1983.

Hallinan, Chris, and Barry Judd, eds. *Native Games: Indigenous Peoples and Sport in the Post-Colonial World.* Bingley, UK: Emerald, 2013.

Hawthorn, H.B. *A Survey of the Contemporary Indians of Canada: A Report on the Economic, Political, Educational Needs and Policies: Part 1.* Ottawa: Indian Affairs Branch, 1966.

———. *A Survey of the Contemporary Indians of Canada: A Report on the Economic, Political, Educational Needs and Policies: Part 2.* Ottawa: Indian Affairs Branch, 1967.

Heine, Michael. *Arctic Sports: A Training and Resource Manual.* Yellowknife: Arctic Sports Association and MACA (GNWT), 1998.

———. *Dene Games: A Culture and Resource Manual, Traditional Aboriginal Sport Coaching Resources, Volume 1.* Yellowknife: Sport North Federation and MACA (GNWT), 1999.

Heine, Michael, and Kevin Wamsley. "Kickfest at Dawson City: Native Peoples and the Sports of the Klondike Gold Rush." *Sport History Review* 27, no. 1 (1996): 72–86.

Hinton, Alexander Laban, Andrew Woolford, and Jeff Benvenuto, eds. *Colonial Genocide in Indigenous North America*. Durham, NC: Duke University Press, 2014.

Johnston, Basil. *Indian School Days*. Toronto: Key Porter Books, 1988.

Johnstone, Lori, and Sydney Millar. *Actively Engaging Women and Girls: Addressing the Psycho-Social Factors, a Supplement to Canadian Sport Life*. Ottawa: CAAWS, 2012.

Kelm, Mary-Ellen. *Colonizing Bodies: Aboriginal Health and Healing in British Columbia, 1900–1950*. Vancouver: UBC Press, 2001.

Kidd, Bruce. "In Defense of Tom Longboat." *Canadian Journal of History of Sport* 14, no. 1 (1983): 43–63.

———. "Springstead, Velma Agnes." In *Dictionary of Canadian Biography*. Vol. 15. Toronto: University of Toronto; Laval: Université Laval, 2005. http://www.biographi.ca/en/bio/springstead_velma_agnes_15E.html.

———. *The Struggle for Canadian Sport*. Toronto: University of Toronto Press, 1996.

———. *Tom Longboat*. Don Mills, ON: Fitzhenry and Whiteside, 1980.

King, Thomas. *The Truth about Stories: A Native Narrative*. Toronto: Anansi, 2003.

Kirk, David. *Schooling Bodies: School Practice and Public Discourse, 1880–1950*. London: Leicester University Press, 1998.

Kirkness, Verna, and Sheena Selkirk Bowman. *First Nations and Schools: Triumphs and Struggles*. Toronto: Canadian Education Association, 1992.

Krasowski, Sheldon. *No Surrender: The Land Remains Indigenous*. Regina: University of Regina Press, 2019.

Lomawaima, Tsianina. *They Called It Prairie Light: The Story of Chilocco Indian School*. Lincoln: University of Nebraska Press, 1994.

Macdonald, Charlotte. *Strong, Beautiful and Modern: National Fitness in Britain, New Zealand, Australia and Canada, 1935–1960*. Vancouver: UBC Press, 2011.

MacIntosh, Donald, Tom Bedecki, and C.E.S. Franks. *Sport and Politics in Canada: Federal Government Involvement since 1961*. Montreal and Kingston: McGill-Queen's University Press, 1988.

MacIntosh, Donald, and David Whitson. *The Game Planners: Transforming Canada's Sport System*. Montreal and Kingston: McGill-Queen's University Press, 1990.

MacLean, Malcolm. "Ambiguity within the Boundary: Rereading C.L.R. James' *Beyond a Boundary*." In *Beyond C.L.R. James: Shifting Boundaries of Race and Ethnicity in Sport*, edited by John Nauright, Alan G. Cobley, and David K. Wiggins, 17–39. Fayetteville: University of Arkansas Press, 2014.

Mangan, J.A. *The Games Ethic and Imperialism: Aspects of the Diffusion of an Ideal*. London: Frank Cass, 1986.

Manuel, Arthur, and Grand Chief Ronald M. Derrickson. *Unsettling Canada: A National Wake-Up Call*. Toronto: Between the Lines, 2015.

McFarlane, Peter. *Brotherhood to Nationhood: George Manuel and the Making of the Modern Indian Movement*. Toronto: Between the Lines, 1993.

McGuire-Adams, Tricia. "Anishinaabeg Women's Stories of Wellbeing: Physical Activity, Restoring Wellbeing, and Dismantling the Settler Colonial Deficit Analysis." *Journal of Indigenous Wellbeing* 2, no. 3 (2018): 90–104.

McGuire-Adams, Tricia D., and Audrey R. Giles. "Anishinaabekweg Dibaajimowinan (Stories) of Decolonization through Running." *Sociology of Sport Journal* 35, no. 3 (2018): 207–15.

McKenzie, Holy A., Colleen Varcoe, Annette J. Browne, and Linda Day. "Disrupting the Continuities among Residential Schools, the Sixties Scoop, and Child Welfare: An Analysis of Colonial and Neocolonial Discourses." *International Indigenous Policy Journal* 7, no. 2 (2016): 1–24.

Mercredi, Ovide, and Mary Ellen Turpel. *In the Rapids: Navigating the Future of First Nations*. Toronto: Viking, 1993.

Miller, Jim. *Shingwauk's Vision: A History of Native Residential Schools*. Toronto: University of Toronto Press, 1996.

——. *Skyscrapers Hide the Heavens: A History of Indian-White Relations in Canada*. Toronto: University of Toronto Press, 2000.

Milloy, John. *A National Crime: The Canadian Government and the Residential School System, 1879–1986.* Winnipeg: University of Manitoba Press, 1999.

Minister's Task Force on Federal Sport Policy. *Sport: The Way Ahead. Minister's Task Force on Federal Sport Policy.* Ottawa: Minister of Supply and Services Canada, 1992.

Mitchell, Michael. *Tewaarathon (Lacrosse): Akwesasne's Story of Our National Game.* North American Indian Traveling College, 1978.

Morrow, Don. "The Knights of the Snowshoe: A Study of the Evolution of Sport in Nineteenth-Century Montreal." *Journal of Sport History* 15, no. 1 (1988): 5–40.

———. "Lou Marsh: The Pick and Shovel of Canadian Sports Journalism." *Canadian Journal of History of Sport* 14, no. 1 (1983): 21–33.

———. "The Strathcona Trust in Ontario, 1911–1939." *Canadian Journal of History of Sport and Physical Education* 8, no. 1 (1977): 72–90.

Morrow, Don, and Kevin B. Wamsley. *Sport in Canada: A History.* 3rd ed. Don Mills, ON: Oxford University Press, 2013.

———. *Sport in Canada: A History.* 4th ed. Don Mills, ON: Oxford University Press, 2017.

National Indian Brotherhood. *History of the AFN.* Ottawa: AFN/NIB, 2001.

———. *Indian Control of Indian Education.* Ottawa: NIB/AFN, 1972.

———. *Tradition and Education: Towards a Vision of Our Future, Volume 1.* Ottawa: NIB/AFN, 1988.

Neu, Dean, and Richard Therrien. *Accounting for Genocide: Canada's Bureaucratic Assault on Aboriginal Peoples.* London: Zed, 2003.

Norman, Moss E., Michael Hart, and LeAnne Petherick. "Indigenous Gender Reformations: Physical Culture, Settler Colonialism, and the Politics of Containment." *Sociology of Sport Journal* 36, no. 2 (2019): 113–23.

Paraschak, Vicky. "Aboriginal Peoples and the Construction of Canadian Sport Policy." In *Aboriginal Peoples and Sport in Canada: Historical Foundations and Contemporary Issues,* edited by Janice Forsyth and Audrey R. Giles, 95–123. Vancouver: UBC Press, 2013.

———. "An Examination of Sport for Aboriginal Females on the Six Nations Reserve, Ontario, from 1968 to 1980." In *Women of First Nations: Power, Wisdom, and Strength*, edited by Christine Miller and Patricia Chuchryk, 83–96. Winnipeg: University of Manitoba Press, 1996.

———. "'Get into the Mainstream': Aboriginal Sport in Canada, 1967–2002." In *2002 North American Indigenous Games Research Symposium Proceedings*, edited by Vicky Paraschak and Janice Forsyth, 23–30. Winnipeg: University of Manitoba, 2003.

———. "Invisible but Not Absent: Aboriginal Women in Sport and Recreation." *Women and Girls in Sport and Physical Activity*, special issue of *Canadian Woman Studies* 15, no. 4 (1995): 71–2.

———. "Native American Games and Sports." In *International Encyclopedia of Women and Sports*, edited by Karen Christensen, Allen Guttmann, and Gertrude Pfister, 788–91. New York: Macmillan, 2001.

———. "The Native Sport and Recreation Program, 1972–1981: Patterns of Resistance, Patterns of Reproduction." *Canadian Journal of History of Sport* 26, no. 2 (1995): 1–18.

———. "Organized Sport for Native Females on the Six Nations Reserve, Ontario, from 1968 to 1980: A Comparison of Dominant and Emergent Sport Systems." *Canadian Journal of History of Sport* 21 (1990): 70–80.

———. " 'Reasonable Amusements': Connecting the Strands of Physical Culture in Native Lives." *Sport History Review* 28, no. 1 (1998): 121–31.

Persson, Diane. "The Changing Experience of Indian Residential Schooling: Blue Quills, 1931–1970." In *Indian Education in Canada, Volume 1: The Legacy*, edited by Jean Barman, Yvonne Hébert, and Don McCaskill, 150–67. Vancouver: UBC Press, 1986.

Pettipas, Katherine. *Severing the Ties that Bind: Government Repression of Indigenous Religious Ceremonies on the Prairies*. Winnipeg: University of Manitoba Press, 1994.

Phillips, Murray, Russell Field, Christine O'Bonsawin, and Janice Forsyth, eds. *Indigenous Resurgence, Regeneration, and Decolonization through Sport History*, special issue of *Journal of Sport History* 46, no. 2 (2019).

Ponic, Pam. "A Herstory, a Legacy: The Canadian Amateur Sport Branch's Women's Program." *Avante* 6, no. 2 (2000): 51–63.

Popular Memory Group. "Popular Memory: Theory, Politics, Method." In *The Oral History Reader*, edited by Robert Perks and Alistair Thomson, 75–86. London: Routledge, 1998.

Satzewich, Victor. "Indian Agents and the 'Indian Problem' in Canada in 1946: Reconsidering the Theory of Coercive Tutelage." *Canadian Journal of Native Studies* 17, no. 2 (1997): 227–57.

Schmidt, Raymond. "Lords of the Prairie: Haskell Indian School Football, 1919–1930." *Journal of Sport History* 28, no. 3 (2001): 403–26.

Schrodt, Barbara. "Federal Programs of Physical Recreation and Fitness: The Contributions of Jan Eisenhardt." *Canadian Journal of History of Sport and Physical Education* 15, no. 2 (1984): 45–61.

———. "The Seeds of Destruction: Factors in the Dissolution of British Columbia's Pro-Rec Programme." In *Proceedings of the 5th Canadian Symposium on the History of Sport and Physical Education*, edited by Bruce Kidd, 431–7. Toronto: University of Toronto, 1982.

Shingwauk, Augustine. *Little Pine's Journal: The Appeal of a Christian Chippeway Chief on Behalf of His People*. Toronto: Copp, Clark, 1872.

Shropshire, Kenneth. "Race, Youth, Athletes, and Role Models." In *Paradoxes of Youth and Sport*, edited by Margaret Gatz, Michael Messner, and Sandra Ball-Rokeach, 135–40. Albany: SUNY Press, 2002.

Szabo, Chris. "Historical Overview of Government Involvement in Aboriginal Sport and Recreation." Leisure Information Network, 2011.

Thompson, Paul. "The Voice of the Past: Oral History." In *The Oral History Reader*, edited by Robert Perks and Alistair Thomson, 21–8. London: Routledge, 1998.

Trennert, Robert, Jr. *The Phoenix Indian School: Forced Assimilation in Arizona, 1891–1935*. Norman: University of Oklahoma Press, 1988.

True Sport Foundation. *Annual Canadian Sport Awards, Nomination Guidelines.* October 12, 2004.

Truth and Reconciliation Commission of Canada. *Honouring the Truth, Reconciling for the Future: Summary of the Final Report of the Truth and Reconciliation Commission of Canada.* Winnipeg: Truth and Reconciliation Commission of Canada, 2015.

——. *Truth and Reconciliation Commission of Canada: Calls to Action.* Winnipeg: Truth and Reconciliation Commission of Canada, 2015. http://trc.ca/assets/pdf/Calls_to_Action_English2.pdf.

Unwin, Peter. "Who Do You Think I Am? A Story of Tom Longboat." *The Beaver,* April–May 2001, 20–6.

Wagamese, Richard. *Indian Horse: A Novel.* Madeira Park, BC: Douglas and McIntyre, 2013.

Weaver, Sally. *Making Canadian Indian Policy: The Hidden Agenda, 1968–1970.* Toronto: University of Toronto Press, 1981.

Woolford, Andrew. *This Benevolent Experiment: Indigenous Boarding Schools, Genocide, and the Redress in Canada and the United States.* Winnipeg: University of Manitoba Press, 2015.

Wotherspoon, Terry, and Vic Satzewich. *First Nations: Race, Class, and Gender Relations.* Regina: Canadian Plains Research Center, 2000.

Zeeman, Brenda. *To Run with Longboat: Twelve Stories on Indian Athletes in Canada.* Edmonton: GMS2Ventures, 1988.

Dissertations and Theses

Ba'abbad, Fatima. "History of Sioux Lookout Black Hawks Hockey Team, 1949–1951." MA thesis, Western University, 2017.

Brown, William. "Remembering Tom Longboat: A Story of Competing Narratives." MA thesis, Concordia University, 2009.

Fiske, Jo-Anne. " 'And Then We Prayed Again': Carrier Women, Colonization, and Mission Schools." MA thesis, University of British Columbia, 1981.

Heine, Michael. "Gwich'in Tsii'in: A History of Gwich'in Athapaskan Games." PhD diss., University of Alberta, 1995.

Lansley, Keith. "The Amateur Athletic Union of Canada and Changing Concepts of Amateurism." PhD diss., University of Alberta, 1971.

O'Bonsawin, Christine. "Failed TEST: Aboriginal Sport Policy and the Olympian Firth Sisters." MA thesis, University of Western Ontario, 2002.

Paora Te Hiwi, Braden. "Physical Culture as Citizenship Education at Pelican Lake Indian Residential School, 1926–1970." PhD diss., Western University, 2015.

Schrodt, Barbara. "A History of Pro-Rec: The British Columbia Recreation Programme, 1934–1953." PhD diss., University of Alberta, 1979.

Film Strips and Videos

Canada. Department of Citizenship and Immigration. Indian Affairs Branch. *Tom Longboat: Canadian Indian World Champion.* National Film Board of Canada, 1952.

Scher, Len, dir., and Joanne Muroff Smale and Michael Allder, prods. *The Un-Canadians.* National Film Board of Canada, 1996. https://www.nfb.ca/film/un-canadians/.

Story, David, dir. *Longboat.* Dereck Van Lint and Associates, 1993.

Tucker, David, dir. *Wildfire: The Tom Longboat Story.* Canadian Broadcasting Corporation, 1993.

INDEX

Page numbers for images and illustrations are listed in italics.

Janice Forsyth, member of the Fisher River Cree Nation, is an associate professor in the Department of Sociology and Director of Indigenous Studies in the Faculty of Social Science at Western University in London, Ontario. She is co-editor of the award-winning multi-author volume, *Aboriginal Peoples and Sport in Canada: Historical Foundations and Contemporary Issues*, published by UBC Press in 2013.